Confucianism and the Chinese Self

Jack Barbalet

Confucianism and the Chinese Self

Re-examining Max Weber's China

palgrave
macmillan

Jack Barbalet
Australian Catholic University
Melbourne, Victoria, Australia

ISBN 978-981-10-6288-9   ISBN 978-981-10-6289-6   (eBook)
https://doi.org/10.1007/978-981-10-6289-6

Library of Congress Control Number: 2017954012

Cover image © Dorling Kindersley, Getty Images
cash © Rockicon, Noun Project
coin © Bakunetsu Kaito, Noun Project
Cover design by Tjaša Krivec

Printed on acid-free paper

This Palgrave Macmillan imprint is published by Springer Nature
The registered company is Springer Nature Singapore Pte Ltd.
The registered company address is: 152 Beach Road, #21-01/04 Gateway East, Singapore 189721, Singapore

For my son,
David

PREFACE

The rise of China over the past 40 years is a global event of major significance. The unexpected transformation of China after the death of Mao Zedong and the speed with which China has achieved economic parity with the other major nations in the world excites the curiosity of a continually growing number of scholars. But European or 'Western' interest in China is not new. The image of China as a 'middle kingdom' isolated from the world beyond East Asia is not an accurate representation of an empire that drew the attention of travelers and traders even before the European Enlightenment of the seventeenth century, from which time it served as a beacon of hope for European philosophers who opposed entrenched privilege and sought to see satisfied opportunities for talent, possibilities which seemed evident in the imperial examination for entry into the Chinese bureaucracy. The early European use of China as emblematic of what was just and right was reversed in the post-Enlightenment engagement with China as a resource to be exploited, peopled with souls in need of salvation. This perspective and the practices commensurate with it encouraged rumblings that, by 1912, burst into a revolutionary transformation of China. These events coincided with Max Weber's preparation of his desk in order to write *The Religion of China*, a book that occupies our concern in the following pages.

Although my interest in *The Religion of China* is relatively recent, I have had a relationship with Weber over the course of my entire adult life. My very first academic publication was a discussion of an aspect of Weber's sociology, and this was followed by a flow of articles and books in which Weber's ideas are treated as central to the particular topic of the publication in question. While Weber has not monopolized my attention in research and writing over what is now a long career, I find myself frequently returning to him. Like all relationships, my relationship with Weber has had its ups and downs. Relationships of the type I mention here are unavoidably one-sided. This is not to say that my interaction with this spectre, 'my' Weber, has not changed over the years. But one constant in it has been my appreciation of Weber's power to inspire thoughtful reaction and new investigation. Indeed, Weber's work is a repository of ideas that can be drawn on and used for further scholarship and research. And his standing as a sociological classic means that engagement with his themes is to engage with core elements not only of the discipline of sociology, but also cognate studies, including history, religion, and regional studies, including China studies.

While my interest in sociology is longstanding, only relatively recently did I develop a research interest in Chinese societies. During a semester stay at the Max Planck Institute for the Study of Societies in Cologne during 2007, while engaged in unconnected research, I began a study of Chinese business practices. But it was not until I went to Hong Kong in 2011 that I could undertake China research on a more focused and full-time basis. Since that time, I have done nothing else, more or less. Although my research since arriving in Hong Kong has not been engaged only with Weber's discussion of China, Weber has been a remarkably effective conduit through which my interest in China has been channeled and developed. My relationship with Weber in this quest, as the following chapters will reveal, has not been to directly borrow from him. Rather, it has been to revisit the terrain he so dominantly occupies, to examine again what he describes and explains, to participate in a dialogue or exchange, or, to put it slightly differently, to engage in a forceful argument with Weber about what he sees in China and how he sees it.

What is written above relates to the subtitle of this book rather than the title, to Weber not Confucius. When I presented my ideas for this book to Sara CrowleyVigneau, the commissioning editor at Palgrave, my title was *Max Weber's China: Confucianism and the Chinese Self*. The marketing people at Palgrave, though, saw the folly in this title and brought my original subtitle to the primary place it now occupies. Weber's *The Religion of China* is many things, including a discussion of Confucianism. This is reflected in the present book in many ways. Half way through the second chapter Weber's 'take' on Confucianism is examined. The whole of the third chapter is occupied with a discussion of the historical development of Confucianism from the beginning up to the present time. The fourth chapter also relates to Confucianism in so far as it is seen by Weber and his sources, and many others, as the orthodox thought tradition of Imperial China. The Confucian basis of the Chinese family and self-image is extensively discussed in Chap. 5. In Chap. 6, the idea that Confucianism is magic-tolerant is examined in detail. In much discussion today, Confucianism is synonymous with Chinese culture, or at least, enduring elements of it. The argument of this book shows why this view requires the most careful critical evaluation. At the same time, discussion of the Chinese self cannot avoid consideration of the influence of Confucianism. This is Weber's view also.

Finally, a note concerning terminology is required. Chinese names, in pre-1980 publications, are typically presented in terms of the Wade-Giles system of Romanization; since the 1980s, though, the Chinese pin yin system is used. Where a source uses a Wade-Giles Romanization in the chapters to follow the pin yin form is placed in parenthesis after it, as in Mao Tse-tung (Mao Zedong).

ACKNOWLEDGEMENTS

This book was conceived and written in Hong Kong, where I was for six years Chair Professor in Sociology and Head of the Sociology Department at Hong Kong Baptist University. The Department and the city provided all sorts of benefits, intellectual and otherwise, that I gratefully acknowledge. In writing a work such as this, many debts of gratitude are incurred. It is not possible to acknowledge everyone who has contributed to this book. Through a common engagement with Weber, and China, I have become indebted to many people. Some have read chapters in various forms and provided comments; some have engaged with me in conversation, face-to-face and through email; others have listened to my seminar presentations and contributed to Q&A; some have done more than one of these. The list to follow is not complete, and it is alphabetical. I wish to acknowledge in this context Martin Albrow, Peter Baehr, Hon Fai Chen, Joshua Derman, (the late) Lin Duan, David Faure, Gary Hamilton, Xiaoying Qi, Wolfgang Schluchter, Po-Fang Tsai, Bryan Turner, David Wank, and Sam Whimster, among others. It goes without saying that none of them is responsible for what is written in the pages to follow. In Chinese tradition, the court practice of magistrates involved both their 'human considerations' (*qing*) and codified law (*fa*). The preceding acknowledgements spring from *qing*. It is also necessary to make acknowledgments that come from something closer to *fa*. Previously published papers are drawn upon in some of the chapters below, although in every instance rewritten for the present book. Part of Chap. 2 derives from my contribution to *The Anthem Companion to Max Weber*, edited by Alan Sica; a version of Chap. 3 originally appeared in the *Revue Internationale de Philosophie*; a version of Chap. 4 originally appeared in the *Journal of Classical Sociology*, and parts of Chap. 5 are drawn from a paper that appeared in the *Journal for the Theory of Social Behaviour* and a paper that appeared in the *Sociological Review*. These publications and their editors are gratefully acknowledged. It is customary for authors to acknowledge the support they receive from their family. I embrace this custom. My wife, Xiaoying, has heard rehearsals of what is written below and unfailingly provided good advice. My appreciation of her wise judgment, which is by no means the only quality she possesses that I treasure, extends well beyond her support for what is written here. Although their contribution has not been so direct, my sons Tom, Felix, and David have extended my scholarly grasp and imagination, in more ways than they appreciate. It is a further pleasure to acknowledge their contribution to the writing of this book.

Jack Barbalet
Hong Kong and Melbourne
2017

CONTENTS

CHAPTER 1

Introduction

Over 100 years ago, the German economic and cultural writer Max Weber saw China as a puzzle. In his survey of Chinese economic institutions and history, he noted a number of conditions that in Europe had favored the development of modern capitalism, but in China, these same conditions failed to produce the effect they had in Europe. While China had experienced various forms of what Weber describes as premodern capitalism, the modern industrial form, he shows, simply eludes China. Weber's resolution of this puzzle is in terms of what he calls the 'Chinese mentality'—the mentality comprising patterns of thought drawn from the works of Confucius as understood by the scholar administrators of Imperial China, the literati. Confucianism, for Weber, was rational to a degree but significantly unlike the rationalism that he postulates is core to European Protestantism. Whereas Protestantism was originally a revolutionary force against the background of conservative and traditional religions in Europe, according to Weber, Confucian rationalism is directed to the adjustment of its adherents to the world and not to their transforming it capitalistically.

Weber's argument concerning the resolution of this puzzle, of why China did not develop an indigenous capitalism, is itself in need of explanation, or at least context. His concern with 'mentality' in considering the transformation of economic relationships is not an obvious focus when most explanations of the emergence of capitalism look to such factors as population growth, changes in agricultural productivity, trade opportunities, the emergence of instruments of credit, and so forth. Weber's

© The Author(s) 2017
J. Barbalet, *Confucianism and the Chinese Self,*
https://doi.org/10.1007/978-981-10-6289-6_1

approach to the development of capitalism is outlined in his famous work first published in 1905, *The Protestant Ethic and the Spirit of Capitalism*, a work that provoked a debate in Germany soon after its appearance that, in many ways, has continued until today. With the publication of its English-language translation in 1930, the so-called Weber thesis became a defining element of the sociological apprehension of economic orientations. For Weber, it is the value orientation of the economic actor that defines the form of the economy, and in its formative manifestation this orientation is underpinned by ethical values that have religious correlates, if not religious origins.

In an endeavor to demonstrate the veracity of his account of the advent of the capitalist spirit in the Protestant Reformation of the sixteenth century, Weber undertook a number of cross-cultural studies. His core theme is the idea that through the Calvinist notion of 'calling', the practices of constancy of worldly activity provide the form and motive of profit-making for its own sake. The argument, then, is that the rise of modern capitalism in Europe is associated with cultural factors that are shaped by the Protestant Reformation, and therefore that those societies which are without Protestant rationalism will fail to experience an indigenous development of modern capitalism. This is the hypothesis that Weber wished to confirm in his studies of non-European societies. At the time of his writing, extensive material concerning the beliefs, customs, and institutions of China and India as well as other regions had been produced by imperial administrators and traders as well as by Christian missionaries. Weber drew upon not only this material but also documentary sources, including translations of the classic works of these cultures, as well as scholarly writings produced by academic orientalists.

In writing on China, Weber was not embarking on a voyage of discovery so much as organizing evidence produced by others to make the case that he, in effect, had already decided. He is quite explicit that his intention is not to present a balanced view. In his 'Introduction' to the studies of the economic ethics of world religions, as he characterizes his project, Weber states:

> The studies [of China and India and other places] do not claim to be complete analyses of cultures, however brief. On the contrary, in every culture they quite deliberately emphasize elements in which it differs from Western civilization. They are, hence, definitely oriented to the problems which seem important for the understanding of Western culture from *this* view-point. (Weber 1991: 27–28; emphasis in original)

In other words, Weber draws upon that evidence available to him which reveals the uniqueness of the West, especially as it relates to the original emergence of modern capitalism in Europe. Weber's purpose in his discussion of China, then, is to validate his argument concerning the formation of the capitalist spirit as it arises out of the ethic of Calvinism, which is outlined in his earlier work, *The Protestant Ethic*.

It can be seen, then, that Weber is perfectly candid concerning his purpose in writing about China. After acknowledging both his lack of expert knowledge and the limitations of his sources, Weber describes the character of his studies as 'definitely provisional' (Weber 1991: 28). Weber says that his treatment of the economic ethics of world religions is 'comparative', a term used repeatedly throughout the 'Introduction'. But given that his account of China, say, is principally to highlight the nature of European developments—especially Calvinist rationalism in contrast to his perspectivally-constructed account of Confucianism—his treatment of non-European cases is, rather than comparative in any meaningful sense, primarily illustrative. Indeed, his characterization of Confucianism is a construct designed as a foil for his representation of Calvinism. It serves to put into clear relief the idea that Calvinism could inspire activities that underlie the advent of modern capitalism while Confucianism, on the other hand, can only prevent its emergence. In so pointed a vision, there are unavoidable omissions as well as distortions, irrespective of the reliability or otherwise of the sources drawn upon in forming the view in question. This being the case, why bother with Weber's treatment of China at all?

In a review of the English-language translation of Weber's *The Religion of China*, after indicating the work's 'inadequate documentation, methodological defects, frequent inaccuracies and occasional wrongheadedness' (van der Sprenkel 1954: 272), the reviewer goes on to say that the book nevertheless 'remains a great work'. He continues:

> Limited by inadequate equipment, and with a hampering linguistic barrier between himself and his sources, Weber was yet able to raise nearly all the important questions, though not to answer them. His essay can still serve today as a programme for the further development of studies in Chinese society and social institutions. (van der Sprenkel 1954: 274)

Indeed, this is the greatness of *The Religion of China*; it is a source the value of which lies in the importance not of its immediate content and approach, but in the terrain it covers and the questions it poses. The status of its argument, as 'definitely provisional', means that through critical engagement with it our understanding can be enlarged regarding significant aspects of Chinese history and society.

The principal statement of Weber's treatment of China is the work referred to above, *The Religion of China*, first published in 1915. But this is not the only text in which China is the focus of Weber's attention. A short time before writing *The Religion of China*, Weber wrote a book that consists of a wide-ranging account of exotic and ancient religions, *The Sociology of Religion*. In interesting ways, the discussion in this work of Confucianism and other elements of Chinese thought and practice are developed and incorporated in *The Religion of China*, as shown in Chap. 6. *The Sociology of Religion* is inserted in Weber's massive tome *Economy and Society* (Weber 1978: 399–634), a work in which, incidentally, there is also a brief but detailed discussion of 'domination' in the Chinese empire (Weber 1978: 1047–51). Another work in which there is mention throughout of various aspects of Chinese economy, urban development, and religion is the compilation of Weber's late lectures, delivered in 1919–1920, published posthumously as *General Economic History* (Weber 1981). While the examination in the present book of Weber's China is chiefly conducted through engagement with *The Religion of China*, his other sources are drawn on where appropriate.

The intellectual background to Weber's interest in China is mentioned above in terms of his endeavor to validate the argument of *The Protestant Ethic* in his broader studies of the economic ethics of the world religions. This is a defining feature of *The Religion of China* and widely appreciated. What is less frequently noted, however, is how closely Weber was occupied with China not only intellectually but through his involvement with Christian religious organizations in Germany, and even more directly through his championing of the acquisition of German concessions and imperial enclaves in China during the closing decades of the nineteenth century and the beginning of the twentieth. This background to Weber's nonacademic interest in China is discussed in Chap. 2. The chapter is conceived in terms of how China is present in the Germany of Weber's time, and it is shown that Weber's writing on China has a context beyond his well-known concern with the historical origins of capitalism and the construction of a capitalist 'spirit' through religious changes during the Reformation and their absence in China.

Chapter 2 not only considers the shaping of perceptions of China available to Weber as a result of the purposes and operations of German institutions—not only religious and economic, but also political—but additionally the historical legacy of the philosophical, literary, and cultural appropriation of China as an exotic source of imagery, inspiration, and derogation, at different times and in different contexts. The chapter goes on to consider Weber's conception of China in *The Religion of China*, his treatment of Confucianism as a vehicle for his own purpose, and his possibly willful misapprehension of it through misstatement of its representation in the sources he draws on. It is also shown in the chapter how the elements of his argument concerning the Protestant ethic and its relationship with the spirit of capitalism take a different form in his exposition in *The Religion of China* than in its original statement, in *The Protestant Ethic and the Spirit of Capitalism*.

The discussion of Confucianism presented by Weber, focused as it is on the idea that Confucianism operates as an ethic of an administrative class, the literati, raises a number of concerns that he acknowledges as important but is not able to fully develop in his discussion, including the role of Confucian ritual in state legitimation. At the same time, it has been remarked that Weber neglects developments in Confucian ideas, especially the formation of neo-Confucianism during the fourteenth and fifteenth centuries, the advent of which arguably had a lasting influence on Chinese practices about which Weber was unaware (Metzger 1977). In addressing these and other issues, Chap. 3 presents a comprehensive historical summary of developments in Confucianism. In doing so it considers characteristically distinctive manifestations of this rich and expansive tradition in different dynasties, indicating what persists and what changes in it.

Two things about Weber's discussion of Confucianism that are brought out in the chapter are noteworthy. The first of these is how strongly Weber's sense of Confucianism was shaped by the Jesuit missionary construction of Confucianism—not necessarily directly but as a result of the influence of the Jesuit apprehension of Confucianism on subsequent treatments, both on Protestant missionary and academic sinological writers, each of whom influenced Weber's account directly. The other thing to mention is that at the time of Weber's writing in 1913, Confucianism was undergoing radical critique from Chinese social movements promoting reform that in many ways paralleled Weber's own assessment of Confucianism, and at the same time Confucianism itself experienced pressures for internal transformation. These currents both confirmed aspects of Weber's assessment of Confucianism and also pointed to significant elements of his treatment of Confucianism that are limited in various ways. There is some evidence that Weber was aware of the transformations in Confucianism but he simply ignored them in his discussion in *The Religion of China*. They did not resonate with the purpose of that book in confirming Weber's argument concerning the original European source of modern capitalism.

Having discussed Confucianism in Chap. 3, Daoism—the other indigenous thought tradition of China—is the obvious subject of Chap. 4. Confucianism and Daoism are treated by Weber as orthodoxy and heterodoxy, respectively. It is noted in Chap. 2 that Weber's understanding of Confucianism as orthodox has a certain importance for his account of Chinese history and institutions. In this chapter, Weber's application of the concepts of orthodoxy and heterodoxy to Chinese institutions is examined. Weber follows a long tradition of missionary and sinological usage of these terms. It is shown in Chap. 4, nevertheless, that the Chinese state (unlike European states) was less concerned with enforcing correct belief, orthodoxy, against its subjects, and more concerned with their correct behavior, orthopraxy. Indeed, it is shown that rather than orthodoxy it is orthopraxy that is key to understanding political rule in Imperial China.

Weber's discussion of Daoism includes an analysis of its leading text, the *Daodejing* (perhaps better known as the *Tao te ching*), as well as reference to later Daoist communities and practitioners. Whereas Weber characterizes Confucianism as rational even though traditional, Daoism, on the other hand, is regarded by him as a mystical force and even more traditional than Confucianism. The evidence for this assessment is examined in the chapter and its place in the overall argument of *The Religion of China*, which purports to show why a native modern capitalism could not emerge in China, is indicated. Weber does acknowledge an association of Daoism with commercial activity and propertied interests but dismisses it as insignificant because of his prior characterization of Daoism as mystical and traditional. The final section of Chap. 4, then, reassesses the possible relationship between Daoism and entrepreneurial engagement. It shows that Daoism entails a conception of the world-in-process that, rather than being inherently traditional, encourages a positive disposition to change and to opportunities for achieving personal advantage.

Reference to an entrepreneurial spirit that may underlie the ethos of capitalism raises the question of how persons conceive the 'self' that animates their understanding of their 'interests' and how these interests direct their relations with others. This and associated questions are extensively treated in Chap. 5. The place of the 'individual' in Imperial Chinese society is typically resolved in favor of the idea that state practice, clan structure, and family relationships, all lead to the subordination of persons so that, as Weber (1964: 173) put it, 'individual interests *per se* remained out of the picture'. In considering the constitution of the self in Chinese discourses and the place of self-interest in the practices of persons in Chinese society, Chap. 5 begins with an exposition of the Confucian self and the structure of the traditional Chinese family. After showing how situational self-interest is important for understanding the dynamism of family life in traditional China, the chapter goes on to look at Chinese approaches to the self in addition to Confucianism.

Previous discussion, of Confucianism in Chap. 3 and Daoism in Chap. 4, prepares the way for an account of distinctive approaches to the self and to self-interest in these different schools of thought. In Chap. 5, it is shown that the Confucian tendency to highlight its antipathy to 'selfishness' relates not to a blanket opposition to the notion of self-interest, but rather, to admonishment of satisfaction of the interests of 'present selves' against those of 'past selves'. This formulation may be construed as referring to relations between living persons on the one hand, and their ancestors, including not only parents but also previous generations, on the other. It is shown in this chapter, however, that as an individual person can be seen to have a present and a past, as well as a future, each temporal phase of self may have a self-interest of its own. This idea is not so remote from what is quite familiar, as when Weber argues that the Protestant ethic serves to direct persons to future-oriented goals or purposes and away from present temptations. It is shown in the chapter that not only in different societies but in different discourses self-interest operates in terms of the priorities of distinct temporal phases of self. Which temporal phase is privileged in this process will depend on what self-cultivation practice is applied, either Confucian or Daoist, or modern business training.

It was mentioned earlier that ideas concerning Confucianism as an ethic of the literati, developed in *The Religion of China*, were first rehearsed in Weber's preceding book, *The Sociology of Religion*. In both works is an examination of the relationship between magic and Confucianism. Confucianism, in Weber's account, is both magic-tolerant and magic-infused, even though Confucianism is, in principle, indifferent—if not opposed—to magic, as he notes. This characterization of Confucianism is particularly important for Weber's argument because of his insistence that Calvinist religious rationalization, on the other hand, entails 'the elimination of magic from the world' because it 'repudiated all magical means to salvation as superstition and sin' (Weber 1991: 105). On this dimension is a clear distinction and polar opposition between Confucianism and Calvinism on which ultimately balances Weber's claim that modern capitalism has a European origin and could not emerge out of Chinese conditions. This issue and various matters related to it are explored in Chap. 6.

Chapter 6 opens with a brief consideration of the difference between the 1905 edition of the *Protestant Ethic* and the 1920 edition, with the latter alone treating the expulsion of magic as defining of Calvinist religious rationalization. The source of this foundational argument and its exposition in *The Sociology of Religion* is then set out, followed by the details of Weber's discussion concerning the compromise of Confucianism through magic. Discussion in the chapter then moves on to an examination of Weber's claims concerning the Calvinist elimination of magic. Weber acknowledges 'superstition' in Calvinism as evidenced by the New England witch trials, which involved events that occupied just over one year. But Weber has nothing to say about the much more extensive witch-hunts of Reformation Europe that lasted for over a century. Indeed, at this time, Calvin and his followers across Europe were obsessed with satanic witchcraft, in which the reality of magic is accepted not only as a force in itself, but constitutive of a spiritual domain subject to the opposed forces of God and Satan on which Calvinist doctrine and practice, belief, and faith rested. This key but neglected aspect of Calvinism, demonstrated in the chapter through examination of Calvin's own writing and the use of biblical sources, corrects Weber's account of a demagicalized Calvinism and the difference he postulates between Calvinism and Confucianism evaporates. The chapter also shows that Weber's account of Chinese magic is partial and misleading. The chapter makes an original and unsettling contribution by undermining the major plank of Weber's famous Protestant Ethic thesis.

In the discussion throughout the chapters described above, with the exception of a small section of Chap. 2, Weber's argument concerning the nature of modern capitalism has been taken for granted. In the final chapter, Chap. 7, the depiction of modern capitalism in Weber's ideal-type conceptualization of it is subjected to careful consideration. The way in which Weber applies his notion of modern capitalism to the institutional data of Imperial China is critically considered in the chapter. The chapter goes on to briefly outline the emergence and form of capitalism in today's

China. This is a difficult topic for a number of reasons, not the least of which is the historically brief period occupied by these developments, which requires that any assessment be tentative in the extreme. This is required because the capitalist economy of modern China is insipient and the approach of the Chinese authorities experimental, pragmatic, and therefore, subject to practices and policies that are liable to be not only impermanent but unexpected, as so much of China's development has been over the last three decades (Ang 2016). Given the distinctive character of China's own modern capitalism, in many ways dissimilar to present-day American and different 'varieties' of European capitalism, to use a now familiar term (Hall and Soskice 2001), Weber's insistence that a native Chinese capitalism is impossible may simply have been premature.

References

Ang, Yuen Yuen. 2016. *How China Escaped the Poverty Trap*. Ithaca: Cornell University Press.

Hall, Peter A. and Soskice, David. 2001. *Varieties of Capitalism: The Institutional Foundations of Comparative Advantage*. Oxford: Oxford University Press.

Metzger, Thomas A. 1977. *Escape from Predicament: Neo-Confucianism and China's Evolving Political Culture*. New York: Columbia University Press.

van der Sprenkel, O.B. 1954. 'Review: Chinese Religion'. *British Journal of Sociology*. 5(3): 272–75.

Weber, Max. 1978. *Economy and Society: An Outline of Interpretive Sociology*, edited by Guenther Roth and Claus Wittich. Berkeley: University of California Press.

Weber, Max. 1981. *General Economic History*, translated by Frank Knight with a new Introduction by Ira J. Cohen. New Brunswick, NJ: Transaction Books.

Weber, Max. 1964. *The Religion of China: Confucianism and Taoism*, translated and edited by Hans H. Gerth, with an Introduction by C.K. Yang. New York: The Free Press.

Weber, Max. 1991. *The Protestant Ethic and the Spirit of Capitalism*, translated by Talcott Parsons. London: Harper Collins.

CHAPTER 2

China in Germany

Introduction

Max Weber's principal writing on China, known in English as *The Religion of China: Confucianism and Taoism*, was first published in 1915. This was a time of enormous transition, both for Weber's Germany and for China. In August 1914, Britain declared war on Germany—an act that effectively removed the possibility of Germany continuing to prosecute its imperial and colonial ambitions, the consequences of which included Germany's loss of concessions and leases it had held in China at least since 1861. Two years before the onset of the European quagmire that was the First World War, on the first day of January in 1912, Sun Yat-sen declared the Provisional Government of the Republic of China in which he accepted the role of president. This was the beginning of a revolutionary transformation of China that was to undermine and replace practically every aspect of Chinese society that Weber treats in his 1915 exposition.

In *The Religion of China*, which Weber later expanded for publication in 1920, there is an attempt to show that Chinese institutions, especially economic, political, and administrative institutions, and also the characteristically Chinese thought traditions of Confucianism and Daoism, made it impossible for the nascent capitalist practices that had operated in China to develop into a form of modern industrial capitalism. Major aspects of Weber's argument will be discussed in the chapters to follow. Weber's book-length attention to China, which touches on many aspects of its social organization and culture, including its reflective literature, required that he have access to

© The Author(s) 2017
J. Barbalet, *Confucianism and the Chinese Self*,
https://doi.org/10.1007/978-981-10-6289-6_2

and discuss extensive source material. At the time of his writing, Weber had available most of the standard texts of the Chinese classics and copious historical documents and analyses as well as reports of various types written by missionaries, diplomats, and travelers (see Yang 1964: xxxviii–xxxix). Sinology by the end of the nineteenth century and the beginning of the twentieth was well developed (Jones 2001: 99–119) and German university departments of sinology flourished in a number of cities, including Berlin, Hamburg, Frankfurt, and Leipzig (Kern 1998: 508).

Weber's wider contribution to sociology can be described as a major element of a broad movement toward German modernism (Ringer 2004; Sica 2004). A feature of German modernism in general includes a widespread, if not commonplace, awareness of and reference to China and things Chinese. In this context, China functioned as a rhetorical measure in representing hidden possibilities and untried options, dark phantoms and bright images, exotic others and exploitable resources. The historical and social science interest in China among German scholars, which is represented in Weber's study, was part of a continuum in which German literary and philosophical writing also had a significant place for Chinese tropes and material (see Bush 2010; Gosetti-Ferencei 2011). Before discussing *The Religion of China*, the following account of China in Germany will provide some background to Weber's argument that is not typically indicated in the secondary literature and to which Weber himself does not draw attention.

THE 'DISCOVERY' OF CHINA

Pointing to a German interest in China is not intended to suggest that Germany alone had such a concern, for there was throughout Europe from at least the thirteenth century a fascination with an exotic Orient in which China had a significant presence. Neither is it true that the German conception of China was unchanging, for it is possible to make a broad distinction between a preoccupation that could be described as sinophilia and one that was of a sinophobic disposition, the first more or less corresponding with the European Enlightenment and the second with post-Enlightenment preoccupations (Steinmetz 2007). While acknowledging that Germany was not isolated from the rest of Europe in terms of currents of taste and perception, the discussion here shall focus on China in Germany, as preparatory to an account of Weber's *The Religion of China*, and therefore, the background and broad context of Weber's thinking about China.

It was mentioned earlier that European interest in China could be seen to have been aroused by the thirteenth century. This is because more than any other single event, Marco Polo's travels, undertaken from 1276 to 1291, generated an interest in distant and remote lands of great wealth, variety, and curiosity. Marco Polo was a Venetian merchant whose extensive travels are reported in a four-volume work, the second volume of which is devoted to China. *Marco Polo's Travels* was originally written in Old French and circulated in manuscript form throughout Europe, copied and translated many times. It is of interest that the first printed edition of *Marco Polo's Travels* was a German translation, published in Nuremberg in 1477, and the second printed edition was also a German translation published in Augsburg in 1481 (Hart 1942: 256). It was not until 1579 that the first English translation appeared. This difference here between Germany and England no doubt simply reflects the fact that the printing revolution, enabling the mass production of books, was begun in Germany, rather than in England. But it does register an early German interest in China and a literary, informative, and also, imaginative presence of China in Germany.

By the late seventeenth century and the early eighteenth, a much more significant manifestation of China in Germany is in the writings of the polymath Gottfried Wilhelm Leibniz (1646 1716). Leibniz had a sympathetic understanding of Confucius and Chinese thought more broadly (Ching and Oxtoby 1992; Leibniz 1994; Perkins 2004) and extolled the virtues of Chinese governance at a time when Europe was subject to aristocracy and inherited privilege (Reichwein 1968: 79–83; Steinmetz 2007: 381; Zhang 1998: 101–104). Leibniz's inspiration and principal source was in correspondence with the Jesuit mission in Beijing, which was established in 1601, although the Jesuit presence in China began in 1579 (Latourette 2009: 91–130). Not only were German intellectual tastes in the eighteenth century tantalized by Chinese thought and institutions but also were German aesthetic commitments significantly 'Chinese'. China, or a version of it that became known as Chinoiserie, was brought into the fabric of design and crafts adopted by German courts and wealthy families from the late seventeenth century. During the eighteenth century variant Chinese styles were applied in European architecture and furniture as well as in porcelain and fine art. French and German interpretations of rococo, the style of soft curves and muted colors borrowed extensively from China—and to a lesser degree Japan—competed with each other in their apprehensions of Chinese influence and representation (Hudson 1961: 270–90; Reichwein 1968: 25–72).

Closer to Weber's time a reminder of the long-standing presence of China in Germany is the attention given to Chinese philosophy by Georg Wilhelm Friedrich Hegel (1770–1831) in his *Lectures on the History of Philosophy* that were delivered over a number of years from 1816. Hegel's theme is the historical progress of consciousness, of an incremental development of awareness of individuality and freedom, from a state of relative absence to its fullest realization in Hegel's own time. Hegel's survey begins with a pre-history of philosophy in the East, in China and India. He writes that 'in the East the element of subjectivity has not come forth, religious ideas are not individualized' (Hegel 1892: 118). The philosophy, or rather, pre-philosophy, of China in Hegel's account consists of the thought of Confucius (Hegel 1892: 120–21), the ideas found in the *Y-king* (*I Ching* or *Yijing*) (Hegel 1892: 121–23), and finally the ideas of the Tao-king (*Tao Te Ching* or *Daodejing*) written by Lao-Tsö (Laozi) (Hegel 1892: 124–25). Hegel describes Confucius as 'only a man who has a certain amount of practical and worldly wisdom' whose reputation 'would have been better [served] had [his original works] never been translated' (Hegel 1892: 121). The *Yijing* similarly fails to impress Hegel; it is a 'collection of concrete principles' in which 'there is not to be found in one single instance a sensuous conception of universal natural or spiritual powers' (Hegel 1892: 122). Hegel engages more seriously with the thought of Laozi, even though disparagingly, asking at the conclusion of a detailed though brief analysis 'if Philosophy has got no further than ... its most elementary stage [in Laozi's thought] what is there to be found in all this learning?' (Hegel 1892: 123).

Hegel's assessment of Chinese thought is as negative as Leibniz's had been positive, as he acknowledges (Hegel 1892: 120). What is important in pointing to Hegel's discussion of Chinese thought is not the errors of fact and judgment he brings to it, especially in his discussion of Laozi (see Wong 2011), but first his need to give attention to it at all, and second his acknowledgement of a long-standing interest in Chinese thought and institutions from at least the time of the Jesuit mission to China in 1579 and during the period of the European Enlightenment from the late seventeenth century up to Hegel's own time. He refers to a translation, or what he describes as a paraphrase, of Confucius published in Paris in 1687 and a series, also published in Paris from 1776 to 1814, *Mémoires concernant l'histoire, les sciences, les arts, les mœurs, les usages, & c. des Chinois: Par les Missionnaires de Pékin*, a compilation of documents prepared by the Jesuit mission in Beijing. Hegel also refers to the discussion of Confucius in Windischmann's book of 1827, *Die Philosophie im Fortgang der Weltgeschichte* (*Philosophy in the Course of World History*). In discussing Laozi, Hegel draws on the translation of Laozi by Abel Rémusat in his *Mémoire sur la Vie et les Opinions de Lao-Tseu* published in Paris in 1823. Hegel (1892: 124) provides a sense of concrete immediacy to his discussion of ancient Chinese thought when he says that Laozi's principal writings 'have been taken to Vienna, and I have seen them there myself'.

Hegel's standing as a leading philosopher was not confined to Germany, of course. And his global approach to philosophy resonated with currents that were developing around the ideas of 'world religions' being formulated in England by the expatriate German Max Müller, a Sanskrit scholar based in Oxford. Müller loosely borrowed from Hegel ideas of the dialect and progress in understanding religious development (Stone 2002: 9–11). He first defends the idea of a comparative study of religion, as successor to his comparative study of language, in a series of four lectures delivered at the Royal Institute in 1870. An acceptance of the practice of a scientific study of religion encompassing if not all religions at least the 'most important', he says, 'is now only a matter of time' (Müller 1873: 34–35). Being a linguist it is not surprising that Müller's conception of the material such a science would explore is the 'sacred books' (Müller 1873: 23) or 'sacred writings' (Müller 1873. 24) of major religions of the world. The inevitability of the coming of a comparative science of religion—that it is 'now only a matter of time'—arises from the fact that the data of the science is already available:

> The ancient religions of China, again, that of Confucius and Laotse, may now be studied in excellent translations of their sacred books by anyone interested in the ancient faiths of mankind. (Müller 1873: 25)

Indeed, by 1879, Müller had launched a series of publications with Oxford University Press, *The Sacred Books of the East*, which by 1910 comprised 50 published volumes.

Those volumes of Müller's series that related to the Chinese sacred books were all written or translated by James Legge (1815–1897), who had served as a China missionary from 1840 until 1873; he became Professor of Chinese at Oxford University in 1876. Legge contributed six volumes to *The Sacred Books of the East*, published from 1879 to 1891, covering the broad literatures of Confucianism and Daoism. This is a larger output than any of the other 21 contributors to the series, with the exception of one other contributor and also the editor, Max Müller, who were also each responsible for six volumes. Legge's translations were drawn upon extensively by Weber, as we shall see later and in other chapters. Our attention here, though, is to the fact that Legge's knowledge of the Chinese classics derived from his 33 years as a missionary in China. Indeed, European colonial incursion into the 'East', to use Müller's term, not only made the 'sacred books' of these regions available for European scientific treatment, but the missionary involvement in Western imperial activity typically came with a linguistic expertise, which generated the translations that Müller acknowledges were readily available by the middle of the nineteenth century (see Wong 2015). Let us turn, then, to missionaries as a conduit of a sense of the presence of China, bringing it directly into German awareness and sensibility.

MISSIONARIES

Richard Wilhelm (1873–1930) was a German missionary scholar who was a contributor to not only German but also European and American awareness of Chinese thought. Wilhelm's famous translations of *Daodejing*, first published in 1910, and, more importantly, *Yijing*, first published in 1913, derived from his work as a Protestant missionary in China from 1897 until he took up a Chair of Chinese at the University of Frankfurt in 1924. The vast majority of missionaries in China were British, with American missionaries constituting the second major national group. The next largest national group of Protestant missionaries were German, although their numbers were significantly smaller that either the British or American, failing to reach even 10 percent of the missionary population in China at any given time. The small numbers of German missionaries was made up for in the influence of German theology, through which 'German missionary ideas often defined the grounds for the debate' (Wu 2016: 10). The German missionary societies that operated in China as a result of opportunities provided by the 1861 Treaty of Tientsin (Tianjin), which opened all of China to missionary activity which had previously been confined to five coastal cities, included the Basel Evangelical Society, the Berlin Missionary Society for China, the Rhenish Missionary Society, and the Berlin Women's Missionary Society for China, although the last of these confined its activities to maintaining a home for Chinese girls in Hong Kong (Latourette 2009: 372–73). In 1884, another German missionary society was formed, The General Evangelical Protestant Missionary Society, soon joined by Ernst Faber who had originally gone to China with the Rhenish

Mission (Latourette 2009: 398). Faber was another missionary scholar who wrote and published extensively in Chinese, English, and German on the work of mission and on Chinese conditions and philosophy (Latourette 2009: 373). Faber's study of Mencius (Faber 1877) is referred to by Weber (1964: 250–52) along with the work of other missionary scholars including Wilhelm, as well as British missionary scholars.

The treaty that opened the interior of China to Christian, largely Protestant, missionaries was forced upon the Chinese Qing government as a consequence of its defeat at the end of the second Opium War of 1858–1860. From this time the numbers of Protestant missionaries rose rapidly, from 81 in 1858 to 189 in 1864; by 1874 the number of Protestant missionaries in China was reported to be 473, and by 1895 over 1000, peaking at over 8000 by 1925 (Latourette 2009: 405–7). While the rate of growth of these numbers is impressive, it must be remembered that the population of China in 1900 was approximately 400 million. The significance of the missionary presence in China was clearly not its numerical magnitude but rather its intrusive force as a proxy for Western imperial military and commercial power that was a constant abrasive assertion of Chinese subservience and humiliation. On the home front also, China missionaries supported by religious societies, congregations, and broader publics enjoying the benefits of empire were a constant presence of China in Germany and other sending countries of the entanglement of domestic advantage and Asian resources, not only souls to be saved but items of trade, dividends of commerce and also national prestige. Weber's involvement with Christian organizations and their publications, while not related directly to foreign mission, indicates the unavoidable presence of church-related activity throughout German society at the time (Aldenhoff 2010; Mommsen 1990: 19–20, 32, 123–27; Swatos and Kivisto 1991; Marianne Weber 1975: 31–37, 188–89, 234–35). German missionaries in particular 'shaped the public imagery of foreign lands' (Wu 2016: 11–12, see also 32) as well as supplied scholars such as Weber with extensive source material on China and Chinese affairs.

The biggest single setback to missionary activity, not simply in China but with regard to Christian missionary activity anywhere, was the Boxer rebellion that lasted from 1899 to 1901. The Boxer (*Yihequan*) movement was proto-nationalist and anti-foreign, and directed its hostility to Christian missionaries and their Chinese converts, among others, killing 136 Protestant and 47 Catholic missionaries and 32,000 Chinese converts as well as the German plenipotentiary in Beijing. The response of European powers, formed as a military Eight-Nation Alliance, including Germany, was overwhelming in the extent of atrocities committed not only against the Boxers but Chinese men and women in general, and in the subsequent looting of Chinese property at all levels of the population (Bickers and Tiedemann 2007; Cohen 1998). The aftermath of the Boxer eruption and its suppression was highly positive for the missionary movement, however, bringing increased interest about and support for the work of Christian missionary activity in China to all supporting countries, including Germany:

> ...the sufferings of missionaries and of Chinese Christians in the Boxer out-
> break ... focused the attention of the Protestant world on China. The appeal
> to the heroic, the challenge to carry on the work of the martyrs, seldom
> failed of a response. (Latourette 2009: 569)

For Germany this upsurge after the suppression of the Boxers of mission-ary activity in China was abruptly halted with the onset of war between the European powers in 1914. German Protestant missions were by no means destroyed by war hostilities, however. While anti-German feeling was strong among some American and British missionaries, their organizations gave monetary support and support in kind to German Protestant mis-sions, which continued to operate in China (Latourette 2009: 743–44), even establishing new missions in China in 1919 (Latourette 2009: 771). But the war reflected an aspect of the national base of missionary activity that is essential to understand and provides detail of German involvement, in particular, as it impinges on an appreciation of the background to Weber's *The Religion of China*.

GERMAN IMPERIALISM

The First World War was not simply between Britain and Germany but between their empires and related to their imperial ambitions. Indeed, European interest in China is inseparable from the question of trade and the prospects of trade that motivated Marco Polo's much earlier travels and that by the late sixteenth century were manifest in stable commercial relations between Europe and China (Findley and O'Rourke 2007: 286–94). German trade with China was originally indirect, through pur-chase of Chinese-sourced items from Dutch and English merchants and also Russian (Findley and O'Rourke 2007: 295–303). By 1752, however, the Royal Prussian Asian Trading Company, known as the Emden

Company because it was based in the seaport of Emden, began trading directly with China through Canton. This was a modest enterprise consisting of four ships, but significant enough to be regarded as a threat by the British East India Company (Simms 2007: 362). The end of the Emden Company was brought about by the disruption of the Seven Years' War, fought between 1754 and 1763 with Britain and Prussia, and their allies, on one side, against France and Austria, and their allies, on the other. One hundred years later, another war prosecuted by Britain, the Second Opium War of 1856 to 1860, generated a new opportunity for Germany to return to directly trading with China. Prussia became a signatory to the Treaty of Tientsin (Tianjin) in 1861, which gave the German Customs Union access to commercial relations with China as well as to opportunities for German missionaries to operate in China, as indicated earlier.

Germany's diplomatic and commercial presence in China during the period immediately after signing the 1861 Treaty was confined to Tianjin, a major port city just over 100 kilometers from Beijing. Foreign concessions in the city were originally taken by Britain and France, soon to be followed by Japan as well as Germany. America had unofficial representation through the British mission. After the turn of the century, from 1901, Austro-Hungary, Italy, and Belgium also were granted concessions in Tianjin. The German enclave proved to be highly profitable for trade and was soon home to a new financial institution, the Deutsche-Asiatische Bank, which quickly established branches in other major Chinese trading cities (Gall et al. 1995). Soon after establishing its settlement in Tianjin, Germany occupied another concession in Hankow (Hankou), a town on the Yangtze River approximately 700 kilometers west of Shanghai. Britain, France, Russia, and Japan also held concessions in Hankou; Germany's was only second in size to the British. But the strongest German presence in China was to come in 1898, when it leased a large area of land from the Imperial Chinese government on Kiaochow (Jiaozhou) Bay. German naval interests had earlier considered this location to be an ideal site for a naval base on the recommendation of Baron von Richthofen, a geologist who traveled extensively in China. Richthofen's diaries, published in 1907, are recommended by Weber (1964: 252) as a 'descriptive introduction to modern Chinese conditions'. It goes without saying that von Richthofen was not a disinterested observer of Chinese affairs (see Wu 2014).

The opportunity for Germany to acquire Jiaozhou Bay in Shandong arose in 1897 with the murder of two German Catholic missionaries. In response to their death German warships were dispatched to the area and a 99-year lease of the land surrounding the bay was secured for Germany (Schrecker 1971: 19–40; see also Gottschall 2003). German development of the area, including the building of railways and mining, was commercially successful and the bay's naval facilities were of enormous strategic as well as commercial value to Germany (Schrecker 1971: 210–46; Wu 2016: 83–84). Weber's awareness of and interest in these developments is not clearly reflected in his writing, but it exists nevertheless. His direct appreciation of the intricacies of global capitalism from the middle of the nineteenth century, and his understanding of industry and transportation (both rail and shipping), as well as a sympathy for business interests, it has been suggested, derive from Weber's family connections, associations, and contacts (Roth 2000). At the same time, Weber's endorsement of German imperial ambition in general, indeed his strident encouragement of it, is clearly expressed in publications that appeared over the span of his adult life. In his inaugural lecture, 'The Nation State and Economic Policy', delivered in 1895, Weber (2000: 20) describes himself as an 'economic nationalist'. Indeed, the lecture is such a strident assertion of the need for the domination of German national power that some scholars hold that Weber did not mean what he said in this work (see Turner and Factor 1984: 15), even though it is consistent with his subsequent views, expressed both in private correspondence and public lectures and publications (Mommsen 1990; see also Zimmerman 2006).

Two years after the inaugural lecture, in a lecture given in Mannheim at the end of 1897, just 35 years after the first German concessions were established in China and a year before German battleships forcefully acquired the quasi-colony at Jiaozhou Bay, Weber made the following prescient announcement:

> With frightening rapidity, we are approaching the point at which the limits of the markets of half-civilized Asiatic peoples will have been reached. Then only power, naked power, will count in the international market. (quoted in Mommsen 1990: 77)

Indeed, Weber wrote articles in support of the naval policy of Admiral Alfred von Tirpitz (Mommsen 1990: 137, 139), a policy which included annexation of Jiaozhou Bay as a base for the German Navy (Gottschall 2003; Schrecker 1971). In reflections on 'The Economic Foundations of Imperialism', written between 1911 and 1914 and published in *Economy and Society*, Weber (1978: 918) muses on the '[i]ncreasing opportunities for profit abroad [that] emerge again today, especially in territories that are opened up politically and economically'. There is no explicit mention of China here, although the description of activities that follows parallels those that were taking place at the time in the German concessions and lease areas in China. To dispel any doubt concerning his focus, though, Weber (1978: 919) goes on to say:

> The safest way of monopolizing for the members of one's own polity profit opportunities which are linked to the public economy of the foreign territory is to occupy it or at least subject the foreign political power in the form of a 'protectorate' or some such arrangement...The universal revival of 'imperialist' capitalism ... and the revival of political drives for expansion are thus not accidental. For the predictable future, the prognosis will have to be made in its favour.

With the onset of the First World War, just a short time after this passage was written, Germany lost its possessions in China. The destruction wrought by the war, a consequence of imperial ambition, did not shake Weber's attachment to his imperial commitments and his vision of the correctness of strident nationalism as an appropriate strategy for the German state.

In the context of Weber's explicit endorsement of German imperial expansionism, including in China, the 'synchronization between Weber's text and external imperial ideology' has been noted (Steinmetz 2012: 866). The claim that this 'was not due to any direct support for the German imperial interests in China' is anomalous in light of Weber's support for von Tirpitz's strategy, mentioned earlier, but the consonance of Weber's position as a consequence of his 'strategic orientation within the German academic field' (Steinmetz 2012: 866) cannot be doubted as a more visible element of Weber's commitment. According to this claim, Weber selected his sources for *The Religion of China* in order to make the case that Chinese economic development was constrained only by internal factors:

> Weber's *Religion of China* was structured around the premise of Chinese economic stagnation, which he explained in terms of shortcomings of Chinese values or national culture. He drew most heavily on the writings of Jan de Groot, who considered the Chinese to be 'semi-civilized' and prone to religious 'fanaticism'. Weber was ignorant of the growth of Chinese capitalism in the late nineteenth century, including in the region around the future German colony in Shandong Province. He also ignored the fettering impact of Western imperialism on Chinese capitalism and of British opium on the Chinese work ethic. (Steinmetz 2007: 416)

Weber seldom referred to or debated works that offered a contrary assessment of Chinese prospects, according to Steinmetz. The argument that China was not static or stagnant, against Weber's assessment, was proposed by the most prominent linguist and sinologist in Germany at the time who incidentally taught de Groot, namely Georg von der Gabelentz (1888), but simply was ignored by Weber in *The Religion of China* which has no reference to Gabelentz (Steinmetz 2007: 415, 2012: 866). Sinologists who were not in high-prestige German institutions were also ignored by Weber, according to Steinmetz (2007: 468–69, 2012: 866), and their arguments, such as those of Ching Dao Wang (1913), are not mentioned or discussed by Weber in *The Religion of China*.

MAX WEBER'S CHINA

Having considered the context or exterior of *The Religion of China*, it is now necessary to turn our attention to its argument, its interior. For this is a work that at the time of its publication brought China into Germany in a decisive and definitive manner, asserting the correctness of the German imperial approach to East Asia and colonized regions in general. Weber's work is a remarkable synthesis, effectively summarizing a broad spectrum of European scholarship and opinion on China up to the time of its being written. It has been noted above that Weber drew on a large literature in writing *The Religion of China*, but because of frequent inaccurate attribution and inadequate referencing, repeated in the English translation (van der Sprenkel 1954: 275), it is not always possible to know what sources he drew on. This situation has been corrected with the modern German edition in which there is a rectified and complete bibliography (Schmidt-Glintzer and Kolonko 1991). A recent English-language discussion provides a useful summary of Weber's sources (Sunar 2016: 86–90). Excluding his own texts, Weber referred to 159 titles in *The Religion of China*, many of which are directly concerned with aspects of Chinese history and society. In that sense, the work represents an encyclopedic foray into German and other European sinology. A long footnote, which constitutes a partial bibliographic essay, concludes with the statement:

> I did not have an expert sinologist to cooperate on the text or check it. For that reason the volume is published with misgivings and with the greatest reservation. (Weber 1964: 252)

This disclaimer aside, there is a consensus among scholars that Weber's discussion remains more or less true to the state of knowledge and historical conventions that run through his sources, including a characterization of Confucianism that is essential for his argument, which shall be briefly addressed later.

Weber's ability to assimilate vast bodies of literature, his attention to detail, and his incessant quest to derive meaning from information leads him to pose questions concerning Chinese history, society, and thought that to some considerable extent have informed discussion in 'China studies' since Weber's writing. At the same time, the limitations not only of Weber's sources but also in his own account that is based upon them have continued to draw attention. The character of the sources Weber draws upon and his acceptance of their rendition of Chinese culture are indicated in the following section, which outlines Weber's apprehension of Confucianism as orthodoxy, on which Weber bases the second half of *The Religion of China*. This theme will be returned to in other chapters. But Weber is concerned not only with what he calls Chinese 'mentality'. *The Religion of China* presents a detailed and often sophisticated outline of political and social institutions, not always appreciated by commentators on Weber's work, which shall also be considered in this chapter. It is often noted that *The Religion of China*, in arguing that the spirit of capitalism could not arise out of Chinese conditions, endeavors to confirm the argument first developed in Weber's much better known work, *The Protestant Ethic and the Spirit of Capitalism*. We shall see, however, that Weber's account in *The Religion of China*, of the relationship between values and economic orientation, is significantly different from the treatment this topic receives in *The Protestant Ethic*. This discussion encourages us to return to Weber's treatment of Confucianism as inherently unsuitable for provision of a capitalist spirit, to inculcate a practice of 'calling', ensuring single-minded devotion to this-worldly orientation. It is shown below that while Confucianism is not directed to the purpose of money-making for its own sake, as in Weber's celebrated depiction of Protestantism, it does entail self-cultivation practices that proved useful for market actors, especially merchants, in Qing dynasty China. It has to be added that such actors were not involved in the construction of modern capitalism, and the final section of the chapter returns to an aspect of Weber's institutional argument to consider how it might contribute to our understanding of why this was so.

CONFUCIANISM REVEALED

An underlying assumption of Weber's account in *The Religion of China*, and a major tenet of his argument concerning the failure of modern capitalism to develop in China, is the claim that Confucianism constitutes an orthodoxy against which all other creeds are heterodox. This theme will be discussed in detail in Chap. 4 below. At this point, it is necessary to indicate that this representation of Confucianism is in many ways an invention of European sinology and betrays the latter's missionary roots. This is not to doubt the historic figure Kongzi (literally Master Kong), a teacher and political aspirant who lived during the Spring and Autumn period (771–476 BC) of Chinese history. This and the subsequent Warring States period (476–221 BC) were marked by political upheaval, realignments of political alliance, and protean statecraft. A feature of these times was the formation of itinerate colleges of political and military advisers, led by a prominent thinker, offering their services to competing states and their princes. Kongzi was one of a number of such thinkers who populated this period of Chinese history.

While Kongzi and Mengzi are relatively unfamiliar names, although known to Weber (1964: 113, 124), their Latin transliterations, 'Confucius' and 'Mencius', respectively, given by members of the sixteenth-century Jesuit mission to Beijing, are universally familiar. The missionary interest in China has been not only to convert the Chinese to Christianity, but also to interpret Chinese traditions in such a manner as to make the Chinese amenable to conversion, finding 'equivalent' Chinese terms for Christian notions and personalities or roles (Wong 2005). Indeed, the figure of Confucius underwent such a transformation:

> For sixteenth-century Chinese, the native entity, Kongzi ... was the object of an imperial cult, the ancient ancestor of a celebrated rhetorical tradition, and a symbol of an honored scholarly fraternity (the *ru*, or 'Confucians') represented by a phalanx of officials who staffed every level of the imperial bureaucracy. But before the eyes of clerics newly arrived from the West he appeared as prophet, holy man and saint. (Jensen 1997: 33)

Although Weber does not relate this history of metamorphosis in *The Religion of China*, he effectively enacts it when he claims that the 'canonization of Confucius is the first certain example of a historical figure becoming a subject of worship' (Weber 1964: 174). The context of this remark is a discussion of the 'functional' deities of the 'official Chinese state cult', but the footnote attached to it provides no source for or elaboration of this unlikely claim, but distractingly refers to canonization in the Catholic Church (Weber 1964: 290 note 3). And yet, this is an appropriate indicator if it implicitly acknowledges the responsibility of Matteo Ricci, the leader of the sixteenth-century Jesuit mission to Beijing, in this 'canonization', rather than that of Chinese officials, as Weber implies. This process will be more fully treated in the next chapter.

The apprehension of Confucian thought, more or less encouraged by the Jesuit approach, was to regard it as a native Chinese ethical monotheism, which therefore took the form of a 'natural religion'. The European Enlightenment notion of natural religion supposed a pagan morality absent of miracle, revelation, or sacrament. As noted above, the Jesuit construction of Confucianism was highly influential in subsequent European thought, especially in the work of Leibniz and also other Enlightenment thinkers, including Quesnay and Voltaire, who extolled the virtues of moral Confucian China against corrupt aristocratic Europe (Hudson 1961: 319–25; Zhang 1998: 99–101). While the eighteenth-century European vision of China lost its political and popular appeal after the French Revolution, as both Europe and China underwent significant transformations that led to a more negative image of China as stagnant and uncivilized (Hudson 1961: 326–28)—an image borrowed by Weber (1964: 55), as we have seen, and explained in terms of bureaucratic ossification (Weber 1964: 60, 151–52)—the missionary and sinological representation of Confucianism, as originally a native Chinese religion, persisted into the nineteenth century and beyond (see de Groot 1910: 89–131; Faber 1897: 34–38, 57–66; Legge 1877, 1880: 1–58).

Weber is both true to this interpretive tradition and also dissents from it. In addition to the supposed canonization of Confucius he holds that Confucius claimed that the 'order of the world ... could not be retained without belief [and therefore] the retention of religious belief was politically even more important than was the concern for food' (Weber 1964: 143). There is no attribution here but the most likely reference is the *Analects* of Confucius Book 12 Chap. 7, in which the belief referred to, according to the Legge translation drawn upon by Weber, is not religious but the people's 'faith in their rulers'; this latter cannot 'be dispensed with' even though 'military equipment ... [and] food' may be 'part[ed] with' (Legge 1971: 254). In spite of these contortions the sacralization of Confucius and Confucianism undertaken by missionaries from the sixteenth to the nineteenth centuries is not completely accepted by Weber who goes on to insist that Confucianism is not a religion (Weber 1964: 146, 156). This is largely a consequence of Weber's rejection of the idea of natural religion and his insistence that religion must operate through explicitly God-embracing beliefs and devotional piety, a theme to be more fully developed in Chap. 6.

Weber's wholesale acceptance of the idea that there is throughout Imperial Chinese history a Confucian orthodoxy blinds him to the significance of Buddhism after the third century and its transformation of Chinese thought and practices (Gernet 1995; Qi 2014: 105–28), a significance one writer sees as a hidden force of modernization in China (Buss 1985: 84). Weber is oblivious to the periods of Buddhist influence, indeed dominance, where he assumes a continuing and undifferentiated Confucian presence (Collins 1990: 59) and philosophical hegemony from the eighth century (Weber 1964: 165). With the exception of a brief, inadequate, confused, and misleading discussion in a mistitled section of Chap. 7 of *The Religion of China* (Weber 1964: 195–96, see also 217), he has nothing to say about Buddhism in China, sinicized from the third century, and its influence on social organization and economy. The closest he comes to recognition of its significance is to acknowledge 'the profound traces' left by 'popular Buddhism' on the 'workaday life of the masses' (Weber 1964: 234).

Weber found the missionary sinological crystallization of a Chinese orthodox 'mentality' in Confucianism to be an ideal device by which to demonstrate his purpose of showing that the cultural basis of modern capitalism is located only in the history of European developments. The missionary contrast of Christianity and Confucianism, their juxtaposition in a common moral universe as distinct but competing ethical discourses, permits Weber's demonstration that Confucianism has a rational dimension, but that 'Confucian rationalism meant rational adjustment to the world' (Weber 1964: 248). What is necessary for the development of capitalism, in Weber's (1964: 248) estimation, however, is 'Puritan rationalism [which] meant rational mastery of the world'. This view is parallel to the seventeenth- and eighteenth-century European complaint against the perceived pacifism and lack of martial courage on the part of Confucian China, against the standard of the European elevation of military power and glory (Hudson 1961: 320–21). Weber (1964: 114–15, 169) not only notices the difference between Chinese quiescence and European valiance and striving, but he insightfully explains it in terms of the unifying and pacifying consequences of China's imperial political structures against the competitiveness and martial conflict between European principalities and states (Weber 1964: 61–62, see also 103). Each formation, he believes, has a commensurate economic dimension, with the European alone leading to market competition and economic rationality.

INSTITUTIONS AND BELIEFS

Weber's discussion of state forms and relations in *The Religion of China* introduces an institutional argument for which he is seldom given sufficient credit. Indeed, Weber's interpreters typically ignore this aspect of *The Religion of China* and almost exclusively focus on his claim regarding the absence of an appropriate religious tradition in explaining China's failure to experience modern capitalism (Giddens 2011: 177–78; Parsons 1968: 541–42, 577; Schluchter 1989: 103–11). Weber's intention, and what unifies the argument of *The Religion of China*, is to demonstrate the uniqueness of the West in its institutions as well as in the patterns of its thought and values. This purpose would be successful in its own terms if Weber were intent on only comparing civilizations, but in attempting to explain the formation of modern capitalism in Europe and its absence in China in terms of religious beliefs and orientations, the institutional argument and the value argument come into a contradictory relationship with each other. Much of the scholarship on *The Religion of China* resolves this contradiction, however, by simply ignoring the institutional argument as providing an alternative framework to the argument concerning religious traditions.

It is not unusual to hear the complaint from writers close to Weber sources that the English title, *The Religion of China*, fails to match the original *Konfuzianismus und Taoismus*, given by Weber to both the originally published essay of 1915 and its augmented form of 1920. Weber's translator, Hans Gerth, writing during the rise of the Cold War in 1951, notes that he 'named this volume *The Religion of China* in order to avoid the isms' of the original title (Weber 1964: ix) although the offending suffixes are retained in the subtitle of the translation, *The Religion of China: Confucianism and Taoism*. A point too frequently ignored, however, is that neither the English title nor the original German indicates the important fact that just over half the book is not primarily concerned with Confucianism or Daoism but with the economic, political, and social institutions of early China. Indeed, even astute Weber scholars continue to focus primarily on the argument about Chinese 'mentality', principally Confucianism, and ignore the institutional argument set out in the work or reduce it to an aspect of the argument concerning Confucian values (Kalberg 2012: 145–64). There is thus a neglected aspect of Weber's approach that is key to his discussion of China (Huang 1994) but not confined to it, namely, that he entertains an unresolved dichotomy of institutional and religious factors in the post-*Protestant Ethic* accounts of historic formations.

Weber's signature argument, first outlined in *The Protestant Ethic and the Spirit of Capitalism*, concerns the 'elective affinity' between elements of the Protestant creed and capitalist motivation, the 'influence of certain religious ideas', as he puts it, 'on the development of an economic spirit, or the *ethos* of an economic system' (Weber 1991: 27). This argument underlies the discussion of Confucian and Daoist 'mentality' in *The Religion of China* in so far as it falls short of the capacity—inherit in Protestantism, according to Weber—to promote the capitalistic ethos. But before writing the *Protestant Ethic*, in his talk on 'The Social Causes of the Decline of Ancient Civilization' delivered in 1886 (Weber 2013), in the discussion of his doctoral dissertation, submitted in 1889, on commercial partnerships in the Middle Ages (Weber 2002), and in key parts of later works, including *Economy and Society* (1978), *General Economic History* (1981), as well as *The Religion of China* (1964), Weber also treats institutional not ideational or value factors as independent variables. In attempting to reconcile the institutional and religious arguments coterminous in *General Economic History,* sociologist Randall Collins (1990: 21, 33) holds that Weber provides an explanatory role to religious organizations, not doctrine. But a cursory examination of the relevant sections of the text reveals that this is not correct (see Barbalet 2008: 166–69). The problem remains of unreconciled contrary arguments concerning the basis of capitalism in *General Economic History,* and as we shall see, in *The Religion of China.*

The methodological schizophrenia of institutional reasoning on the one hand and arguments based on the causal efficacy of mentality and values on the other—presented together in a single text—is especially clear in *The Religion of China* because in it Weber develops a negative case of why modern capitalism did not develop in the Chinese empire. Weber writes that 'bourgeois industrial capitalism might have developed from the petty capitalist beginnings' in China but for a number of reasons 'mostly related to the structure of the state' it was prevented from doing so (Weber 1964: 100). After setting out the details of this position Weber changes direction and argues instead that it was the absence of an appropriate religious tradition that prevented the advent of industrial capitalism in China.

In addition to recognizing the problematic dualism of the unreconciled institutional and religious arguments in *The Religion of China*, two further remarks are called for, one relating to the problematic nature of Weber's institutional argument and the other to a certain coarsening of the religious argument as it is presented in *The Religion of China*, against the standard of *The Protestant Ethic*. First, Weber's discussion of Chinese institutions is conducted in a largely historical narrative that is source to the construction of a number of important ideal-type conceptualizations, especially concerning variant bureaucratic and state forms. But as a number of commentators have shown (Collins 1990: 58–73; Creel 1977; Faure 2013; Hamilton 1984; van der Sprenkel 1965; Yang 1964), Weber's historical account is seriously flawed, partly because of the limitations of the sources on which he drew but also because of some of his own assumptions. Some of the relevant problems with Weber's institutional argument will be explored here, but before those matters are dealt with, it can be noted how the argument concerning the religious element in the development of modern capitalism is significantly different in *The Religion of China* from the presentation in *The Protestant Ethic and the Spirit of Capitalism*.

THE RELIGIOUS ARGUMENT SIMPLEX

The continuity of Weber's approach is in the endeavor, in his discussion of the consequences of Confucianism, to explore 'the influence of certain religious ideas', as he says in *The Protestant Ethic and the Spirit of Capitalism*, 'on the development of an economic spirit' (Weber 1991: 27). In the *Protestant Ethic*, Weber not only distinguishes but separates the ethos of capitalism from the economic system of capitalism. This is not simply in the fact that the historically novel ethic, of earning money 'purely as an end in itself' conjoined with 'the strict avoidance of all spontaneous enjoyment of life' (Weber 1991: 53), may be 'present before the capitalistic order' (Weber 1991: 55). More to the point, in *The Protestant Ethic and the Spirit of Capitalism*, Weber not only regards the advent of the capitalistic ethic as an unintended consequence of the Protestant Reformation (Weber 1991: 90), but he, at the same time, insists that he has 'no intention whatever of maintaining such a foolish and doctrinaire thesis as that the spirit of capitalism … could only have arisen as the result of certain effects of the Reformation, or even that capitalism as a system is a creation of the Reformation' (Weber 1991: 91). Yet he seems to abandon this qualification in *The Religion of China* in the detail of his claims that it is 'the lack of a particular mentality' which has 'handicapped' the emergence of 'rational entrepreneurial capitalism' in China (Weber 1964: 104). Indeed, the last chapter of his work is a finely argued and entirely tendentious demonstration that Confucianism is not identical with European reform religions. Of particular interest in this account is an entirely novel idea that the Puritan ethic goes directly to a capitalistic ethos and that the Christian devout is the capitalist entrepreneur (Weber 1964: 243, 247), a position never entertained in *The Protestant Ethic and the Spirit of Capitalism*.

In his original account of the elective affinity of Calvinist asceticism and capitalist entrepreneurial motivation, Weber links the two through the historical development of the practice of 'calling' or 'vocation' associated with this-worldly or mundane commitments and engagements. He says that a person's calling is in their 'fulfilment of the obligations imposed upon [them] by [their] position in the world' and that this 'valuation of the fulfilment of duty in worldly affairs [is] the highest form which the moral activity of the individual could assume' (Weber 1991: 80). In the *Protestant Ethic*, Weber indicates that this sense of a calling operates differentially for the Calvinist ascetic than it does for the capitalistic entrepreneur (Weber 1991: 118–19, 69), and elsewhere, in the vocation lectures (Weber 1970a, b), he applies the notion of calling without a prior religious dedication to vocation, both scientific and political (see Barbalet 2008: 46–74). The point to be made here is that in the *Protestant Ethic*, the religious element is in the historical construction of a representation of self as engaged in a vocation and the capitalistic element is an adaptation of this form to money-making. There is no supposition of identity between the religious ethic and the capitalist ethos except in that each of them assumes the form of a mode of self-control in which impulses are overcome and firmly held this-worldly convictions are realized through a particular 'clarity of vision and ability to act' (Weber 1991: 69). There is a further element of the argument in the *Protestant Ethic* that is absent from *The Religion of China*.

The link, between the Calvinist this-worldly religious calling and the capitalistic ethos, that Weber postulates in *The Protestant Ethic and the Spirit of Capitalism* as arising from an historical accident, he says has no continuing role in the development and operation of capitalist economies. Weber (1991: 70) writes that in a society dominated by ongoing capitalist activities any 'relationship between religious beliefs and conduct is generally absent, and where it exists ... it tends to be of the negative sort'. He goes on to add that the 'devotion to the calling of money making' which underpins the spirit of capitalism 'no longer needs the support of any religious forces' and that any 'attempts of religion to influence economic life' are experienced as 'unjustified interference' (Weber 1991: 72). Weber's understanding in 1905, when the *Protestant Ethic* first appeared, is that 'the capitalism of to-day, which has come to dominate economic life, educates and selects the economic subjects which it needs', and in doing so, it draws 'on a way of life common to whole groups of men [and women]' (Weber 1991: 55). But less than a decade later, Weber shifts his views about the moral capacity of those imbued with the capitalist ethos to remain true to the requirements of upstanding conduct he ascribes as necessary for the capitalist system.

In *The Religion of China*, Weber spells out the 'indispensable ethical qualities of the modern capitalist entrepreneur' (Weber 1964: 247) in a manner that places the religious component firmly within the economic sphere in a manner at odds with the treatment in the *Protestant Ethic*. The relevant ethical qualities are described as including a 'radical concentration on God-ordained purposes' (Weber 1964: 247). In the context this is required for and supports 'a horror of illegal, political, colonial, booty, and monopoly types of capitalism … as against the sober, strictly legal and the harnessed rational energy of routine enterprise' (Weber 1964: 247). In this way, Weber draws a very clear line between the Chinese merchant and manufacturing class of his day and the incipient capitalists of seventeenth-century Protestant Europe. In the *General Economic History*, originally given as lectures in 1917, Weber provides a similar assessment of require-ments for capitalism. Weber says that the development of the concept of calling gave to the 'modern entrepreneur' an ability to provide to his workers who were subject to 'ecclesiastical discipline', by virtue of his employing them, 'the prospect of eternal salvation' (Weber 1981: 367–68). Here is an acknowledgement that while the religious element did not nec-essarily operate for the capitalist, the effectiveness of his 'ruthless exploita-tion' of workers he employed was facilitated by their faithful devotion. But Weber's formulation is ironic, pointing to a religiously informed life 'inconceivable to us now, [which] represented a reality quite different from any it has today' (Weber 1981: 368). He continues by noting that the historically earlier mark of 'ethical fitness … identified with business honour' was achieved through religious acceptance within Protestant communities (Weber 1981: 368). All of this is now eclipsed in the most unfortunate manner, according to Weber: 'Ascetic religiosity has been dis-placed by a pessimistic though by no means ascetic view of the world … [in which] private vices may under certain conditions be for the good of the public' (Weber 1981: 369). Weber concludes the *General Economic History* with a pessimism about capitalism which brings together a now-impossible requirement of a conjunction of religion and economics for which the *Protestant Ethic* has little space:

> Economic ethics arose against the background of the ascetic ideal; now it has been stripped of its religious import. It was possible for the working class to accept its lot as long as the promise of eternal happiness could be held out to it. When this consolation fell away it was inevitable that those strains and stresses should appear in economic society which since have grown so rapidly. (Weber 1981: 369)

Through exposure to a war economy, with its felonious opportunities of profiteering and racketeering for capital and its infelicitous consequences for labor, Weber effectively revises the schema of differential forms of 'vocation' or 'calling', religious and economic, set out in the *Protestant Ethic*. In the *General Economic History*, and slightly earlier in *The Religion of China*, he uncomfortably melds together religious ascetic and capitalist entrepreneur, at least in his narrative of everyday participation if not in his general ideal type of the conditions necessary for modern capitalism (Weber 1981: 276–78), to which we shall soon return. It should be noted that *The Religion of China*, published during the war in 1915, was written before the war in 1913. The remerging of religious and economic orientation in Weber's account of capitalism in his discussion of China does not therefore come out of a war consciousness but an imperial consciousness of German enterprise in Shandong, China, as discussed earlier.

Confucianism Redux

In the 'Confucianism and Puritanism' chapter of *The Religion of China*, Weber requires a more or less direct Protestant religious contribution to capitalism that Confucianism is necessarily unable to provide. This is a departure from the methodology of the *Protestant Ethic*, although not from the moralizing pragmatics of the *General Economic History*, indicated earlier, in failing to articulate a differentiation in the form and impetus of distinct callings, religious and economic, each of which corresponds to a respectively distinct 'value sphere'. This latter consideration is a matter which Weber discusses with nuanced sensitivity elsewhere (Weber 1970a: 147). The conflation of religious and economic engagements in *The*

Religion of China may be a reflection of Weber's broader preoccupations brought by awareness of European imperial incursion in China and, later, experience of wartime profiteering, as suggested earlier, but in any event it reduces the value of his discussion here for understanding the prospects of a Chinese capitalism. Even more apparent is the distortion of his characterization of Confucian ethics. Weber's purpose in attempting to demonstrate the impossibility of capitalism under conditions of Confucian ethical norms is to show the veracity of his account of Western capitalism and its historical uniqueness in terms of the singular European Reformation from the late sixteenth century. But his characterization of Confucianism in this account is a distortion and it reveals the need for appreciating not the ethical but the institutional context, which Weber had earlier attempted to portray in the work but then abandoned.

In addition to Weber's misleading representation of Confucian ethics, the discussion here shall briefly treat the irrelevance of those ethics for consideration of the prospects of capitalism in China. Weber (1964: 235) characterizes Confucianism as imbibing only 'adjustment' to the 'conditions of the "world"' so that any person under its influence 'does not constitute a systematic unity but rather a complex of useful and particular traits'. He goes on to say that the Confucian way of life:

> ...could not allow a man an inward aspiration toward a 'unified personality' ... [because] life remained a series of occurrences. It did not become a whole placed methodically under a transcendental goal. (Weber 1964: 235)

In his pacific acquiescence the Confucian is merely an outcome of circumstances and without any integrity of his own. This is a theme elaborated by Weber in his chapter on 'The Confucian Life Orientation' in which it is stated that 'Confucianism means adjustment to the world' (Weber 1964: 152), that 'equilibrium of the soul should and could be attained only if man fitted himself into the internally harmonious cosmos' (Weber 1964: 153), and that 'Confucianism was only interested in affairs of this world such as it happened to be' (Weber 1964: 155). All of this, the quiescence and malleability of the Confucian self, is, according to Weber, socially realized in Confucius' dictum that 'I bow to the majority' (Weber 1964: 163). The difficulty with this assessment is that it cannot be substantiated and it is not even clear that Weber himself fully believes it to be credible.

Beginning with the last quotation in the above paragraph, Weber infers an injunction to 'bow to the majority' from a passage from Confucius which he quotes as 'Where we are three I find my master' (Weber 1964: 163). There is no attribution here, but this text is close to *Analects* Book 7 Chap. 21 in the Legge translation that Weber draws upon, which reads:

> The Master said, 'When I walk along with two others, they may serve me as my teachers. I will select their good qualities and follow them, and their bad qualities and avoid them. (Legge 1971: 202)

Weber's bowdlerization of Confucius' statement and meaning may serve his purpose in characterizing Confucianism as pragmatically unprincipled but the text itself reveals a stable commitment which assumes a firm discernment, uninfluenced by the flow of events, between appropriate and inappropriate behavior. Learning from others, as Confucius puts it, is decidedly not a matter of passively following the crowd, as Weber would have it. This removes support from the image of the Confucian as a vacillating uncentered individual without an inner core. Indeed, Weber does acknowledge that there are 'all sorts of particularized affinities to be found between Confucianism and the sober rationalism of Puritanism' (Weber 1964: 161).

When considering the 'Central Concept of Propriety' in Confucianism Weber notices the 'self-control, self-observation and reserve' of the Confucian who 'thought of prudently mastering the opportunities of this world through self-control' (Weber 1964: 156). This brief description indicates an orientation parallel to the idea of a calling in Protestantism that Weber so clearly elaborates in the *Protestant Ethic*. But in *The Religion of China* the self-control of the Confucian is sharply contrasted with that of the Puritan (Weber 1964: 236–48). Weber's discussion here is turgid, passionate, and frankly loaded against the possibility of a Chinese capitalism because Confucianism is without the theologically driven angst of the Puritan who in his God-given despair must change the world capitalistically, according to Weber, while the Confucian can only adjust to it. In this contrast 'Nothing conflicted more with the Confucian ideal of gentility than the idea of a "vocation"' (Weber 1964: 248). Weber achieves this convenient conclusion by making the Puritan ascetic directly into a capitalist entrepreneur, a move that is not part of the original argument in the *Protestant Ethic* (Weber 1991: 68–71) and requires historical conjuring. At the same time he excludes the possibility of the Confucian construction of calling or 'vocation' itself being transposed from an ethical or bureaucratic practice to a commercial practice involving different sets of people and purposes with a consequent rationalization of the secondary non-Confucian arena, much as he had argued in the *Protestant Ethic* when pursuing the 'influence of certain religious ideas on the development of an economic spirit' (Weber 1991: 27). But in *The Religion of China* Weber's articulation of a direct transformation of a community of worshipers into a class of capitalist entrepreneurs collapses the incremental iteration and social relocation of calling treated in *The Protestant Ethic and the Spirit of Capitalism*, a development that actually occurs in China, unnoticed by him.

Weber's denial of a Confucian calling analogous to a Protestant calling is supported by his idea that only the Puritan but not the Confucian experiences tension with the world. But this claim results not only from a lapse of investigation on Weber's part but also of imagination. Any system of thought that postulates a condition from which a present experience departs, to its detriment, generates a type of tension analogous to the Puritan experiences of the difference between the heavenly and earthly kingdoms (Yang 1964: xxxvii). Confucius' inspiration and ethic is premised on such a difference between an ideal state of being, from which present conditions have departed. Weber's insistence on a Puritan value-tension in the generation of a capitalist spirit is problematic on a number of levels, however. First, the argument itself is unique to Weber; it does not correspond with reported experiences of early Calvinists nor with the studies Weber drew upon in constructing his argument (Barbalet 2008: 54–56). Second, alternative accounts of the development of an originating capitalistic entrepreneurial spirit do not rely on a value-tension of the type Weber describes but on opportunities for profit-making through investment of time, effort, and capital and associated practices of deferred gratification and community affirmation of profit-making as an esteemed activity (Barbalet 2008: 118–24). In this context a cognitive and affective sensitivity to changing circumstances and how to cope with them, an inclination to find new opportunities for money-making where others see only constraints and declining present fortunes, can be construed as the basis of the entrepreneurial ethos underlying the spirit of capitalism (Schumpeter 2000, 2008).

It is of particular interest that Weber reports entrepreneurial inclinations in China (1964: 183, 188, 205) among traders, merchants, and the propertied classes (1964: 186, 204, 224). But the drive for gain he notes in these and similar sources is dismissed as inefficacious because by hypothesis they have a pedigree irrelevant for entrepreneurship in being 'contemplative' rather than 'asceticist' (1960: 337, 1964: 188, 243). In these complaints Weber confuses the underlying drive for profit with the structure of the economy within which it operates. He had already explained the absence in Imperial China of modern industrial capitalism in institutional terms. To dismiss Chinese imperatives to profit-making as devoid of the ethos of capitalism because they were not based on the internal tensions he believed he had located in early modern European Protestantism is unnecessary.

While Weber does not entertain the possibility and his approach in *The Religion of China* precludes it, the self-discipline of the Confucian calling was in fact applied by Chinese merchants during the Qing dynasty (1644–1912). At this time a number of handbooks were published and circulated which were based on Confucian principles but directed to the guidance of merchants in pursuit of their pecuniary careers. In drawing on Confucian self-cultivation practices, merchants advanced their commercial interests against their spontaneous impulses and distractions from the purposes of profit-making. This is similar to the way in which the development of calling among Calvinists and Puritans was borrowed by early entrepreneurs and applied not to congregational rectitude but to enterprise. Whereas Calvinist doctrine and practice 'led to a fearful demand for economic restriction (and political control) rather than the entrepreneurial activity as Weber has described it' (Walzer 1976: 304), the self-restraint and vocational single-mindedness associated with it enhanced pursuit of profit-making when applied to market engagements. Similarly, while Confucian values could not consistently legitimize the profit motive and market activities (Brook 1997: 33–38), the Confucian self-cultivation practices and sense of calling inculcated by them were effectively applied by businessmen who operated outside the institutional range of the Confucian literati (Lufrano 1997).

The merchant handbooks of Qing China effectively transferred the traditional Confucian practices of self-cultivation from the institutions of filial piety and bureaucratic administration to the extraneous non-Confucian practices of the market. The 'inner mental attentiveness' (*jing*) central to Confucian self-cultivation in this new context functioned to firstly dispel or at least manage the external distractions which might lead 'honourable merchants' to errors of judgment in business and, secondly, to renounce the appeals of 'gambling, whoring and opium smoking' to which 'petty merchants were particularly attracted' (Lufrano 1997: 64). The importance of self-control in suppressing such 'natural' impulses in promoting money-making is explicit in these manuals (Lufrano 1997: 63–67). The question of capitalistic interest formation in Chinese society will be returned to in Chap. 5.

INSTITUTIONS WITH CHINESE CHARACTERISTICS

The failure of the Chinese economy at this time to move from a merchant to a modern industrial form cannot be attributed to the absence of a sense of self-control and the purpose of money-making associated with Weber's idea of calling. Nor can the predominance of Confucian values be entirely held responsible. While it is possible to show that such values existed, it is more difficult to specify how they may inhibit the activities of those who not only fail to share them but also their exponents. As Weber (1964: 85–86) shows, imperial office permitted the accumulation of varying amounts of wealth. Those officials without mercantile background typically entrusted their accumulated funds to merchants who would manage their investments for them (Elvin 1973: 291–92). At the same time, land-holding families and, especially after the seventeenth century, merchant families routinely financed an able son's study for the imperial examination. In this sense, then, any 'sharp dichotomy between "officials" and "merchants"', according to Elvin (1973: 292), 'is therefore misleading'. Indeed, value impermissibility is itself likely to be either irrelevant for economic activity or, if effective, will counter-intuitively have a positive rather than an inhibitory effect.

In discussing the negative values regarding enterprise of the Russian aristocracy, which are in many ways similar to those of Chinese mandarins, the economic historian Alexander Gershenkron (1962) shows that the prevailing pre-industrial value system did not prevent industrialization and that the research question might be focused not on how values inhibit entrepreneurial activity but on the propensity of values to change and in response to what factors they may do so (Gershenkron 1962: 68). Gershenkron (1962: 68–69) regards entrepreneurs as 'men who by definition … may not be orientated in their action by any discernible set of values' who experience 'a far-reaching divorce between their actions and the general value system to which they may still adhere'. In this vein, it should be remembered, according to Schumpeter (2008: 190), that anti-capitalist values were rampant during the period of capitalist emergence in Europe, a point he incidentally directs against Weber's *Protestant Ethic* argument and its underlying ideal-type methodology (Schumpeter 2008: 191).

It is typical of Weber's ambiguity, concerning what he sees as the factors responsible for the failure of China to experience modern industrial capitalism, that he vacillates between Chinese mentality and Chinese institutions as the determining factors. After treating at length Confucian orthodoxy as the basis of China's economic traditionalism, he concludes the second part of *The Religion of China* with an apparently definitive statement that the Confucian 'mentality' was 'strongly counteractive to capitalist development' because of its 'autonomous laws' (Weber 1964: 249). But immediately preceding this final sentence of the work Weber says that the mentality which can be characterized by these 'autonomous laws' is in fact 'deeply co-determined by political and economic destinies'. This ambiguity parallels his conclusion of the first part of the book in which it is claimed: 'Rational entrepreneurial capitalism … has been handicapped' in China 'by the lack of a particular mentality' but also 'by the lack of a formally guaranteed law, a rational administration and judiciary, and by the ramifications of a system of prebends' (Weber 1964: 104). Given that '[b]oth economic and intellectual factors were at work' (Weber 1964: 55), it is important to consider what Weber has to say about the former as well as the latter.

The Religion of China opens with a discussion of the history of money in China, moves on to an account of the Chinese city, and then provides an important discussion of the development of the organization of the imperial state and the characteristically Chinese bureaucracy, followed by a treatment of the institutions and organization of rural society, which is then followed by a discussion of the sib or patrilineal kinship clan that concludes the first part of the book. The first chapter of the second part is also occupied with a consideration of a particularly Chinese institution, the literati. This extensive treatment of institutions attempts to be comparative insofar as Weber interposes the account of Chinese elements with analogous and contrasting cases drawn from the histories of European and ancient civilizations. Weber's account of Chinese institutions has given rise to reflection and criticism of variable illumination and intensity. It is not possible here to review Weber's complete argument and the discussion it has provoked. The following brief account will be confined to his treatment of the sib (although in what follows, the term 'clan' will be used) and its relationship to the prospects of capitalist development. This is because Weber is clearly adamant that the clan is an undisputed inhibitor of capitalist organization, and yet, it is implicated in the capitalistic revolution that has gripped China since the 1980s.

Weber points out that kinship, through the clan organization, is the source of not only personalized business dealings, but local or village administration and civic regulation involving the maintenance of ceremonies, education, credit provision, and welfare as well as protection and the maintenance of order. The clan as a corporate entity owned property, the profit from which was distributed to household heads. Weber says that the form of property held by the clan was confined to landed property as the clan was too irrational to engage in capital investment (Weber 1964: 89, 103). Indeed, Weber's assessment of the clan, and the business of Chinese individuals in general, is that the solidarity of relations through kinship meant that there was 'no rational depersonalization of business' so that for 'the economic mentality, the personalist principle was … a barrier to impersonal rationalization' (Weber 1964: 85, 236). To this general assessment, Weber provides a series of particular instances. Because the clan supported household self-sufficiency, Weber (1964: 90) says, it was responsible for 'delimiting market developments'. Through kinship relations the clan supported its members against discrimination and thus 'thwarted' labor discipline characteristic of 'modern large enterprise' and the 'free market selection of labour' associated with it (Weber 1964: 95, see also 97). Finally, the kinship clan was inherently opposed to innovation, and fiscal innovation, in particular, 'met with sharp resistance' (Weber 1964: 95–96).

Historical research since Weber's time has revised many of his empirical claims. Two points in particular relate to those concerning market inhibition and fiscal innovation. The full extent of market development in China was not appreciated by Weber's sources. It is now known that China experienced significant market generated growth from the late Song dynasty (960–1279) which lasted until the beginning of the nineteenth century (Elvin 1973; Pomeranz 2000). Indeed, Elvin provides much evidence concerning the reach of markets in rural China. He writes that '[i]ncreased contact with the market made the Chinese peasantry into a class of adaptable, rational, profit-orientated, petty-entrepreneurs' and that 'in the course of the seventeenth century the number of market towns … began to multiply at a rate exceeding that of the population increase' (Elvin 1973: 167, 268). It is by no means clear, therefore, that the lineage clan delimited market developments. Indeed, the clan operated as a market actor and, against the assessment Weber provides and his sources urged, there is evidence that innovative financial devises were developed by clan managers. Lineage trusts operated from the beginning of the seventeenth century with an express purpose 'to amass and incorporate business property and protect it from the predations of household division' (Zelin 2009: 627).

The trust was a device for the rational protection of investment folios based on the lineage organization and which overcame its fiscal limitations:

While lineage trusts themselves remained closed corporations whose membership was determined by birth, trusts behaved like individuals in the market place, buying and selling salt manufacturing shares and developing portfolios that included both wholly owned family firms and shares in a variety of non-kin ventures ... by the Qing [dynasty], the institution of the lineage trust ... had become a popular device for the protection of investable assets. By creating a trust a successful merchant could keep his company intact, allowing each of his sons to succeed not to bits and pieces of the firm, but to equal shares in an undivided pool of assets that could likewise be passed on to their heirs. (Zelin 2009: 627)

Thus, the problem of the clan, noted by Weber (1964: 82–83), of the dissipation of capital stock through a 'democratic' inheritance regime, was overcome by a rational innovation unnoticed by his sources.

But not only is there a factual problem with Weber's account of Chinese kinship institutions, his interpretation of the family as an inherently traditional form of organization interferes with his appreciation of its role in enhancing economic prospects, not only Chinese. The idea, forcefully stated in *The Religion of China*, that through kinship obligation the family is a source of traditional constraint that inhibits the capitalist ethos of profit-making for its own sake can also be found in *The Protestant Ethic and the Spirit of Capitalism* when Weber writes that Protestant calling generates emotional detachment and depersonalizes family relations, and where he presents early modern European entrepreneurs as individuals free of family ties and traditional obligations (Weber 1991: 70, 107–8; see Barbalet 2008: 216–18). And yet the unit of enterprise and the major proximate sources of entrepreneurial attainment in early modern Europe was not the individual entrepreneur free of family responsibility and commitment, but individuals who were economically enriched by kinship networks and marital alliances who thereby had immediate access to reputation, credit, and uniquely reliable associates (Grassby 2000), a pattern of familial capitalism that has a continuing history (Church 1993; La Porta et al. 1999; Zeitlin 1974).

Weber excludes consideration of these possibilities indicated in the previous paragraph by hypothesis. In *The Religion of China*, he writes that 'the ascetic sects of Protestantism ... established the superior community of faith and a common ethical way of life in opposition to the community of blood, even in a large extent in opposition to the family' (Weber 1964: 237). It is correct to note that while the clan was 'completely preserved' in China, 'in the occidental Middle Ages it was practically extinct' (Weber 1964: 86). But it was the Catholic Church not the Protestant faith that first discouraged adoption, concubinage, marriages without the woman's consent and similar practices that sustain kinship organization so that by the ninth century in Europe, the nuclear family predominated over the joint or extended family (Greif and Tabellini 2010: 137). Weber's misapprehension of the role of the family in capitalist prospects and his treatment of the particularism of kinship as necessarily opposed to rationality of enterprise has a further, methodological dimension. This is his conflation of formalism and rationalization that derives from his application of the ideal type form.

In an important discussion in which the economically rational contribution of lineage to present-day Chinese capitalist development is outlined, sociologist Yusheng Peng (2005) shows that Weber erroneously assumes that formalism necessarily underwrites rationalism and that, in fact, informal and personalist factors may contribute to rational economic activities (Peng 2005: 347–49). Clan organization or kinship lineage can function to rationalize and protect property rights, to facilitate transactions, and reduce transaction costs and to provide network benefits, including bridging ties (Peng 2005: 338–39). The general point, that Weber's insistence that the 'personalist principle was ... a barrier to impersonal rationalization' (Weber 1964: 236), has met widespread criticism in the context of his theory of organization. Philip Selznick's pioneering observation that 'individuals have a propensity to resist depersonalization, to spill over the boundaries of their segmentary roles, to participate as *wholes*' led him to appreciate the interplay of 'informal associations' and 'the formal system' through 'unwritten laws' and the corollary that to 'recognize the sociological relevance of formal structures is not, however, to have constructed a theory of organization' (Selznick 1948: 26–28). Organization theorists have continued to point to the non-contradictory and possibly facilitating relations between informal and rational organizational elements, against Weber's insistence on the necessary and exclusive association of only formal and rational elements.

CONCLUSION

This is not the place to present an argument concerning the development of modern capitalism in China since the post-Mao reforms of the 1980s, led by Deng Xiaoping. Consideration of the capitalist economy in China, developed over the past 30-odd years, and how it relates to Weber's understanding of capitalism will be treated in the final chapter. But in concluding the present chapter, it is appropriate to ask about the consistency of Weber's argument concerning the impossibility of the development of a native capitalism in China.

In *The Religion of China*, Weber's argument is directed to the question of why modern capitalism, that is to say industrial capitalism, did not emerge in China. His consideration of the supposed inability of Confucianism to provide an ethic supportive of a capitalist ethos does not properly address this question but relates rather to market or commercial capitalism, which Weber acknowledges in different ways did indeed operate in Imperial China. The advent of industrial capitalism since the 1980s, because it operates with 'personalist' social forms both familial and political that Weber dismissed as irrational and therefore non-capitalistic, cannot satisfy Weber's claim that the Chinese 'would be quite capable ... of assimilating capitalism which has technically and economically been fully developed in the modern cultural area' (Weber 1964: 248). The question of the absence of modern industrialization in Imperial China requires consideration of the conditions for application of advanced technology to production. Historian Mark Elvin (1973: 298–99) shows that throughout the Ming and Qing dynasties, resourcefulness associated with innovation was present and entrepreneurship was well developed, but there was an absence of technologically-driven production in late Imperial China for the following reason:

> ...a rational strategy for peasant and merchant alike tended in the direction not so much of labour-saving machinery as of economizing on resources and fixed capital...This situation might be described as a 'high-level equilibrium trap'. In the context of a civilization with a strong sense of economic rationality, with an appreciation of invention ... it is probably a sufficient explanation of the retardation of technological advance. (Elvin 1973: 314–15)

It can be noted here that the argument concerning a 'high-level equilibrium trap' has been critically appraised as misdirected, that it uses 'Western models of capitalism to characterize China's late imperial economy' (Hamilton 2006: 99). Hamilton (2006: 100–1) does not reject the fact of a devolution in production technology, however, but wishes to show that an emphasis on whether the Imperial Chinese economy was tending to capitalism or not ignores the organizational features of that economy and the 'evolution of the system over the past 500 years' (Hamilton 2006: 121). Hamilton's focus on the importance of commerce in the organization of China's late imperial economy is salutary and is intended to sidestep both the issue raised by Weber regarding why a native capitalism did not emerge in China and therefore also Elvin's response to Weber.

The economic decline of China in the late Qing was no doubt due to institutional factors as well as others that Weber discusses, especially those connected with government capacities. The weakness of the Qing court, in dealing with foreign debt especially following the Opium Wars of the mid-nineteenth century and China's defeat by Japan in 1895, reflected only the most visible limitation of the Chinese regime. Population surplus, which rendered labor-saving innovation and therefore industrialization unnecessary, according to Elvin, eventually led to a disruption of both cultivation and commerce. The autonomy of provincial administration seriously undermined the central government's ability to implement any reforms it initiated (see Weber 1964: 47–50). The collapse of the last imperial dynasty with the 1911 Republican revolution bequeathed these institutional problems to its successors (Bergère 1984). From the middle of the twentieth century, the command economy and population control devised by the Communist Party sufficiently overcame these and associated problems to permit capitalist development from the 1980s. In this sense Weber's dismissal of the prospects of Chinese capitalism was simply premature. That part of Weber's argument which is useful in understanding the institutional limitations on the historic trajectory of modern capitalist development in China is typically ignored or underemphasized by his readers. Weber's argument concerning the inability of the Chinese mentality to develop a capitalistic orientation, when it is not positively misleading, seems to offer little for an understanding of China's path to the 1980s. But then, the purpose of Weber's analysis in *The Religion of China* is to demonstrate the correctness of his arguments concerning the uniqueness of the West and the supposed veracity of his claims concerning the singular power of Protestant asceticism to found modern capitalism. In this endeavor, Imperial China is simply drawn upon as a negative case. Weber's image of China as backward and dominated by traditional or non-rational thought systems is consistent with the missionary and German imperialist mentality discussed at the beginning of this chapter, even though it goes beyond them as an endeavor to provide support for his own argument concerning the cultural basis of the singular origins of modern capitalism in Europe.

REFERENCES

Aldenhoff, Rita. 2010. 'Max Weber and the Evangelical-Social Congress'. Pp. 193–202 in *Max Weber and his Contemporaries*, edited by Wolfgang J. Mommsen and Jürgen Osterhammel. London: Routledge.

Balazs, Etienne. 1966. *Chinese Civilization and Bureaucracy*. New Haven: Yale University Press.

Barbalet, Jack. 2008. *Weber, Passion and Profits: 'The Protestant Ethic and the Spirit of Capitalism' in Context*. Cambridge: Cambridge University Press.

Bergère, Marie-Claire. 1984. 'On the Historical Origins of Chinese Underdevelopment'. *Theory and Society*. 13(3): 327–37.

Bickers, Robert A. and Tiedemann, R. G. (eds). 2007. *The Boxers, China, and the World*. Lanham: Rowman & Littlefield.

Brook, Timothy. 1997. 'Profit and Righteousness in Chinese Economic Culture'. Pp. 27–44 in *Culture and Economy: The Shaping of Capitalism in Eastern Asia*, edited by Timothy Brook and Hy V. Luong. Ann Arbor: University of Michigan Press.

Bush, Christopher. 2010. *Ideographic Modernism: China, Writing, Media*. Oxford: Oxford University Press.

Buss, Andreas E. 1985. *Max Weber and Asia: Contributions to the Sociology of Development*. Cologne: Arnold-Bergsträsser-Institut. Materialien Zu Entwicklung und Politik.

Ching, Julia and Oxtoby, Willard G. (eds). 1992. *Moral Enlightenment: Leibniz and Wolff on China*. Nettetal: Steyler Verlag.

Church, Roy. 1993. 'The Family Firm in Industrial Capitalism: International Perspectives on Hypothesis and History'. *Business History*. 35 (4): 17–43.

Cohen, Paul A. 1998. *History in Three Keys: The Boxers as Event, Experience, and Myth*. New York: Columbia University Press.

Collins, Randall. 1990. *Weberian Sociological Theory*. Cambridge: Cambridge University Press.

Creel, Herrlee G. 1977. 'The Beginnings of Bureaucracy in China: The Origin of the *Hsien*'. Pp. 121–59 in his *What is Taoism? And Other Studies in Chinese Cultural History*. Chicago: University of Chicago Press.

de Groot, Jan Jakob Marie. 1910. *The Religion of the Chinese*. New York: Macmillan.

Elvin, Mark. 1973. *The Patterns of the Chinese Past*. Stanford, CA.: Stanford University Press.

Faber, Ernst. 1877. *Eine Staatslehre auf ethischer Grundlage oder Lehrbegriff des chinesischen Philosophen Mencius. Aus dem Urtexte übersetzt, in systematische Ordnung gebracht und mit Anmerkungen und Einleitungen versehen*. Elberfeld: Friderichs.

Faber, Ernst. 1897. *China in the Light of History*. Shanghai: American Presbyterian Mission Press.

Faure, David. 2013. 'Commercial Institutions and Practices in Imperial China as Seen by Weber and in Terms of More Recent Research'. *Taiwan Journal of East Asian Studies*. 10(2): 71–98.

Findley, Ronald and O'Rourke, Kevin H. 2007. *Power and Plenty: Trade, War and the World Economy in the Second Millennium*. Princeton: Princeton University Press.

Gabelentz, Georg von der. 1888. *Confucius und seine Lehre*. Leipzig: F.A. Brockhaus.

Gall, Lothar, Feldman, Gerald D., James, Harold, Holtfrerich, Carl-Ludwig, Büschgen, Hans E. 1995. *The Deutsche Bank, 1870–1995*. London: Weidenfeld and Nicolson.

Gernet, Jacques. 1995. *Buddhism in Chinese Society: An Economic History from the Fifth to the Tenth Centuries*. New York: Columbia University Press.

Gernet, Jacques. 1996. *A History of Chinese Civilization*. Cambridge: Cambridge University Press.

Gershenkron, Alexander. 1962. 'Social Attitudes, Entrepreneurship, and Economic Development'. Pp. 52–71 in his *Economic Backwardness in Historical Perspective*. Cambridge, MA: Harvard University Press.

Giddens, Anthony. 2011. *Capitalism and Modern Social Theory*. Cambridge: Cambridge University Press.

Gosetti-Ferencei, Jennifer Anna. 2011. *Exotic Spaces in German Modernism*. Oxford: Oxford University Press.

Gottschall, Terrell D. 2003. *By Order of the Kaiser: Otto von Diederichs and the Rise of the Imperial German Navy, 1865–1902*. Annapolis, MD: Naval Institute Press.

Grassby, Richard. 2000. *Kinship and Capitalism: Marriage, Family and Business in the English-Speaking World, 1580–1740*. Cambridge: Cambridge University Press.

Greif, Avner and Tabellini, Guido. 2010. 'Cultural and Institutional Bifurcation: China and Europe Compared'. *American Economic Review*. 100(2): 135–40.

Hamilton, Gary G. 1984. 'Patriarchalism in Imperial China and Western Europe: A Revision of Weber's Sociology of Domination'. *Theory and Society*. 13(3): 393–425.

Hamilton, Gary G. 2006. 'The Importance of Commerce in the Organization of China's Late Imperial Economy'. Pp. 93–126 in his *Commerce and Capitalism in Chinese Societies*. London: Routledge.

Hart, Henry H. 1942. *Venetian Adventurer: Being an Account of the Life and Times and of the Book of Messer Marco Polo*. Stanford: Stanford University Press.

Hegel, Georg Wilhelm Friedrich. 1892. *Lectures on the History of Philosophy*, Volume 1, translated by E.S. Haldane. London: Kegan Paul, Trench and Trüber.

Huang, Su-Jen. 1994. 'Max Weber's *The Religion of China*: An Interpretation'. *Journal of the History of the Behavioral Sciences*. 30(1): 3–18.

Hudson, G.F. 1961. *Europe and China: A Survey of their Relations from the Earliest Times to 1800*. Boston: Beacon Press.

Jensen, Lionel. 1997. *Manufacturing Confucianism: Chinese Traditions and Universal Civilization*. Durham, NC: Duke University Press.

Jones, David Martin. 2001. *The Image of China in Western Social and Political Thought*. London: Palgrave.

Kalberg, Stephen. 2012. *Max Weber's Comparative-Historical Sociology Today: Major Themes, Modes of Causal Analysis, and Applications*. London: Ashgate.

Kern, Martin. 1998. 'The Emigration of German Sinologists 1933–1945: Notes on the History and Historiography of Chinese Studies'. *Journal of the American Oriental Society*. 118(4): 507–29.

La Porta, Rafael, Lopez-de-Silanes, Florencio and Shleifer, Andrei. 1999. 'Corporate Ownership around the World'. *Journal of Finance*. 54 (2): 471–517.

Latourette, Kenneth Scott. 2009. *A History of Christian Missions in China*. Piscataway, NJ: Gorgias Press.

Legge, James. 1877. *Confucianism in Relation to Christianity*. Shanghai: Kelly and Walsh.

Legge, James. 1880. *The Religions of China: Confucianism and Taoism Described and Compared with Christianity*. London: Hodder and Stoughton.

Legge, James. 1971. *Confucius: Confucian Analects, The Great Learning & The Doctrine of the Mean*. New York: Dover Publications.

Leibniz, Gottfried Wilhelm. 1994. *Writings on China*, translated by Daniel Cook and Henry Rosemont, Jr. Chicago: Open Court.

Lufrano, Richard John. 1997. *Honorable Merchants: Commerce and Self-Cultivation in Late Imperial China*. Honolulu: University of Hawai'i Press.

Metzger, Thomas A. 1977. *Escape from Predicament: Neo-Confucianism and China's Evolving Political Culture*. New York: Columbia University Press.

Mommsen, Wolfgang J. 1990. *Max Weber and German Politics 1890–1920*. Chicago: University of Chicago Press.

Müller, Max. 1873. *Introduction to the Science of Religion: Four Lectures Delivered at the Royal Institution with Two Essays on False Analogies, and the Philosophy of Mythology*. London: Longmans, Green, and Company.

Parsons, Talcott. 1968. *The Structure of Social Action. Volume 2*. New York: The Free Press.

Peng, Yusheng. 2005. 'Lineage Networks, Rural Entrepreneurs, and Max Weber'. *Research in the Sociology of Work*. 15: 327–55.

Perkins, Franklin. 2004. *Leibniz and China: A Commerce of Light*. Cambridge: Cambridge University Press.

Pomeranz, Kenneth. 2000. *The Great Divergence: China, Europe, and the Making of the Modern World Economy*. Princeton, NJ: Princeton University Press.

Qi, Xiaoying. 2014. *Globalized Knowledge Flows and Chinese Social Theory*. New York: Routledge.

Reichwein, Adolf. 1968. *China and Europe: Intellectual and Artistic Contacts in the Eighteenth Century*. New York: Barnes and Noble.

Ringer, Fritz. 2004. *Max Weber: An Intellectual Biography*. Chicago: University of Chicago Press.

Roth, Guenther. 2000. 'Global Capitalism and Multi-ethnicity: Max Weber Then and Now'. Pp. 117–30 in *The Cambridge Companion to Max Weber*, edited by Stephen Turner. Cambridge: Cambridge University Press.

Schluchter, Wolfgang. 1989. *Rationalism, Religion and Domination: A Weberian Perspective*. Berkeley: University of California Press.

Schmidt-Glintzer, Helwig and Kolonko, Petra. (eds). 1991. *Max Weber: Die Wirtschaftsethik der Weltreligionen. Konfuzianismus und Taoismus. Schriften 1915–1920*. Tübingen: J.C.B. Mohr.

Schrecker, John E. 1971. *Imperialism and Chinese Nationalism: Germany in Shantung*. Cambridge, MA: Harvard University Press.

Schumpeter, Joseph A. 2000. 'Entrepreneurship as Innovation'. Pp. 51–75 in *Entrepreneurship: A Social Science View*, edited by Richard Swedberg. Oxford: Oxford University Press.

Schumpeter, Joseph A. 2008. 'Capitalism'. Pp. 189–210 in his *Essays: On Entrepreneurs, Innovations, Business Cycles, and the Evolution of Capitalism*, edited by Richard V. Clemence with an Introduction by Richard Swedberg. New Brunswick, NJ: Transaction Books.

Selznick, Philip. 1948. 'Foundations of the Theory of Organization'. *American Sociological Review*. 13(1): 25–35.

Sica, Alan. 2004. *Max Weber and the New Century*. New Brunswick, NJ: Transaction Publishers.

Simms, Brendan, 2007. *Three Victories and a Defeat: The Rise and Fall of the First British Empire*. London: Allen Lane.

Steinmetz, George. 2007. *The Devil's Handwriting: Precoloniality and the German Colonial State in Qingdao, Samoa, and Southwest Africa*. Chicago: University of Chicago Press.

Steinmetz, George. 2012. 'Imperial Entanglements of Sociology and the Problem of Scientific Autonomy in Germany, France and the United States'. Pp. 857–71 in *Transnationale Vergesellschaftingen*, edited by Hans-Georg Soeffner. Berlin: Springer.

Stone, Jon R. 2002. 'Introduction'. Pp. 1–24 in *The Essential Max Müller: On Language, Mythology and Religion*, edited by Jon R. Stone. London: Palgrave Macmillan.

Sunar, Lutfi. 2016. *Marx and Weber on Oriental Societies: In the Shadow of Western Modernity*. London: Routledge.

Swatos, William H. and Kivisto, Peter. 1991. 'Max Weber as "Christian Sociologist"'. *Journal for the Scientific Study of Religion.* 30(4): 347–62.

Turner, Stephen P. and Factor, Regis A. 1984. *Max Weber and the Dispute over Reason and Value: A Study of Philosophy, Ethics and Politics.* London: Routledge and Kegan Paul.

van der Sprenkel, Otto B. 1954. 'Chinese Religion'. *British Journal of Sociology.* 5(4): 272–75.

van der Sprenkel, Otto B. 1965. 'Max Weber on China'. Pp. 198–220 in *Studies in the Philosophy of History: Selected Essays from History and Theory*, edited by George H. Nadel. New York: Harper.

Walzer, Michael. 1976. *The Revolution of the Saints: A Study in the Origins of Radical Politics.* New York: Athenium.

Wang, Ching Dao. 1913. 'Die Staatsidee des Konfuzius und ihre Beziehung zur konstitutionelle Verfassung'. *Mitteilungen des Seminars für Orientalische Sprachen zu Berlin.* 16(1): 1–49.

Weber, Marianne. 1975. *Max Weber: A Biography*, translated by Harry Zohn. New York: John Wiley.

Weber, Max. 1960. *The Religion of India: The Sociology of Hinduism and Buddhism*, translated and edited by Hans H. Gerth and Don Martindale. New York: The Free Press.

Weber, Max. 1964. *The Religion of China: Confucianism and Taoism*, translated and edited by Hans H. Gerth, with an Introduction by C.K. Yang. New York: The Free Press.

Weber, Max. 1970a. 'Science as a Vocation'. Pp. 129–56 in *From Max Weber: Essays in Sociology*, edited by H.H. Gerth and C. Wright Mills. London: Routledge.

Weber, Max. 1970b. 'Politics as a Vocation'. Pp. 77–128 in *From Max Weber: Essays in Sociology*, edited by H.H. Gerth and C. Wright Mills. London: Routledge.

Weber, Max. 1978. *Economy and Society: An Outline of Interpretive Sociology*, edited by Guenther Roth and Claus Wittich. Berkeley: University of California Press.

Weber, Max. 1981. *General Economic History*, translated by Frank Knight with a new Introduction by Ira J. Cohen. New Brunswick, NJ: Transaction Books.

Weber, Max. 1991. *The Protestant Ethic and the Spirit of Capitalism*, translated by Talcott Parsons. London: Harper Collins.

Weber, Max. 2000. 'The Nation State and Economic Policy (Inaugural lecture)'. Pp. 1–28 in *Weber: Political Writings*, edited by Peter Lassman and Ronald Speirs. Cambridge: Cambridge University Press.

Weber, Max. 2002. *The History of Commercial Partnerships in the Middle Ages*, translated by Lutz Kaelber. Lanham, MD: Rowman & Littlefield.

Weber, Max. 2013. 'The Social Causes of the Decline of Ancient Civilizations'. Pp. 387–412 in his *The Agrarian Sociology of Ancient Civilizations*, translated by R.I. Frank. London: Verso.

Wong, Man Kong. 2005. 'The Use of Sinology in the Nineteenth Century'. Pp. 135–54 in *Colonial Hong Kong and Modern China: Interaction and Reintegration*, edited by Lee Pui Tak. Hong Kong: Hong Kong University Press.

Wong, Kwok Kui. 2011. 'Hegel's Criticism of Laozi and its Implications'. *Philosophy East & West*. 61(1): 56–79.

Wong, Man Kong. 2015. 'Nineteenth Century Missionary-Scholars at Work: A Critical Review of English Translations of the *Daodejing* by John Chalmers and James Legge'. *Monumenta Serica: Journal of Oriental Studies*. 63(1): 124–49.

Wu, Shellen Xiao. 2014. 'The Search for Coal in the Age of Empires: Ferdinand von Richthofen's Odyssey in China, 1860–1920'. *American Historical Review*. 119(2): 339–63.

Wu, Albert Monshan. 2016. *From Christ to Confucius: German Missionaries, Chinese Christians, and the Globalization of Christianity, 1860–1950*. New Haven: Yale University Press.

Yang, C.K. 1964. 'Introduction'. Pp. xiii–xliii in Max Weber, *The Religion of China: Confucianism and Taoism*. New York: The Free Press.

Zelin, Madeleine. 2009. 'The Firm in Early China'. *Journal of Economic Behavior and Organization*. 71(3): 623–37.

Zeitlin, Maurice. 1974. 'Corporate Ownership and Control: The Large Corporation and the Capitalist Class'. *American Journal of Sociology*. 79(5): 1073–119.

Zhang, Longxi. 1998. *Mighty Opposites: From Dichotomies to Differences in the Comparative Study of China*. Stanford, CA: Stanford University Press.

Zimmerman, Andrew. 2006. 'Decolonizing Weber'. *Postcolonial Studies*. 9(1): 53–79.

CHAPTER 3

Confucianism

INTRODUCTION

It was shown in the previous chapter that Weber regards Confucianism as an orthodox tradition that fails to meet the requirements of rationalization necessary for modern capitalism. It was also shown that Weber's grasp of Confucianism is less than complete. In this chapter, the nature of Confucianism will be discussed more fully, leaving detailed discussion of Weber's construction of Confucianism to the remaining chapters. In the present chapter, an overview of Confucianism is presented that covers the period from Confucius's own lifetime to the end of the last dynasty of Imperial China in 1912 and the beginning of the Republican period.

At the beginning of the twentieth century, Confucianism was widely regarded as a (world) religion, emblematic of and encompassing Chinese culture, and a barrier to social, political, and economic development. The last of these propositions is no longer accepted, certainly not as a general or necessary truth, but the consensus regarding the first two propositions is possibly strengthened. At the beginning of the nineteenth century, however, there was no Chinese equivalent term for religion and Confucian teaching existed alongside Daoist and Buddhist teachings. These latter are traditions from which Confucianism had borrowed over a long period of historical time. Such borrowing, though, did not deplete these other traditions nor did Confucian thought lose its identity to them. Indeed, it was the lattice of interchange between these three principal teachings that was seen as distinctive of Chinese civilization, rather than Confucian teaching alone bearing the load of Sinic culture. These changes in the perception of Confucianism, or in its substance (the two may be only loosely connected), are arguably characteristic features of Confucianism itself. As shown here, Confucianism is a complex phenomenon with different constitutive elements manifest in different ways at different times and under different circumstances.

Interpretations of Confucianism vary enormously concerning its *modus operandi*, whether it is principally a philosophical, spiritual, socioethical, administrative, or some other form of discourse, and also concerning its content, claims, and values. Given the long history of Confucianism and its diverse roles in different settings, this is not surprising. It is possible, nonetheless, to point to certain texts and even particular passages in them that represent its core. One such passage, from the *Daxue* (*Great Learning*), is likely to be accepted in this regard by the majority of interested discussants:

> Things being investigated, knowledge became complete. Their knowledge being complete, their thoughts were sincere. Their thoughts being sincere, their hearts were then rectified. Their hearts being rectified, their persons were cultivated. Their persons being cultivated, their families were regulated. Their families being regulated, their States were rightly governed. Their States being rightly governed, the whole kingdom was made tranquil and happy. (Legge 1971: 358–59)

Here is the notion of sincerity as a core value, self-cultivation as a required activity, filial piety as a necessary responsibility, and political order and world peace as imperative goals or purposes. Confucianism arguably entails each of these, even though there has been variation in the balance between them.

While the text, *Daxue*, from which the above quotation is taken, has been regarded as one of the Four Books (*Sishu*) crystalizing Confucian thought since 1190, it is originally a chapter of the *Liji* (*Book of Rites*). *Liji* is a compilation of loosely connected documents of unknown authorship describing Zhou dynasty (1046–256 BC) ritual and administrative practices. Yet, it is not anomalous that the Confucian canon should include material Confucius (551–479 BC) did not write or which predated him; he was, in words attributed to him: 'A transmitter and not a maker, believing in and loving the ancients' (Legge 1971: 195). Indeed, that the so-called Confucian tradition includes texts predating Confucius and that are extraneous to him as a person indicates that he was part of a current broader than the terms 'Confucian' and 'Confucianism' endeavor to capture. This broader current is that of the 'scholars' or 'classicists', the *ru*.

The term *rujia* (*ruists*, 'scholars') refers to a body of intellectuals and administrators that originated in the Zhou dynasty court, which has continued to play a significant role in all subsequent dynasties. The *ruists* were responsible for *ru* teaching (*rujiao*) and *ru* learning (*ruxue*), later drawing on Confucius's sayings recorded in the *Analects* and the ideas of his major interpreters, Mencius (372–289 BC) and Xunzi (ca. 310–230 BC), in the development of imperial court ideology and practices. From the late Han dynasty (206 BC–220 AD), *ruists* or literati preserved Confucian thought by reconfiguring it in various ways, and from that time, the imperial court practiced rites that included sacrifices to Confucius. The merging or mutual identification of the *ru* tradition with Confucius did not occur until at least a generation after Confucius's lifetime. Through a critique of Confucius, as representative of the *ru*, the philosopher Mozi (470–391 BC) and his school effectively identified one with the other in a polemic that changed the perception of both (Harbsmeier 2013). Mozi opposed Confucius's advocacy of ritual and tradition as the basis of morality, and emphasized instead personal endeavor and universal love (Johnston 2010: 351–69). In doing so, Mozi identified a body of thought sufficiently coherent in Confucius that it could be regarded as an embodiment of the *ru* tradition.

Weber's influential commentary on Confucianism, *The Religion of China*, written during the early period of the Chinese Republic (1912–1949), confines its discussion to the imperial dynasties of China and draws extensively on contemporary European sinological sources, as indicated in the previous chapter. In treating Confucianism as a class ethic of the literati, the scholar-administrators of Imperial China, Weber draws three conclusions. First, because it is a traditional ethic, Confucianism 'meant adjustment to the world, to its orders and conventions' (Weber 1964: 152). Second, Confucian self-perfection was achieved in compliance with mundane powers, especially 'the requirements of social life … [through] ceremonial and ritualist propriety' and through 'family piety … [or] organically given, personal relations' (Weber 1964: 228, 236). Third, then, while family piety 'rested on the belief in spirits' (Weber 1964: 236), the mundane-ethical and this-worldly orientation of Confucianism had no place for a 'doctrine of salvation, or any striving for transcendental values and destinies … [and] lacked individual prayer' so that Confucianism, according to Weber, 'lacked the notion that men are differently qualified in a religious way, and beyond these reasons Confucianism was indifferent to religion' (Weber 1964: 145–46).

In this way, against the measure of a modern European notion of religion, entailing personal devotion and belief, sacrament, an organized clergy, and so on, Weber argues that Confucianism is not a religion. Nevertheless, he compares Confucian values with Protestant values in order to demonstrate that only the latter could underpin a vocation generative of modern industrial capitalism (Weber 1964: 226–49). This is because 'Confucian rationalism meant rational adoption to the world [while] Puritan rationalism was rational mastery of the world' (Weber 1964: 248). Modern capitalism failed to emerge in Imperial China, according to Weber, because of the limitations of Confucian 'mentality' (Weber 1964: 55, 104). Weber's views regarding the character and limitations of Confucianism overlap with those of the contemporary Chinese 'New Culture Movement' (1913–1917), which rejected Confucian traditionalism. The New Culture Movement held Confucian traditionalism and the Qing court, which upheld it, to be responsible for China's subordination to Western powers and sought national regeneration in a rejection of Confucianism and a negotiated embrace of Western values (Weston 1998).

A contrasting view to Weber's estimation of the nonreligious nature of Confucianism is the idea that Confucius founded an original religion of the Axial Age (Jaspers 1953), an idea that has become increasingly influential (Bellah and Joas 2012; Eisenstadt 1986; see also Provan 2013). The idea of an Axial Age, a period in ancient civilizations during which there were coterminus religious revolutions of lasting significance, is indirectly related to Weber's own writing through his inspiration of philosopher Karl Jaspers by way of Weber's account of the 'age of prophets' (Weber 1978: 439–50). Ironically, though, Weber (1978: 442, 447) excludes Confucius from the pantheon of prophets by instead referring to the 'ethics of the pre-Confucian period' and 'the Taoists'. More recently, the American sociologist of religion Robert Bellah (2011: 409–23) has returned Confucius to the pantheon of the Axial Age. In doing so, Bellah drew on the ideas of the philosopher Herbert Fingarette (1972) regarding Confucius's supposed transcendentalism. Fingarette (1972: 12) is correct in finding *li* (rite, ritual) at the center of Confucius's concerns and the source of a 'binding power' that requires neither force nor legislation. He is also right to connect the core Confucian notion of *ren* (nobility of character, benevolence) with *li* in so far as *ren* refers to the person who 'pursues' a 'pattern of conduct and relationships' that is *li* (Fingarette 1972: 42). But to associate *li* with not only moral but magical, spiritual, and religious energy (Fingarette 1972: 3–10, 15–16, 20, 46, 77–78) is unwarranted. Confucius—and more thoroughly Mencius and Xunzi—explain the power of ritual and its connection with *ren* through the notion of *xin* (heart/mind) in which cognitive and affective qualities coexist (Qi 2014: 172–76). This prefigures the argument developed by the sociologist Randall Collins (2004) when he shows that interactive rituals generate emotional energy through which morality and moral communities are formed. Religion may be read into this situation but it is not inherent in it. We shall consider the connections between Confucius and religion later, but can here note that there is no basis in the idea that religion or magical power is implicit in Confucius's understanding of *li* and *ren*.

Over its long history, Confucian thought and practice have changed considerably, sometimes through internal development and sometimes through foreign influence, both direct and indirect. In tracing key developments in Confucianism, including its possible association with religion, the following discussion will pay attention to some of Weber's observations regarding the nature of Confucian thought, but without focusing on his comprehensive treatment of Imperial Chinese institutions and ideas, which is undertaken in other chapters of this book. The goal of the following discussion, rather, is to indicate the variable and contrasting expressions and representations of Confucianism, and the different purposes it has attempted to achieve, and to show that Confucianism is not a singular and unified phenomenon, as Weber tends to treat it, but a mix of diverse ideas and practices, which change and develop over time.

One of Many: Confucianism in the Han and Tang Dynasties

The intellectual currents of the Warring States period (475–221 BC) of China's early history were rich and diverse, comprising a number of retrospectively named 'schools'. The best known of these (and their ascribed leading thinkers) are the *ruists* (Kongzi [Confucius], Mengzi [Mencius]), Mohists (Mozi), Legalists (Shang Yang, Han Feizi), and Daoists (Laozi, Zhuanzi). The Warring States period, during which seven major and a number of minor states struggled for dominance, concluded with the victory of the Qin state in 221 BC and the founding of the Qin dynasty, with which the Chinese empire began. The Qin court's ruling doctrine was Legalism, supporting state-centric utilitarian authoritarianism. The Qin court effectively rendered irrelevant other Warring States teachings, especially the ideas associated with Mozi and Confucius, through a combination of neglect and repression, culminating in the 'burning of books and burying of scholars' episode (213–210 BC). The fortunes of *ruists* improved in the subsequent Han dynasty (206 BC–220 AD).

Much can be made of the success of Dong Zhongshu, a high official of the Han court who allegedly convinced Emperor Wu (rule: 141–87 BC) to implement Confucian principles to the exclusion of all others. The late Han adoption of Confucianism is apparently confirmed with the inauguration of a cult in the Wu court in 136 BC honoring Confucius (Jensen 1997: 6). This inaugurated a practice of the ritual formation of what might be called a Confucian 'orthodoxy' that continued as long as there was an imperial household in China (Wilson 1996). The application of such ritual foundations has encouraged the view not simply of a state orthodoxy centered on Confucian thought but the establishment of an 'official' Chinese imperial religion (Granet 1975: 97–119) in which the literati are functionally equivalent to priests, their canon a scripture, and their training academies serving the same religious purpose as monasteries (Goossaert and Palmer 2011: 20–22).

Indeed, sacrifices and supplications to Confucius by both literati and emperors occurred throughout the Imperial period, and many emperors bestowed titles and other honors in memorializing Confucius. These practices are associated with the metaphysics of imperial rule in China, summarized as the Mandate of Heaven. Heavenly Mandate operates in terms of the acquisition of the rightness of rule through a ruler's able performance of his role and duties, rather than his lineage. While a standard of secular statecraft and administration are necessary in achievement of the Heavenly Mandate, they are not sufficient. Other relevant performances include the emperor's participation and leading role in ritual practices that ensure legitimacy, especially when establishing a new ruling house, and also in rituals associated with the consolidation of the worldly order for which the emperor is held to be responsible.

Is it possible to describe these imperial cults and *ruist* rituals as religious? An answer to this question will be contingent on what is meant by religion (Asad 1983; Ashiwa and Wank 2009; Nongbri 2015). Certainly the participants in these rituals had no term equivalent to the modern notion of religion. The sacrifices to Confucius, by both emperors and literati, expressed respect for a man and did not constitute sacramental offerings to a god. Also, the imperial court rites involved no congregation or communal observance but were exclusive to the imperial household.

Another factor, which cannot resolve the religion question but discounts the strong claim of Confucian orthodoxy, is that not only Confucian but also Daoist rituals, temples, and liturgies were engaged by the imperial court during the Han dynasty and the following Tang dynasty, and from the mid-Tang, Buddhist rituals were also introduced into the imperial court (Wang 2012a: 274–75; Welch 2003: 153–56).

There are two separate issues that emerge from this consideration. First, there is the question of whether Confucianism can be regarded as a religion, and second, in what sense, if any, can Confucianism be regarded as an orthodoxy in Imperial China. While the rituals of the literati have been described as 'religious-like' if not explicitly religious by a number of authors, and it may be possible to describe the literati approach to the Confucian canon in terms of 'faith', the issue becomes one of interpretation and semantics, given the absence of any self-designated description of Confucianism as a religion (see Chen 2012; Sun 2013; Yao 2000). On the question of Confucian orthodoxy, it is important to consider the various literati uses of Daoist texts and the Daoist trope more generally. The post-Han *xuanxue* movement attempted a revitalizing interpretation of Confucianism through the lens of philosophical Daoism (Chua 2010; Hon 2010). This has led to the misdescription of the movement as neo-Daoist even though Confucius remained through it the highest sage. Its purpose was to correct perceived distortions of Confucian teachings in the continuing quest for a secure basis of an essentially Confucian political order. In later dynasties, literati cultivated Daoist approaches and affectations designed to complement their *ruist* or Confucian personae (Zhou 2013: 67–135). But apart from such 'compromises' to 'orthodoxy', it is erroneous to think of the literati as a religious or priestly group or the imperial academy as a religious institution.

The literati were not a monastic order and their engagement was not pastoral, neither directed to saving souls, theirs or others, nor evangelical or doctrinally proselytizing. Rather, their training was for imperial administration and their Confucian creed and rituals maintained their professional or status solidarity. Weber is correct to dispel the idea that the imperial examination and the associated inculcation of Confucian principles were designed to establish or maintain orthodoxy, religious or otherwise; rather, they promoted 'the *ways of thought* suitable to a cultured man' (Weber 1964: 121) that both preserved privilege and encouraged status group formation (Weber 1964: 117). Indeed, the original implementation of only Confucian principles in state administration, instigated by Dong Zhongshu, was less an exclusionary effort and more a requirement of administration. Other schools focused on social and political philosophy, from which Confucians readily borrowed. Confucians, on the other hand, were adept in maintaining state records, understood the conduct and significance of ritual and the management of institutions (Fung 1952: 405–7; see also Wright 1971: 11–16). The question of Confucian orthodoxy, which, incidentally, Weber advocates, will be treated more fully in the following chapter.

EXPELLING AND INCORPORATING BUDDHIST TROPES: SONG-MING CONFUCIAN INNOVATION

By accommodating to the practical needs of imperial administration and the political structure of the Han state, the *ruists* borrowed extensively from Daoist and Legalist thought. Their attention to stability and hierarchy provided the conditions for economic prosperity, which in turn generated competing bases of social and political power. In these circumstances, Confucians found themselves increasingly marginalized and discredited as the Han dynasty began to collapse under the strain of its own success. The transformations undertaken by Confucian thought in the subsequent reorganization of the Chinese empire depended on continued borrowing from the Daoist classics, especially in the *xuanxue* movement, which effectively lasted from the third to the sixth century. This rectification of Confucian thought continued during most of the Tang dynasty (618–906 AD). Confucian intellectual exchanges with extraneous Chinese traditions were disrupted, however, in the late Tang through the influence of alien teachings in the form of Buddhism.

Buddhism arrived in China in the first century, during the Han dynasty, through the efforts of Indian missionaries. At this time, Chinese reactions to Buddhism were dismissive; it was an uninvited import, irrelevant to local concerns, and it failed to achieve a foothold in the Chinese imagination. By the third century, however, through the endeavors of Chinese converts who melded Buddhist doctrine with Confucian and Daoist concepts, thus harmonizing it with Chinese principles (Keenan 1994), a sinicized Buddhism emerged that attracted increasing interest from peasant, landowning, and merchant classes as well as from members of the imperial court (Qi 2013: 352–59). Indeed, the post-Han decline of Confucianism contributed to a climate in which the appeal of Buddhism, with its adopted local Chinese vocabulary, was increasingly attractive

(Wright 1971: 21–41). It was noted in the previous chapter that Weber's acceptance of the idea that a Confucian orthodoxy held throughout the imperial period of China's history leads him to ignore the importance of Buddhism after the third century.

Confucian objections to Buddhism were directed to its social philosophy and its metaphysics. Confucians believed that Buddhism, in promoting individual salvation, undermined filial piety, the centrality of the family, and the five bonds (*wulun*) in social relations. Metaphysically, the Buddhist notion of 'emptiness', the Confucians believed, contravened the idea that Heaven (*Tian*) and Earth (*Di*) are foundational constituents of reality, and therefore, ultimately undermined the basis of imperial rule. Confucian antipathy to Buddhism was expressed in the late Tang by the essayist Han Yu (786–824) and in the early Song dynasty (960–1279) by the statesman Ouyang Xiu (1007–1072). But it was only with the Song dynasty scholar and teacher Zhu Xi (1130–1200) that a direct Confucian challenge to Buddhism was mounted, through a reordered canon and a reconstituted philosophy, which has become known as *Song-Ming Lixue* (neo-Confucianism). The problem for the neo-Confucians was that a Buddhism that had incorporated key Daoist and Confucian notions so infused the intellectual universe that they were required to deal with issues unknown to pre-Han thought and therefore issues which the original Confucian doctrines were unable to accommodate.

Although by no means the only contributor to neo-Confucianism, Zhu Xi was its most important exponent. From 124 BC, the Five Classics (*Wujing*) of the *ruist* canon were incrementally augmented until, by the early Song, there were Thirteen Classics (*Shisan jing*), including two texts previously absent—namely, the *Lunyu* (*Analects* of Confucius) and the *Mengzi* (*Mencius*). Zhu Xi performed a defining editorial fiat in 1190 by simplifying this canon to consist of Four Books—namely, the *Lunyu*, the *Mengzi*, and two short chapters from the *Liji* (*Book of Rights*), which was a part of the original *Wujing*. These chapters, the *Daxue* (*Great Learning*) and the *Zhongyong* (*Doctrine of the Mean*), were reedited by Zhu and he provided each of the Four Books with detailed commentaries (Gardner 2007). This simplification of the *ruist* canon, to consist only of the text of Confucius and his major interpreter Mencius, along with these two short chapters, was consolidated as a lasting contribution to Chinese thought by Zhu's adoption of them as the exclusive texts for the imperial civil service examination, ensuring an approach to Confucianism that would last until the imperial examination was abolished in 1905.

There is much irony in the fact that while Zhu's Four Books for the first time places Confucius's *Analects* at the center of the *ruist* canon, his interpretation of Confucian thought would have been unrecognizable to the sage he memorializes. In confronting the Buddhist preaching of individual salvation, Zhu returns to the Confucian concept of Heavenly Mandate, but in a manner that emphasizes individual self-cultivation (Wang 2012a: 280). In its classic form, the idea of Heavenly Mandate is core to the notion and practice of imperial sovereignty. In Zhu's neo-Confucian revision, the harmonization of the human realm through self-cultivation effectively bypasses the political domain of imperial legitimacy and concentrates on individual practices that those familiar with Buddhist meditation would have seen as a direct Confucian alternative. Indeed, Zhu advocated daily meditation (*jingzuo*) paralleling Buddhist practice but focused on principles of Confucian morality in a form unknown to Confucius (Needham 1956: 454).

In metaphysics also, Zhu borrowed from Buddhist as well as Daoist ideas to bolster the intellectual basis of a revised Confucian outlook. The advent of Buddhism in China introduced a set of philosophical questions, concerning human nature, mind, self-realization, and humankind's relation to the cosmos, that were unknown to Warring States thinkers (Gardner 2007: xxiii; Qi 2014: 111). Zhu engaged a double agenda in his appropriation of aspects of Buddhist metaphysics to dispel what he regarded as the mystical elements of Daoist and Buddhist thought that he saw infused in Han Confucianism. In particular, Zhu developed a dialectic of interaction between the principles of *qi* and *li*. Everything in the universe comprises these two elements, he claimed, one consisting of vital energy, *qi*, and the other, *li*, representing absolute law-like principles that govern form (Fung 1953: 546–50). Whereas one is the source of growth, the other entails an element of rational order. In this way, neo-Confucianism ironically borrowed from Buddhism in asserting a rationalist ethic designed to supersede it.

The intellectual reasoning that was a hallmark of Song-Ming neo-Confucianism contrasts with its courtly practices, especially rituals introduced at this time which elevated Confucius with new titles and associated sacrificial ceremonies. This more intense focus on the figure of Confucius is in part a consequence of his concentrated presentation in the Four Books (Wang 2012a: 281–83). And yet, the focus on individual self-cultivation and moral rectitude was connected not only with ritual or 'spiritual' engagements but also with commercial practices. During the Song dynasty, agriculture grew in scope and yield, increasing the size and significance of markets and market towns and expanding the numbers of wealthy landed and commercial families (Elvin 1973: 164–78; Gernet 1996: 316–26). These developments promoted a synergy with neo-Confucian ethical individualism and the rationality of profit orientation and entrepreneurship (Elvin 1973: 167).

The theme of a rationalizing ethical outlook in neo-Confucianism and its commercial consequences is taken up by the twentieth-century Chinese-American historian Yu Ying-shih (1987). Yu regards neo-Confucianism as a functional equivalent of European Protestantism in a direct challenge to Weber's argument concerning the inhibiting qualities of Confucianism on capitalist development. It is not possible here to explore Yu's contribution and its limitations (see Barbalet 2014: 319–20). The individualistic ethical tensions within neo-Confucianism are discussed also by the American historian of ideas Thomas Metzger (1977), who argues that in failing to consider these crucial aspects of neo-Confucianism, Weber's argument in *The Religion of China* must be regarded as at least incomplete. It can be acknowledged that Weber was simply blind to developments in Confucian thought during the Song-Ming period. Indeed, Weber's lapse here reflects an absence in European sinology at the time generated through Jesuit missionary interpretations of Confucianism that pervaded European thought during the eighteenth and nineteenth centuries and which affected Weber's understanding of China in general and Confucianism in particular.

JESUIT CONFUCIANISM

A Jesuit mission arrived in China in 1583. By 1594, its members presented themselves, through their dress, expressed interests, and engagements, as *ruists* or literati (Latourette 2009: 91–98). The Catholic Church's missionary orientation of 'accommodation' with the local belief system was taken to mean by the Jesuits in China that they should adapt Confucianism to the needs of their mission to 'save' China. This generated an interpretation of Confucianism that effectively narrowed the tradition of *ruxue*, the 'learning of the scholars', so that Confucius alone was the source of a gospel, the *Analects*, and, as the exemplar of the tradition associated with his name, a figure of saintly comportment. This transformation has been controversially described as the Jesuit 'manufacturing' of Confucianism (Jensen 1997).

Some readers have taken Jensen literally and misunderstood his claim regarding the Jesuit manufacturing of 'Confucianism' (Standaert 1999; Sun 2013: 37–38). Jensen is aware that the term 'Confucianism' was first used as late as 1862 (Jensen 1997: 4), long after the Jesuit intervention. Jensen's argument, however, concerns not the development of a neologism but a distinctive interpretation or presentation of Confucian thought that is a catachrestical invention in the claims it makes concerning the singular role of that thought in the Chinese tradition, the dimensions of that body of thought and the significance of its author, Confucius (Elman 2002: 525–26; Kuo 2013: 239–40). As Jensen (1997: 33) says:

> In Jesuit hands the indigenous Kongzi was resurrected from distant symbolism into life, heroically transmuted and made intelligible as 'Confucius', a spiritual confrere who alone among the Chinese—so their version has it— had preached an ancient gospel of monotheism now forgotten.

It is well known that the Jesuit image of China and the place of Confucianism in it influenced European Enlightenment thought, that it extolled the virtues of moral Confucian China against corrupt aristocratic Europe. This is especially clear in the works of three eighteenth-century luminaries—the French economist, François Quesnay, and the German and French philosophers, Gottfried Wilhelm Leibniz and François-Marie Voltaire (Hudson 1961: 319–25; Zhang 1998: 99–101), as indicated in the previous chapter. While the eighteenth-century European vision of China lost its political and popular appeal after the French Revolution, a number of its features continued to be accepted, both in Europe and in China.

The Jesuit interpretation of Confucius and Confucianism in many ways reflects the nature and purpose of the Jesuit order as an organization. The Company of Jesus, the Jesuits, was formed by the Spanish priest Ignatius Loyola in 1534 with the express purpose of struggling for Catholic reform, of leading the Church's Counter-Reformation (Mullett 1984: 22–25). This latter was the Catholic Church's response to the religious anxieties that occupied Christian Europe during the sixteenth and seventeenth centuries, especially through the dual challenge of the new Protestantism in northern Europe and the non-Christian forces in Spain and other parts of Europe as well as in the newly discovered Americas, Africa, and Asia. The Counter-Reformation was thus possessed by two moods—one defensive and repressive, expressed in the Inquisition; the other, confident and adventurous, that gave rise to Catholic Mission. For both of these engagements, a new priesthood was required, replacing the medieval piety of harsh and debilitating self-punishment. Counter-Reformation priests were specially trained and prepared for active engagement in the world, as a manifestation of the New Testament ideal, *miles Christi* (soldier of Christ); their seminaries provided professional training directed to the performance of clear and strict duties concerning the moral and spiritual elevation of the laity, from whom the priesthood remained remote. The clergy of the Counter-Reformation Church was thus 'an élite corps of highly disciplined and trained priests' (Mullett 1984: 16), and none more so than the Jesuits.

It was not simply a vain conceit that led the Jesuits in China to regard themselves as literati, to dress as Chinese scholars, and to believe themselves to be *ruists*, trained in a seminary they saw as paralleling the *ruist* academy (Brockey 2007). While those the Jesuits imitated were scholar-administrators rather than priests, the Jesuits nevertheless adapted from their Chinese 'counterparts' a sense of responsibility for *ru* teaching (*rujiao*) (Jensen 1997: 48, 50). The particular Jesuit contribution, though, was to reduce the main dimensions of that tradition to the ideas of one man, namely, Kongzi—Latinized as Confucius—who they elevated to a prominence he had previously lacked, and purified the Confucian system, raising it to the 'essence' of Chinese civilization. The ultimate purpose of this immense construction was to save Chinese souls. Its more proximate outcome, though, was an interpretation of Confucianism that not only influenced European conceptions of China but also Chinese understandings of Confucian thought.

The Jesuits, through the investigations of Matteo Ricci, who led the China mission, discovered in Confucius the New Testament ethic that 'you should love your neighbour as yourself'. The Jesuits thus held that Confucius operated through an implicit ancient monotheism (Jensen 1997: 33, 59–60). It was denied by the Jesuits, however, that Confucius's teachings, and indeed the imperial cults associated with Confucius, were religious. In order to maintain a Catholic accommodation with Confucianism and avoid religious opposition between the two approaches, it was necessary to insist that Confucianism was a moral code and that the imperial rituals associated with his name were civic. According to Jensen (1997: 69), 'Ricci … did not so much displace religion as redefine it, emphasizing its character as an ethical system governing all of Chinese social and political life'. For it to embrace 'all of Chinese social and political life', Jesuit Confucianism would first have to be purified of the other forces that were current in China, both before the Jesuits arrived and after they were expelled from China in 1724.

The Jesuits regarded Buddhism, first, to be an idolatrous heathen force which, second, had a corrupting influence on Chinese society, subverting native Confucianism (Jensen 1997: 47). In some ways, this was close to the view of many literati who opposed Buddhism, as indicated earlier. But the Counter-Reformation Jesuits read the Buddhist presence in the Confucian space not simply as an intrusive competitor but as a heresy, an 'evil cult' (*xiejiao*), a concept previously unknown in China but central to Christian discernment and exaggerated by the Inquisition. Indeed, Weber (1963: 45) similarly laments the absence of a 'concept of radical evil' in Confucianism and therefore of 'any integral diabolical power of sin'. Daoism, in Chinese thought, was different from Confucianism but not contradictory with it, in the manner of Yin and Yang as complementary polarities generative of change through harmonious interplay (see Zhang 2002: 83–94). In the Jesuit mind, however, Daoism was another heresy to be purged from the Chinese spiritual space. As we have seen, neo-Confucianism absorbed elements of Buddhism in confronting it. The Jesuits thus regarded neo-Confucianism as tainted, requiring its expulsion from the fold of 'orthodox' Confucianism, this latter 'misunderstood and betrayed' by the revisionist and synthesizing neo-Confucian scholars of the Song dynasty (Zhang 1998: 103).

The notion of Confucian orthodoxy in this sense, of not merely an accepted and sanctioned but an uncontaminated system of belief, is thus a Jesuit construction in which competing traditions are viewed through a European Christian lens forged in the Counter-Reformation. The idea, though, of Confucianism as the orthodoxy of Chinese spiritual and ethical discourse, with Daoism and Buddhism relegated to heterodox ascription, was continued by nineteenth- and twentieth-century sinologists (Legge 1880; de Groot 1910) and advocated by Weber (1964: 173–225), who follows their example. Weber so closely adopts the missionary sinologists' approach that he disregards or is unaware of neo-Confucianism. His insensitivities to developments in Confucian thought have given rise to criticism (Metzger 1977), mentioned earlier, although others, while acknowledging the fact, see it as methodologically explicable (Schluchter 1989: 112). But the notion of orthodoxy itself in this context is a Western projection, with Weber (1964: 214–15) reading Chinese developments through the prism of European history. Imperial Chinese rulers were not concerned with the mental constructs of their subjects, with orthodoxy, but with the rightness of their practices, with orthopraxy (Watson 1993), as we shall see in the following chapter. The Confucian tradition of the literati was based on correct ritual, not faith, orthodox or otherwise.

In the creation of a Confucian orthodoxy, posited against the hetero-doxy of Buddhism, Daoism, and contaminated neo-Confucianism, the Jesuits were enacting European Counter-Reformation engagements with Chinese pieces. The identification of their purified Confucianism with Chinese culture and their self-identity as exponents of the true faith against heresy indicates how thoroughly the Jesuit mission required the terminol-ogy of inquisition. While the interpretation of Confucius developed by Ricci was not always accepted in Rome (Jensen 1997: 67–69), this should not distract from the fact that the Jesuit modeling of Confucianism was a construction paralleling the form of the universal church of pre-Reformation Catholicism—a church, already lost in Europe, that both encompassed European civilization and institutionally monopolized the spiritual and intellectual life of the faithful, necessarily denying alternate doctrine or practice. This form of Jesuitical Confucianism was attractive to elements of the contemporary literati and later generations of Chinese nationalists. When Confucianism takes the form of 'Confucianity', in the late Qing, the universal church shifts its form to that of a national church, as we shall see later.

QING CONFUCIANISM: ANTINOMIES OF A MODERNIZING STATE

After the Manchu conquest of China in the seventeenth century, the new Qing dynasty, from 1644, paradoxically extended Confucian ideological dominance and at the same time weakened literati Confucianism. As non-Han rulers of China, the Qing court's need for legitimacy led to observa-tions of ritual protocols, including tributes to Confucius, at a rate in excess of all previous dynasties (Wang 2012a: 284–86). The Manchu rulers appreciated, though, that the literati presented the single most significant challenge to their rule. By the early eighteenth century, the place of Confucius in court ritual was relatively reduced by unprecedentedly grant-ing high title to five of Confucius's ancestors but not to Confucius. This development was consonant with an earlier initiative, in 1657, when the Qing court issued a new version of the *Xiaojing* (*Classic of Filial Piety*). The *Xiaojing* had been excluded from civil examination preparation since 1190 through Zhu Xi's revision of the Confucian canon but reintroduced by the Qing court in 1660 as required reading for candidates, thus effec-tively reducing the relative importance of the Four Books.

The Qing emphasis on filial piety had a number of consequences. First, the 1657 version of the *Xiaojing* was designed to be accessible not only to the literati, but principally to ordinary people. Indeed, the Qing court's emphasis on filial piety was to introduce a direct line of spiritual communication between the emperor and his imperial subjects by linking his role of ruler with that of teacher, previously the province of the literati. Second, the literati thus found their intellectual role reduced and their carriage of the Confucian tradition compromised relative to that of the neo-Confucians of the Song-Ming period. Third, the imperial promotion of filial piety enhanced the position of patriarchal clans in the structure of dynastic rule. Although the self-protection and social organizational roles of rural clans began to increase during the Ming dynasty, this process was enhanced and consolidated by the Qing, during which time, clans effectively took responsibility for security, welfare, education, and taxation in rural communities. Weber is aware of the importance of clan organization and its basis in the relations of filial piety (Weber 1964: 86–95, 157–58), but he assumed that the patriarchal principle was a constant of imperial rule and not something subject to developmental tendencies culminating in its refined manifestation during the Qing (see Hamilton 1984).

Weber's purpose in writing *The Religion of China* in 1913 was to demonstrate the uniqueness of the West in the advent of modern industrial capitalism. The failure of the latter to emerge in China, he argues, was because of the inherent traditionalism of Confucianism, among other things. While Weber acknowledges the cultist sacrifices to Confucius in imperial court rituals, his notion of religion, as consisting of a congregation united in faith and organized by a specialist clergy, led him to insist that Confucianism is not a religion (Weber 1964: 146, 156), as indicated earlier. And yet, at the time of his writing, there were efforts in China to develop a Confucian religion along the lines of the Protestant Church, endeavors undertaken as part of a program to modernize China's economy and society and address some of the limitations, incidentally identified by Weber, of Chinese institutions and 'mentality'. It is an unfortunate omission in Weber's discussion, then, that those Chinese efforts to deal with problems that were of interest to Weber are not discussed or even mentioned by him, for they indicate something of the complexity of and possibilities in Confucianism that significantly touch his argument.

China's Self-Strengthening Movement, during 1861–1895, encompassed a number of initiatives of the Qing government in response to its defeat in the Opium Wars of 1839–1842 and 1856–1860, the subsequent unequal treaties, and the concessions imposed by the British and other foreign powers. A contemporary slogan, *Zhongxue weiti, xixue weiyong* (Chinese learning for substance, Western learning for function), captures the idea that borrowing from the West in defense of Chinese interests required some adoption of Chinese 'substance' to Western forms. This came to have a number of consequences for the development of Confucian thought and practice. The Self-Strengthening Movement, however, was an expression of Confucian conservatism in the sense that it was uninterested in enacting social and political reform and primarily concerned with the transfer of modern technology, including military technology, to China. The next phase of official reform, *Wuxu Bianfa* (Hundred Days Reform) of 1898, had much wider consequences.

Before discussing *Wuxu Bianfa*, in which religionizing developments arose within Confucianism, it is important to briefly consider the anti-Christian incidents in China from the 1860s, known as the Missionary Litigation Cases or, more directly, the Religious Cases (*jiaoan*). These were often led by local gentry, degree-holders, or literati. This anti-foreign and anti-Christian movement arose after the right of Christian churches to evangelize was granted by the 'unequal treaties' of 1860, in the wake of China's defeat in the second Opium War. The 1860 Convention of Peking opened all of China to missionary activity, whereas the previous 1842 Treaty of Nanking limited foreign missionaries to the ports of foreign concessions—namely, Amoy (Xiamen), Canton (Guangzhou), Foochow (Fuzhou), Ningpo (Ningbo), and Shanghai. As missionary activity spread through China, disputes ensued between missionaries on the one hand and local people and authorities on the other, concerning land and property acquisition for the purpose of building churches and missionary hospitals. These disputes, and the possibility of violence against missionaries and their property, and sometimes Chinese converts, has been characterized by Cohen (1963) as a conflict between Confucianism and Christianity that is merely one expression of the enduring assertion of Confucian orthodoxy against heterodoxy, an interpretation that has been contested (Mino 1965) and in light of the remarks earlier is not accepted here. It is widely agreed that Confucian antipathy to Christian missionaries was directly related to the missionaries' links with foreign embassies and military power which undermined Qing political authority. This was a continuing theme throughout the nineteenth and early twentieth centuries. The Confucian dismissal of Christianity as 'superstition' was entirely consistent with Weber's observation that, as a bureaucratic stratum, the

Confucian literati were 'only interested in the affairs of this world', and thus, rejected otherworldly religiosity (Weber 1964: 155, see also 1963: 90, 122, 1964: 203). What is of interest here, though, is that while this charge of Christian superstition was commonplace after 1860, it was hardly uttered after 1898. From that time there was a shift in the self-image and purpose of Confucianism.

Wuxu Bianfa effectively introduced a modernizing trend within Confucianism through acceptance of two concepts previously unknown in China—*zongjiao* (religion) and *mixin* (superstition). From this time, religion was seen by the Qing court as a key element in the strength of Western powers, both in their state and economy, a proposition with which Weber would concur. The Qing government therefore in effect promoted religion in its commitment to rid China of superstition. The perpetrators of attacks on superstition continued to be literati, but now less directed to missionaries. From this time, Confucian literati encouraged the destruction of Buddhist, Daoist, and local cult temples in order to confiscate their income and property, to be used in financing new school buildings and thereby ultimately to strengthen the state (Goossaert 2006). This manifestation of the antisuperstition posture of late Qing Confucianism raised two contradictory possibilities. Prior to *Wuxu Bianfa*, Confucianism was a socially embedded set of practices tightly associated with an ethical-ritual core based on filial piety. With the religion-superstition distinction as part of state strengthening, Confucianism could itself take a religious form, institutionally distinct, hierarchically organized with a clergy over a congregation, and with worship of Confucius as a god. Alternatively, Confucianism could be a nonreligious civic faith, expressing the Chinese national essence independent of the religious or doctrinal commitment of individual *guomin* (literally, nation's people) or citizens. Both possibilities acquired support in late Qing and early Republican China but neither succeeded.

A leading Confucian intellectual of the period, Kang Youwei (1858–1927), a principal exponent of Confucian antisuperstitionism, attempted to correct the perceived feebleness of literati Confucianism and its inability to strengthen the Chinese state by creating a Confucian church, modeled on European Protestantism. Kang's *Kongjiaohui* (Confucian Church) was designed to transform Confucius into a Christ-like figure in the context of a church with an organized clergy and a congregation of faithful believers (Kuo 2013). Although Kang's success was limited, attracting few adherents, versions of his model were tried a number of times and persisted in various forms from the 1890s and into the Republican period (1912–1949) up to the 1920s (Fan 2010).

The *Kongjiao* (Confucian religion) movement met a number of obstacles. It never acquired support from the majority of Confucian literati, who objected to the notion that Confucianism could be disembedded from the fabric of ritual and convention and turned into an institutionally distinct organizational form founded on doctrine and faith. Also, Chinese modernizers, including many sympathetic to Confucianism, accepted that a modern political constitution required a separation of church and state. This meant that the Confucian heritage could be preserved by the state only by avoiding an official endorsement of Confucianism as a religion. It is for this reason that in 1893, the Qing official Peng Guangyu argued at the First World Congress of Religion in Chicago that Confucianism is not a religion, understood as a sectarian tradition, but rather a 'state doctrine' (Yang 2008: 15). Similarly, the drafters of the Republican constitution in 1912–1913 'struck down the Bill of National Religion and chose instead to write Confucianism into the constitution as the foundation of national education' (Kuo 2013: 263). Both Peng and the drafters of the Republican constitution followed the example of Meiji Japan in its construction of State Shintō as a civic rather than a religious expression of Japanese nationality (Hardacre 1989).

The second possibility of modernized Confucianism, then, was to provide it with a central role in the educational reforms of 1902–1904 and extending into the final days of the Qing dynasty. The creation of a national school system, partly connected with the campaign of temple destruction, was designed to strengthen the nation by providing training in modern vocational skills and disciplines, including science and mathematics, and also to inculcate patriotism and political loyalty in students. The curriculum was, therefore, a mix of both Western learning and Confucian learning, including recitation of Confucian texts and worship of Confucius in the classroom (Kuo 2008). The use of Confucian teaching to foster patriotism was also a lesson learned from Meiji Japan, where Shintō was elemental in a 'national learning' that inculcated a sense of national identity (Hardacre 1989). The importance of Meiji Japan as an example to Chinese reformers has been widely noted. But the Meiji Restoration occurred through regional or domain elite groups displacing, in 1868, the feudal Tokugawa shogunate. The dominant modernizing elites that emerged in China, however, were not associated with traditional society, as they were in Japan.

The New Culture Movement (1913–1917) and May Fourth Movement (1919–1921) were led by emergent elites disassociated from the elite of established Qing society. They identified Confucianism with the failed Qing dynasty, they rejected court ritual, and in dispelling superstition, they had no place for its coupled opposite religion, certainly not Confucian religion. A leader of the May Fourth Movement, Chen Duxiu (1879–1924), who went on to cofound the Communist Party in 1921, famously declared in 1919 his generation's support for 'Mr. Democracy and Mr. Science' and its rejection of Confucianism:

> In order to advocate Mr. Democracy, we are obliged to oppose Confucianism, the codes of rituals, chastity of women, traditional ethics (loyalty, filial piety, chastity), and old-fashioned politics (privileges and government by men alone); in order to advocate Mr. Science we have to oppose traditional arts and traditional religion (ghosts and gods); and in order to advocate both Mr. Democracy and Mr. Science we are compelled to oppose the cult of 'national quintessence' and ancient literature. (quoted in Chow 1960: 59)

Some form of Confucianism may not necessarily be antithetical to a modern Chinese nation and society (Wang 2012b). At the time that China attempted to first achieve a modern nation and encourage development of a modern society, however, Confucianism was so inextricably connected with the failed attempts to transform the Qing empire from within that Confucianism itself was rejected by the new modernizers as inherently traditional. This was also Weber's view, of course, that Confucianism was inextricably linked with the bureaucratic administrators of traditional China. He failed to appreciate, though, that Confucianism is and always has been a mix of possibilities. We are reminded of the veracity of this last claim by the advent of Confucian Institutes since 2004, established around the world and financed from Beijing, which for four decades from 1949 had vilified Confucius and his feudal thinking; today in mainland China there is a rise of New Confucianism (*xinrujia*) (Song 2003; Tan 2008).

CONCLUSION: MODERN TIMES AND NEW CONFUCIANISM

The account above of developments in Confucianism, occupying over 2000 years from the Han dynasty to the beginning of Republican China, indicates emergent themes and also sharp contrasts. One concerns the tension between Confucian borrowing from other traditions and claims regarding its 'orthodoxy' based on its association (until 1911) with state administration, providing Confucianism with ideological dominance through its role in the maintenance of imperial rule. The notion of orthodoxy applied to Confucianism during this period fails to grasp the nature of its dominance, however, given the emphasis Confucianism places on correct behavior—including ritual behavior—rather than correct belief, on orthopraxy rather than orthodoxy properly understood. At the same time, literati antipathy to Buddhism and Daoism can be related to the former's responsibilities in imperial administration rather than to competition between these different traditions in doctrine and for influence, although these latter cannot be simply dismissed. This last point arises from the fact that among the Confucian scholars were thinkers who were 'purifiers' and also scholars who were 'borrowers'. Jesuit transformation of Confucian 'orthodoxy', on the other hand, implies heresy in Buddhist and Daoist 'heterodoxy'. Late Qing literati antisuperstition campaigns introduced yet another understanding of Confucian orthodoxy in which heterodox sects were not merely doctrinally heretical, but politically illegitimate.

A notable contrast in consideration of Confucianism is the possible ascription to it of either religious or civic characterization. European observers disagreed whether imperial Confucian cults were religious or civic, a concern largely stimulated by Christian missionary intentions. There was agreement, however, that literati Confucianism was socially embedded, consisting of rituals and codes concerning filial piety and ancestor 'worship', rather than based on a distinct organizational form in the manner of European churches. This situation changed, however, during the late Qing and early Republican periods when there were attempts to establish Confucian churches and the state, in a contrary move, sought to found Confucianism as a nonreligious civic faith supportive of a modern Chinese cultural nationalism, both new departures in Confucian possibilities, neither of which survived beyond the Republican period. It is not possible to discuss in detail the advent of New Confucianism, developed during the twentieth century in Hong Kong, Taiwan, Singapore, and Boston. The construction of this socially disembedded and intellectually formed version of Confucianism, with carriage of a 'spiritual' and semireligious dimension as well as representing a form of Greater-China cultural nationalism, takes the possibilities in Confucianism so far discussed even further (Dirlik 2011; Makeham 2008; Rošker 2016). At the same time, these developments, like the earlier Song-Ming neo-Confucian appropriations of Buddhist elements, qualify the idea that Confucianism remains an indigenous Chinese tradition.

New Confucianism as an academic discourse (*xinruxue*) is a diverse force with much variation in approach and direction that ranges from disinterested scholarly reinterpretation of established ideas to more politically pointed interventions (Angle 2012; Chan 2014). The scholarly endeavors of intellectual and cultural elites must be distinguished from a very different type of Confucian revival with its putative but hidden roots in the *Kongjiao* (Confucian religion) movement of Kang Youwei, mentioned earlier. The self-identification of New Confucian believers or followers (*xinrujiao*) is manifestation of another form of Confucian revivalism, associated with Confucian Temples in mainland China and Taiwan (Sun 2013; Fan and Chen 2015). This difference between elite and popular New Confucianism—one intellectual and one religious—parallels the distinction Weber (1963) draws in his *The Sociology of Religion* between religious virtuosi and religious masses, one elaborating systems of belief and the other simply consuming them. The difference here, though, in the case of Confucian revival, is that the virtuosi and the masses are not only relating to different constructions of Confucianism that at best have only a remote connection with each other, but also that the numerical proportion of virtuosi and masses is inverse to what might be expected in terms of the literal meaning of these categories. The number of *xinrujiao* participants is too small to constitute a 'mass', if not in Weber's sense, at least in their constituting a diminutive population of 'believers'. There is a third form of New Confucianism, very different from the two just mentioned, that should also be identified in this context. This is the state-advocated Confucianism associated with assertion of Asian values by particular political elites in South East Asia as well as East Asia.

The Asian values debate began with the 'survival ideology', emphasizing discipline and organization (Khong 1995: 124), initiated by the Singaporean state elite. This ideology was designed to counter the supposed negative influence on Singaporeans of ideas 'from abroad'—difficult to monitor and control—in which 'Asian values' were advanced as a positive antidote to 'Western values', namely, values that encouraged bad behavior and poor mentality. The Asian values most desirable for Singaporeans were encapsulated in Confucianism (Khong 1995: 125–26). At the beginning of 1982, the Singapore government announced that Confucianism would be introduced into the school system, to be taught as moral education. Advisers to the Singapore Minister of Education for curriculum design were leading scholars of New Confucianism (Dirlik 2011: 110). It has been argued that the official rehabilitation of Confucius and the promotion of New Confucianism in China also has political nationalist purposes, including acknowledgment of a common heritage which brings mainland China together with Hong Kong, Taiwan, and

Singapore, and thereby facilitates the participation of overseas Chinese in the mainland economy, which was particularly important in the period from the late 1980s to the mid-1990s, when investors from Hong Kong, Taiwan, and Singapore contributed over 75 percent of foreign capital to China. Additionally, New Confucianism is thought to provide moral guidance in place of the now eclipsed Marxist certainties that operated during the Mao era, which is to say that New Confucianism is introduced by the Communist Party to provide legitimation to post-Mao capitalist development. The broader East Asian recruitment of Confucian values to legitimate extraneous economic and political arrangements is arguably consistent with the original state apprehension of Confucianism during the Han dynasty. In an insightful polemic, the Chinese dissident writer Liu Xiaobo argues that while the historical Confucius may have been a 'stray dog', unable to find a 'master' who would employ him in state service, the sage Confucius, venerated by those in political power and their intellectual servants, becomes a 'guard dog' in defending state legitimacy (Liu 2012).

An account of the historical development of Confucianism and its present-day forms reveals a dynamism and plasticity that is simply missing from Weber's detailed examination in *The Religion of China*. Weber confined his investigation to literati Confucianism during the imperial period and his interpretation of its role in the inhibition of a native Chinese capitalism. It can be noted, however, that he wrote at a time of fundamental revolutionary transformation in China. Indeed, Weber was not oblivious to these developments. In *The Religion of China,* he uncharacteristically refers to 'K'ang Yu-wei's modern school' of Confucianism, mentioned earlier, that was contemporary with Weber's own writing. But he does so in order to dismiss an interpretation of a passage from Confucius that Kang 'for understandable reasons' offers to support a modernizing trend and refers approvingly to de Groot's reassertion of the passage's traditional and orthodox roots (Weber 1964: 212). At about the time that he wrote *The Religion of China,* Weber (1978: 924) observes in a discussion of 'The Nation' in *Economy and Society* that:

> Only fifteen years ago, men knowing the Far East still denied that the Chinese qualified as a 'nation'; they held them to be only a 'race'. Yet today, not only the Chinese political leaders but also the very same observers would judge differently. Thus it seems that a group of people under certain conditions may attain the quality of a nation through specific behaviour, or they may claim this quality as an 'attainment'—and within short spans of time at that.

The 'attainment' of national aspiration in China that Weber refers to here occurred through 'specific behaviour' in which Confucianism took on historically new roles and developed forms previously inconceivable. It is a matter of record that Weber neglected these and associated events. The consequences, though, for the relevance of his analysis of Confucianism for continuing research cannot be ignored. It can be seen in the foregoing that not only does Weber fail to appreciate the dynamic elements in Confucianism, but also that his discussion of literati Confucianism is based on sources and interpretations that are in need respectively of supplementation and revision.

REFERENCES

Angle, Stephen C. 2012. *Contemporary Confucian Political Philosophy: Toward Progressive Confucianism*. Cambridge: Polity.

Asad, Talal. (1983). 'Anthropological Conceptions of Religion'. *Man.* 18(2): 237–259.

Ashiwa, Yoshiko and Wank, David. 2009. 'Making Religion, Making the State in Modern China'. Pp. 1–21 in *Making Religion, Making the State: The Politics of Religion in Modern China*, edited by Yoshiko Ashiwa and David Wank. Stanford: Stanford University Press.

Barbalet, Jack. 2014. 'Confucian Values and East Asian Capitalism: A Variable Weberian Trajectory'. Pp. 315–28 in *Routledge Handbook of Religions in Asia*, edited by Bryan Turner and Oscar Salemink. London: Routledge.

Bellah, Robert N. 2011. *Religion in Human Evolution*. Cambridge: Harvard University Press.

Bellah, Robert N and Joas, Hans (eds). 2012. *The Axial Age and its Consequences*. Cambridge: Harvard University Press.

Brockey, Liam Matthew. 2007. *Journey to the East: The Jesuit Mission to China, 1579–1724*. Cambridge: Harvard University Press.

Chan, Joseph C.W. 2014. *Confucian Perfectionism: A Political Philosophy for Modern Times*. Princeton: Princeton University Press.

Chen, Yong. 2012. *Confucianism as Religion: Controversies and Consequences*. Leiden: Brill.

Chow, Tse-tsung. 1960. *The May Fourth Movement: Intellectual Revolution in Modern China*. Cambridge: Harvard University Press.

Chua, Jude Soo-Meng. 2010. 'Tracing the Dao: Wang Bi's Theory of Names'. Pp. 53–70 in *Philosophy and Religion in Early Medieval China*, edited by Alan K.L. Chan and Yuet-Keung Lo. Albany: SUNY Press.

Cohen, Paul A. 1963. *China and Christianity: The Missionary Movement and the Growth of Chinese Antiforeignism, 1860–1870*. Cambridge, MA: Harvard University Press.

Collins, Randall. 2004. *Interaction Ritual Chains*. Princeton: Princeton University Press.

de Groot, Jan Jakob Marie. 1910. *The Religion of the Chinese*. New York: Macmillan.

Dirlik, Arif. 2011. 'Confucius in the Borderlands: Globalization, the Developmental State, and the Reinvention of Confucianism'. Pp. 97–155 in his *Culture and History in Post-revolutionary China*. Hong Kong: The Chinese University Press.

Eisenstadt, Shmuel N. 1986. *The Origins and Diversity of Axial Age Civilizations*. Albany: SUNY Press.

Elman, Benjamin A. 2002. 'Rethinking "Confucianism" and "Neo-Confucianism" in Modern Chinese History'. Pp. 518–54 in *Rethinking Confucianism: Past and Present in China, Japan, Korea and Vietnam*, edited by Benjamin A. Elman, John B. Duncan and Herman Ooms. Los Angeles: UCLA Asian Pacific Monograph Series.

Elvin, Mark. 1973. *The Pattern of the Chinese Past*. Stanford: Stanford University Press.

Fan, Cunwu. 2010. 'Confucian "Religion" in the Early Republican Period'. *Chinese Studies in History*. 44(1–2): 132–55.

Fan, Lizhu and Chen, Na. 2015. 'The Religiousness of "Confucianism", and the Revival of Confucian Religion in China Today'. *Cultural Diversity in China*. 1(1): 27–43.

Fingarette, Herbert. 1972. *Confucius: The Secular as Sacred*. New York: Harper.

Fung, You-lan. 1952. *A History of Chinese Philosophy. Volume 1: The Period of the Philosophers*. Princeton: Princeton University Press.

Fung, You-lan. 1953. *A History of Chinese Philosophy. Volume 2: The Period of Classical Learning*. Princeton: Princeton University Press.

Gardner, Daniel K. 2007. *The Four Books: The Basic Teachings of the Later Confucian Tradition*. Indianapolis: Hackett Publishing.

Gernet, Jacques. 1996. *A History of Chinese Civilization*. Second Edition. Cambridge: Cambridge University Press.

Goossaert, Vincent. 2006. '1898: The Beginning of the End for Chinese Religion'. *Journal of Asian Studies*. 65(2): 307–36.

Goossaert, Vincent and Palmer, David A. 2011. *The Religious Question in Modern China*. Chicago: University of Chicago Press.

Granet, Marcel. 1975. *The Religion of the Chinese People*. Oxford: Basil Blackwell.

Hamilton, Gary G. 1984. 'Patriarchalism in Imperial China and Western Europe: A Revision of Weber's Sociology of Domination'. *Theory and Society*. 13(3): 393–425.

Harbsmeier, Christoph. 2013. 'The Birth of Confucianism from Competition with Organized Mohism'. *Journal of Chinese Studies*. 56: 1–19.

Hardacre, Helen. 1989. *Shintō and the State, 1868–1988*. Princeton: Princeton University Press.

Hon, Tze-Ki. 2010. 'Hexagrams and Politics: Wang Bi's Political Philosophy in *Zhouyi zhu*'. Pp. 71–96 in *Philosophy and Religion in Early Medieval China*, edited by Alan K.L. Chan and Yuet-Keung Lo. Albany: SUNY Press.

Hudson, G.F. 1961. *Europe and China: A Survey of their Relations from the Earliest Times to 1800*. Boston: Beacon Press.

Jaspers, Karl. 1953. *The Origin and Goal of History*. New Haven: Yale University Press.

Jensen, Lionel M. 1997. *Manufacturing Confucianism: Chinese Traditions and Universal Civilization*. Durham: Duke University Press.

Johnston, Ian (translator). 2010. *The Mozi: A Complete Translation*. Hong Kong: The Chinese University Press.

Keenan, John P. 1994. *How Master Mou Removes our Doubts: A Reader-Response Study and Translation of the* Mou-tzu Li-huo lun. Albany: SUNY Press.

Khong, Cho-Oon. 1995. 'Singapore: Political Legitimacy Through Managing Conformity'. Pp. 108–35 in *Political Legitimacy in Southeast Asia: The Quest for Moral Authority*, edited by Muthiah Alagappa. Stanford: Stanford University Press.

Kuo, Ya-pei. 2008. 'Redeploying Confucius: The Imperial State Dreams of the Nation'. Pp. 65–84 in *Chinese Religiosities: Afflictions of Modernity and State Formation*, edited by Mayfair Yang. Berkeley: University of California Press.

Kuo, Ya-pei. 2013. '"Christian Civilization" and the Confucian Church: The Origin of Secularist Politics in Modern China'. *Past and Present*. 218: 235–64.

Latourette, Kenneth Scott. 2009. *A History of Christian Missions in China*. Piscataway, NJ: Gorgias Press.

Legge, James. 1880. *The Religions of China: Confucianism and Taoism Described and Compared with Christianity*. London: Hodder and Stoughton.

Legge, James. 1971. *Confucius: Analects, The Great Learning & The Doctrine of the Mean*. New York: Dover.

Liu, Xiaobo. 2012. 'Yesterday's Stray Dog Becomes Today's Guard Dog'. Pp. 188–200 in his *No Enemies, No Hatred: Selected Essays and Poems*, edited by Perry Link, Tienchi Martin-Liao and Liu Xia. Cambridge, MA: Harvard University Press.

Makeham, John. 2008. *Lost Soul: 'Confucianism' in Contemporary Chinese Academic Discourse*. Cambridge, MA: Harvard University Press.

Metzger, Thomas A. 1977. *Escape from Predicament: Neo-Confucianism and China's Evolving Political Culture*. New York: Columbia University Press.

Mino, Wang Erh. 1965. 'Review of China and Christianity by Paul A. Cohen'. *Bulletin of the School of Oriental and African Studies*. 28(1): 184–85.

Mullett, Michael. 1984. *The Counter Reformation: The Catholic Reformation in Early Modern Europe*. London: Routledge.

Needham, Joseph. 1956. *Science and Civilization in China. Volume 2, History of Scientific Thought*. Cambridge: Cambridge University Press.

Nongbri, Brent. 2015. *Before Religion: A History of a Modern Concept*. New Haven: Yale University Press.

Provan, Iain. 2013. *Convenient Myths: The Axial Age, Dark Green Religion and the World that Never Was*. Waco, TX: Baylor University Press.

Qi, Xiaoying. 2013. 'Intellectual Entrepreneurs and the Diffusion of Ideas: Two Historical Cases of Knowledge Flow'. *American Journal of Cultural Sociology*. 1(3): 346–72.

Qi, Xiaoying. 2014. *Globalized Knowledge Flows and Chinese Social Theory*. New York: Routledge.

Rošker, Jana S. 2016. *The Rebirth of the Moral Self: The Second Generation of Modern Confucians and their Modernization Discourses*. Hong Kong: The Chinese University Press.

Schluchter, Wolfgang. 1989. *Rationalism, Religion and Domination: A Weberian Perspective*. Berkeley: University of California Press.

Song, Xianlin. 2003. 'Reconstructing the Confucian Ideal in 1980s China: The "Culture Craze" and New Confucianism'. Pp. 81–104 in *New Confucianism: A Critical Examination*, edited by John Makeham. New York: Palgrave Macmillan.

Standaert, Nicolas. 1999. 'The Jesuits did NOT Manufacture Confucianism'. *East Asian, Science, Technology, and Medicine*. 16: 115–32.

Sun, Anna. 2013. *Confucianism as a World Religion: Contested Histories and Contemporary Realities*. Princeton: Princeton University Press.

Tan, Sor-Hoon. 2008. 'Modernizing Confucianism and "New Confucianism"'. Pp. 135–54 in *The Cambridge Companion to Modern Chinese Culture*, edited by Kam Louie. Cambridge: Cambridge University Press.

Wang, Chaohua. 2012a. 'Old Sage for New Age? The Revival of Religious Confucianism in China'. *Politics and Religion in Contemporary China*. 6(2): 269–98.

Wang, Gungwu. 2012b. 'Nationalism and Confucianism'. Pp. 23–48 in *Confucianism, Chinese History and Society*, edited by Wong Sin Kiong. Singapore: World Scientific Publishing.

Watson, James L. 1993. 'Rites or Beliefs? The Construction of a Unified Culture in Late Imperial China'. Pp. 80–103 in *China's Quest for National Identity*, edited by Lowell Dittmer and Samuel S. Kim. Ithaca: Cornell University Press.

Weber, Max. 1963. *The Sociology of Religion*, translated by Ephraim Fischoff. Boston: Beacon Press.

Weber, Max. 1964. *The Religion of China: Confucianism and Taoism*, translated and edited by Hans H. Gerth, with an Introduction by C.K. Yang. New York: The Free Press.

Weber, Max. 1978. *Economy and Society: An Outline of Interpretive Sociology*, edited by Guenther Roth and Claus Wittich. Berkeley: University of California Press.

Welch, Holmes. 2003. *Taoism: The Parting of the Way*. Boston: Beacon Press.

Weston, Timothy B. 1998. 'The Formation and Positioning of the New Culture Community, 1913–1917'. *Modern China*. 24(3): 255–84.

Wilson, Thomas A. 1996. 'The Ritual Formation of Confucian Orthodoxy and the Descendants of the Sage'. *Journal of Asian Studies*. 55(3): 559–84.

Wright, Arthur F. 1971. *Buddhism in Chinese History*. Stanford: Stanford University Press.

Yang, Mayfair. 2008. 'Introduction'. Pp. 1–40 in *Chinese Religiosities: Afflictions of Modernity and State Formation*, edited by Mayfair Yang. Berkeley: University of California Press.

Yao, Xinzhong. 2000. *An Introduction to Confucianism*. Cambridge: Cambridge University Press.

Yu, Ying-shih. 1987. *Zhongguo jinshi zongjiao lunli yu shangren jingshen* (The Modern Chinese Religious Ethic and the Spirit of Merchants). Taipei: Lianjing chuban gongsi.

Zhang, Dainian. 2002. *Key Concepts in Chinese Philosophy*, trans. Edmund Ryden. Beijing: Foreign Languages Press.

Zhang, Longxi. 1998. *Mighty Opposites: From Dichotomies to Differences in the Comparative Study of China*. Stanford: Stanford University Press.

Zhou, Zuyan. 2013. *Daoist Philosophy and Literati Writings in Late Imperial China: A Case Study of the* Story of the Stone. Hong Kong: The Chinese University Press.

CHAPTER 4

Daoism

INTRODUCTION

In the title of both Weber's original German book-length discussion of China's early institutions and traditions, *Konfuzianismus und Taoismus*, and its English translation, *The Religion of China: Confucianism and Taoism*, 'Confucianism' and 'Taoism' (Daoism) are indicated together. It is of particular interest, therefore, that commentaries tend to focus on Weber's treatment of Confucianism in the work and simply ignore his account of Daoism (see, for example, Kalberg 2012: 145–64; Schluchter 1989: 85–116; but also see Bendix 1966: 126–34). The neglect of Daoism in these studies is unfortunate because consideration of Weber's treatment of this important stream of Chinese thought raises significant questions regarding his approach. In the previous chapter, discussion of Confucianism followed the historical manifestation of its ideas and their relation with its carriers, the literati, over a long period of historical time, focusing on the different ways that Confucianism could be characterized and the ways that it changes in its form and practices. The manner in which Weber approaches Confucianism was only lightly touched on in that chapter. Details of Weber's treatment of Confucianism are provided elsewhere in this book, in Chap. 2, as we have seen, and in Chap. 6. Discussion of Daoism and Weber's apprehension of it shall be in a different register in the present chapter than was employed in the previous one, focusing more fully on the details of Weber's particular grasp of Daoism and how he draws on the sources he employs in making sense of it.

© The Author(s) 2017
J. Barbalet, *Confucianism and the Chinese Self*,
https://doi.org/10.1007/978-981-10-6289-6_4

In the discussion to follow, three aspects of Weber's treatment of Daoism will be examined. First, it will be shown that Weber's selection and use of sources in his construction of Daoism, which parallels the way in which he constructs the concepts of 'Puritanism' and 'ascetic Protestantism' in selectively drawing on source material in order to methodologically design the representation of phenomena rather than empirically 'find' them (Ghosh 2008), primarily serves his prior understanding and purpose. Second, it will be shown that Weber's contrast of Daoism and Confucianism in terms of a distinction between orthodoxy and heterodoxy reflects a misunderstanding of the means of imperial Chinese state rule. Finally, it will be shown that Weber's interpretation of Daoist thought prevents appreciation of a key element of Chinese entrepreneurship that was evident at the time of his writing *The Religion of China*.

DAOISM IN *THE RELIGION OF CHINA*

Weber holds that Daoism is a heterodox doctrine in contrast with orthodox Confucianism. Weber also insists that Confucianism and Daoism share a number of features in common, even though they became antagonistic over time. The source of Daoist thought and therefore Chinese heterodoxy is the *Tao te ching* (*Daodejing*), a text traditionally attributed to Laozi, although in reality a composite work (Emerson 1995), but nevertheless often called the *Laozi*. Weber says that the meaning of Laozi's doctrine 'originally ... did not differ in the main from that of Confucianism' (Weber 1964: 177). Weber virtually copies this point of view from the Dutch sinologist Jan Jakob Maria de Groot (1854–1921), who holds that the original gods of ancient China, Heaven and Earth, are acknowledged by both Confucianism and Daoism, although Daoism later increased the number of gods, and as the augmented gods were false from the Confucian perspective, worship of them was therefore heterodox (de Groot 1910: 134). According to this line of argument, the principal idea of an order of nature, as represented in the concept *dao*, continues to be shared by both traditions. Additionally, de Groot holds that Confucianism and Daoism share the doctrine of inactivity or *wuwei* (de Groot 1910: 142). All of these propositions are repeated by Weber (1964: 180–82) and incorporated into his discussion.

Perhaps the most important point for Weber, to be addressed below, is the 'famous doctrine of inactivity, or *wuwei*, preached by Lao-tszĕ [and] warmly recommended by Confucius' (de Groot 1910: 142). Before taking up the question of Weber's discussion and understanding of *wuwei*, the supposed original closeness of Daoism and Confucianism can be addressed. While it is misleading to suggest an identity or equivalence of the extensive treatment of *wuwei* in the *Laozi* and its single mention by Confucius (Lau 1979: 132), the idea that the original meaning of Laozi's doctrine and Confucianism 'did not differ in the main', as Weber (1964: 177) says, is to ignore the strongly anti-Confucian thrust of not only the *Laozi* but also the other early leading source of Daoist thought, the *Chuang Tzu* (*Zhuangzi*) (Chan 1963: 17–19; Mote 1989: 60–63). The idea, that both Confucius and the *Laozi* teach that 'life is equal to the possession of a "*shen*" [love of humankind] ... but [that] the means differ' (Weber 1964: 180), is not an adequate statement of their respective positions, and nor does the qualification regarding their different 'means' properly distinguish between them. The supposition of a unifying base of worship common to both Confucianism and Daoism is not only false in itself, but views these very different approaches through a religious lens that is wholly distorting of each of them. The understanding of *wuwei* by de Groot, and also by Weber, is similarly misleading.

Weber is not entirely correct to say that the 'theories of non-intervention', which he sees as common to both Confucianism and Daoism, 'could be deduced ... from the idea of providential harmony (the *Tao*) in the world' (Weber 1964: 188). Confucianism places a premium on social harmony, as Weber says, but Daoism instead focusses on process, through which harmony is neither an objective or purpose nor a necessary outcome (Fung 1952: 180–83). But Weber (1964: 181, 182) is completely mistaken to say that *wuwei* through the *Tao* 'means abstention from all action' and 'release from all activity'. As we shall see, this interpretation of radical inaction as *wuwei* serves Weber's imputation of mysticism in the *Laozi* and Daoism in general, but it is not unequivocally supported by Weber's sources. It is true that *wuwei* is typically translated as 'non-action', although recent commentators point out that it is better understood as 'effortless action' (Slingerland 2007) or 'non-coercive action' (Ames and Hall 2003). Weber recommends the Oxford Professor of Chinese and one-time China missionary, James Legge, as an authority on Daoist texts (1964: 290 n 1). Legge's translations of the Chinese classics, including the Daoist sources, the *Laozi* and the *Zhuangzi*, were published in Max Müller's important series of *Sacred Books of the East*, mentioned in Chap. 2, which exemplifies the comparative approach to the study of world religions drawn upon by Weber. In his translation of the *Laozi*,

Legge is careful to point out that 'the Tâoistic "do nothing" was not an absolute quiescence and inaction, but had a method in it'; namely, that *wuwei* is nonpurposive because the 'Tâo forbids action with a personal purpose [for] all such action is sure to fail' (Legge 1962: 107, 72). The validity of this interpretation aside (Barbalet 2011: 340–47), *wuwei*, according to Legge's approach, is correctly understood not as the absence of action, but action which accommodates to rather than confronts what it is directed toward; *wuwei* is action as synchronicity, rather than forcefulness. This is action which is more mindful of the way in which things change, than it is of the direct interests of the actor; it is a nonwillful form of action directed to realizing the potential in events and in others.

Weber's particular construction of Laozi's doctrine of *wuwei* is important to him because of the way it indicates and confirms Laozi's mysticism (Weber 1964: 180), and it is this characteristic, Weber says, which sets Laozi and his school apart from Confucius and his school. As we have seen, Weber understands *wuwei* as being a release from action, which he now extends to a release from activity, in which case 'one's self is absolutely void of worldly interests' and the suspension of action or at least its minimization through *wuwei* is the 'only proof of the mystic's state of grace' (Weber 1964: 182). The idea here, that Laozi sought a state of grace, begs the question of his intentions and of the nature of the *Laozi* in particular, and 'philosophical' Daoism in general. The function of the proposition is to justify Weber's description of Laozi as engaging in 'contemplative mysticism', a term he uses a number of times (Weber 1964: 182, 183, 186). While Weber believes that Laozi and Confucius shared much, as we have seen, this is the principal point of distinction between them, according to Weber, for the 'Confucians ... were not mystics' (Weber 1964: 182). This difference does not embrace all of the opposition between Daoism and Confucianism, but it does alert us to some crucial distinctions.

The political differences between Daoism and Confucianism are significant. Whereas Daoism is associated with the idea that political rule is to provide a context for the spontaneity of its subjects, including freedom of economic activity, Confucianism advocates extensive administration and political management of the economy. Weber says that this difference springs from the mystical content of Daoist thought and its absence in Confucianism:

> ...the mystic advocated the greatest possible autonomy and self-sufficiency for the individual parts of the state, those small communities which might

form a locus of plain peasant or civic virtue. The mystics upheld the slogan: as little bureaucracy as possible, for their self-perfection could not possibly be promoted by the busy state policy of civilization. (Weber 1964: 184)

The other consequences of Daoist mysticism that Weber identifies promote a difference with Confucianism of degree rather than kind. That the *Laozi* represents a contemplative mysticism means that it lacks a 'religiously motivated, active antagonism to the world' (Weber 1964: 186). According to Weber, Protestantism manifests such an antagonism; it is out of this that modern capitalism arises. Confucianism lacks such an antagonism, according to Weber, although not because it embraces mysticism. Indeed, Confucianism shares with Protestantism a rationalism which Daoism lacks, but as the Confucian ethic reduces tension with the world, it is necessarily traditional in its consequences (Weber 1964: 235–36). Daoism, on the other hand, because it is regarded by Weber as a mystical creed and therefore inherently irrational, 'was even more traditionalist than Confucianism' (Weber 1964: 200, 205). Through its mysticism, then, and instrumentally because of its characteristic doctrine of *wuwei*, Daoism both lacks the 'active motive of a "vocational ethic"' and, correlatively, undermines the possibility of introducing innovation (Weber 1964: 188, 205). While the first of these claims is open to a qualifying interpretation, to be considered shortly, the second is empirically not sustainable as numerous and important technological inventions emanate from Daoist sources (Needham 1956: 115–32).

For Weber, then, much hinges on the argument that Laozi is a contemplative mystic and that Daoism is a mystical creed. A version of this argument, incidentally, is the typical complaint of Confucian literati (Hansen 1992: 7) who are confounded by the characteristically paradoxical form of argument that runs through the *Laozi* (Legge 1962: 26, 107), although there is nothing inherently mystical about an engagement with paradox, either in general or for Daoism in particular (Hansen 1992: 227–29; Csikszentmihalyi 1999: 44–51). In the estimation of one commentator, there have been, both in China and the West, 'attempts to put undue emphasis on the mysterious elements in the Lao tzu' (Lau 1963: xxxviii), but the basis varies on which such emphasis is placed. Whereas Weber imputes contemplative mysticism to *wuwei* as inactivity, Arthur Waley (1958: 59), an early twentieth-century British sinologist, instead associates what he sees as mystical thinking in the *Laozi* with the 'incommunicability' of *dao* doctrines in the text. Another and dissimilar assessment is that the leading Daoist ideas are 'more intellectual than mystical' (Granet quoted in Creel 1977: 15).

Lau's considered summary of the supposed mystical elements of *Daodejing* is to dismiss them as misinterpretations; the sense of the work, he says, is 'only a rather down-to-earth philosophy aimed at the mundane purpose of personal survival and political order' (Lau 1963: xxxviii). Indeed, in a more recent close examination of major arguments concerning the supposed mysticism of the *Laozi*, the conclusion is reached that:

> Not only are explicit references to mystical experiences lacking in the text, but it does not seem that the earliest commentators even read the text as an attempt to express knowledge implicitly gained through such experience ... it is not possible to state authoritatively that the *Laozi* is a mystical text. (Csikszentmihalyi 1999: 51)

Attributions of mysticism, including Weber's, constitute a contrary assessment to the ones presented here. The discussion to this point has been directed to the terms on which Weber constructs Laozi's mysticism and the sources on which he draws.

Lau's reference earlier to the 'philosophical' nature of the *Laozi*—more critical-practical than doctrinal or propositional philosophy (LaFargue 1998), it should be added—is a reminder that in European languages the term 'Daoism' may refer to both a school of thought as well as a body of religious teachings. Chinese language, however, distinguishes between them with different names—respectively, *daojia* and *daojiao* (literally, *dao*-family and *dao*-teaching). Those who argue that the *Laozi* and the other Daoist classic, *Zhuangzi*, are 'philosophical' texts tend also to hold that *daojia* is itself without religious significance and at best only remotely, if at all, meaningfully connected with the cultist ritual practices and teachings that constitute *daojiao* (Chan 1963; Creel 1977; Welch 2003). Indeed, the historical and social circumstances of the development of *daojiao* or Hsien Daoism—as the American scholar Herrlee Creel calls it, in distinguishing it from the 'purposive' Daoism of the *Laozi* (Creel 1977: 4–7)—are quite different. The practices of the folk immortality cults that contributed to the advent of *daojiao* entertain orientations and means ridiculed in the *Laozi* (Creel 1977: 8–9), written some 500 years earlier. The historical circumstances generative of *daojiao* include the advent of a sinicized Buddhism domesticated through assimilation of Daoist and Confucian idiom which provided, in turn, a monastic organizational form to *daojiao* which was previously unknown in China.

The distinction between *daojia* and *daojiao* is lost in much of Weber's discussion of Daoism, as it was for many of the missionary sinologists of the nineteenth century who regarded the *Laozi* as a sacred text which was measured against Christian sources, as when de Groot (1910: 138) describes the 'writings of Lao and Chwang ... as the holy books of Taoism'. Legge's treatment insists on the distinction between *daojia* and *daojiao*, but acknowledges subsequent inclinations to turn Laozi into a god:

> Taoism is the name both of a religion and a philosophy. The author of the philosophy is the chief god, or at least one of the chief gods, of the religion; but there is no evidence that the religion grew out of his book ... any relation between the two things is merely external, for in spirit and tendency they are antagonistic. (Legge 1880: 159–60)

An account of the development of Daoism in distinct phases, from singular reclusive scholars and holy men to monastic communities to temples and festivities and magic, is outlined by de Groot (1910: 144–54). Weber follows this developmental chronology and notices that the later Daoist magicians were not properly speaking '"successors" or "disciples" of Laozi' even though they may have considered themselves to be so (Weber 1964: 188–89, see also 202), largely because of an intellectual degeneration in their understanding of Laozi's thought (Weber 1964: 204). This latter claim is a frequently repeated theme of the missionary and lay sinologists of Weber's historical period. We shall see that Legge offers ambiguous support to the nonreligious complexion of the philosophy of the *Laozi*. Indeed, both he and de Groot are of the view that the *Laozi* is religiously infused through its possible advocacy of both yogic breathing practices and aspirations for longevity and immortality. These are the areas in which Weber also finds the religious content of the *Laozi*.

Weber regards aspirations for longevity as pertaining more to later Daoists than to the *Laozi*, although he seems to believe it is incipient in the latter. He says that the mystic's state of grace can be revealed through a 'demonstrat[ion] that the world cannot touch him ... [a] guarantee for the permanence of one's life on earth', a notion that is 'in accord with Lao-tzu's theories' (Weber 1964: 182). Weber immediately adds that Laozi 'did not develop a true doctrine of immortality; this seems to be a product of later times' (Weber 1964: 183). De Groot (1910: 148), on the other hand, does believe that the *Laozi* advocates a doctrine of longevity, but Legge is more circumspect. In reference to Chap. 50 of the *Laozi*, which he says 'sets forth the Tâo as an antidote against decay and death', Legge goes on to ask whether the author 'in ascribing such effects ... is "trifling" ... or indulging the play of his poetical fancy? or simply saying that the Tâoist will keep himself out of danger?' (Legge 1962: 93). In commenting on a passage in Chap. 52, Legge does feel 'obliged to conclude that even in Lâo-tze's mind there was the germ of the sublimation of the material frame which issues in the ascetism and life-preserving arts of the later Tâoism' (Legge 1962: 96), which is Weber's point, noted earlier. But the passage in question only refers to the claim that the follower of the Dao will 'to the end of his life ... be free from all peril' (Legge 1962: 95). In commenting on a later chapter, Legge acknowledges that a projected reading of the *Laozi's* infrequent remarks on long life to the 'later Tâoist dreams about the elixir vitae' is an 'abuse of [this] and other passages' of the text (Legge 1962: 103).

Weber (1964: 198) also refers to the 'old breathing technique which the *Tao Teh Ching* advised', and which he appreciates is the physiological basis of mystical practices (Weber 1964: 179). Certainly, de Groot (1910: 153) believes that 'the *Tao-teh-king* [was] the first book that taught [man] about immortality and divinity by the discipline of the breath'. In fact, though, it is difficult to locate any advice about breathing techniques of any sort in the *Laozi*. At best, there are metaphorical references to breathing, but these are very infrequent and function as images without imperative and too vague to reveal a preference or a practice. The most explicit reference to breathing is in Chap. 10, which states in Legge's translation that 'When one gives undivided attention to the (vital) breath, and brings it to the utmost degree of pliancy, he can become as a (tender) babe' (Legge 1962: 53–54). The chapter goes on to state that 'In the opening and shutting of the gates of heaven', one can take on the female role (Legge 1962: 54). Legge (1962: 54) acknowledges that 'this chapter is one of the most difficult to understand and translate in the whole work', a point confirmed by the wildly opposite interpretations of the text provided by standard commentators (Chan 1963: 116; Duyvendak 1954: 36–39; Waley 1958: 153–54). Legge's statement regarding the first quoted passage above, that it suggests that by 'management of his vital breath [one can] bring his body to the state of Tâoistic perfection' seems to be an over interpretation, but in any event, the perfection that might obtain is likely to be in a physical suppleness of the body rather than its mystic transcendence. Regarding the second passage, Legge (1962: 54) notes that 'The "gates of heaven" ... is a Tâoistic phrase for the nostrils as the organ of breath'. But again, there is no mystical connotation here as the image of the female role in the *Laozi*, to which such breathing may give access, refers to both fecund potency and the strategic advantage of weakness, neither of which is mystical.

The only other possible references to breathing in the *Laozi* are in Chaps. 42, 52, and 55, but they are without the significance we might be led to expect on the basis of Weber's pronouncement. Legge offers no associated commentary on them. The reference to breathing in Chap. 52 is particularly interesting in terms of the discussion here. From the point of view of Weber's supposition, it is entirely anomalous as it says that keeping the mouth and nostrils closed will exempt one from a life of exertion whereas opening one's portals in promotion of his affairs means there is no safety in his life (Legge 1962: 95). Legge says that the meaning of the chapter is obscure. A possible reading of this passage is that it is an ironic ridicule of the yogic breathing practices that Weber sees as given exposition in the *Laozi*, but as we shall see, a more meaningful explanation is available. Finally, although there is no reference to breathing in the text of Chap. 6, Legge's comments on it claim that the chapter provides foundation 'for the development of the later Tâoism, which occupies itself with the prolongation of life by management of the breath' (Legge 1962: 51). While this assertion is itself without foundation, it does reinforce the idea that advocacy of yogic breathing postdates the *Laozi* and cannot be located in it.

The persistence of the idea that yogic breathing is indicated or even advocated in the *Laozi* is in fact encouraged by Legge's acknowledgement of the authority of the He-shang Gong (Ho-shang Kung) commentary on the *Laozi*, dating from approximately 200 AD. This commentary contains an explicitly pneumatic interpretation of the text associated with the formation of alchemic and magical temple Daoism and an influence from Buddhist sources as they accommodate to Chinese mores. Legge draws extensively on this source. In the Ho-shang Kung commentary on Chap. 6, the chapter which Legge (1962: 51) says lays 'a foundation … for the development of a later Tâoism, which occupies itself with the prolongation of life by the management of the breath or vital force', mentioned earlier, there is an interpretation of the line, 'The gates of the dark one and of the female … are called the root of heaven and earth' (Erkes 1950: 22). It is claimed in this interpretation that 'gates' here refers to 'nose and mouth' which 'inhale and exhale' (Erkes 1950: 22). This is repeated in Kung's commentary on Chap. 52 (Erkes 1950: 92–93). Legge follows suit in his translation, as indicated earlier. The irony, though, is that the

Ho-shang Kung text indicates 'barring' [blocking] the mouth rather than opening it; if breathing was implied, opening is more likely. And yet, this provides a clue to a more meaningful interpretation of these passages in the *Laozi*.

At the time that the *Laozi* or *Daodejing* was written, *qi* was understood to refer to 'both energy and matter' and it had 'unquestioned dynamic properties' (Schwartz 1985: 181). But the term has wider application because an additional 'one of its meanings is ... "breath"' (Schwartz 1985: 180). *Qi* is central in the fourth-century BC cosmology of China. This cosmology, as described by Lau (2003: xxiv–xxvi), holds that the universe is made of *qi*, of varying consistency. Grosser and therefore heavier *qi* makes up the earth; refined and therefore lighter *qi* rises and is the sky or heaven. Humankind, as situated between the earth and the sky, is a harmonious mixture of the two kinds of *qi*, with the body consisting of grosser *qi* and the heart/mind holding refined *qi*. Lau reports that at the time there were different understandings regarding human endowments of *qi*, one school holding that more *qi* could be acquired over the course of a lifetime, and another holding that a person's *qi* is limited to their original endowment, and that it is depleted by expenditure of mental energy; death results from an exhaustion of a person's supply of *qi*. On the basis of the teachings of the first school, a person should keep their apertures open to admit additional *qi;* on the basis of the second school, on the other hand, blocking one's apertures is necessary to avoid loss of *qi*. Assuming this cosmology, the *Laozi* represents a version of the second school of thought concerning the limited supply of *qi* a person possesses over a lifetime. Chapter 52 simply states the obvious—it is best to block, bar, or close the mouth and nostrils. Reference to *qi* in the other chapters of the *Laozi* mentioned can also be understood entirely in terms of this early cosmology, and the yogic breathing interpretation adopted by Weber, and his sources, is not only unnecessary but misleading.

ORTHODOXY AND HETERODOXY

Weber differentiates between the *Laozi* and later Daoists; as we have seen, he holds that the *Laozi* is a mystical text but also that the '*Tao Teh Ching* was apparently largely free of magic' and that 'Taoist doctrine may also be differentiated from these magical crudities' (Weber 1964: 185, 200). Later Daoism, on the other hand, 'was merely an organization of magicians' and 'sorcerers' (Weber 1964: 224–25, 203). But both the *Laozi* and the later Daoists are together classified by Weber as a 'heterodox tradition', an appellation employed by Legge (1880: 200–2) and de Groot (1910: 134), as these traditions stand in relation with and in contrast to what these writers regard as 'orthodox' Confucianism. Weber argues that this particular distinction between orthodoxy and heterodoxy is relatively permeable, however, especially with regard to magic, which Confucian orthodoxy tolerates. In considering the relation between Confucianism and Daoism, Weber says that while the Confucian literati failed to understand the 'original meaning of Lao-tzu's philosophy' and also 'sharply rejected' its 'consequences', they nevertheless 'treated with tolerant disdain' the magic of Daoist priests, which they 'regarded as a diet suitable for the masses' (Weber 1964: 204). The theme of magic is pursued in detail in Chap. 6, but it is necessary to here note its importance to Weber's account of Confucianism.

The Confucian attitude to Daoist magic, as Weber describes it, indicates both the political rationale of orthodoxy in state rule and its acquiescence in the face of the beliefs of the population over which that rule is exercised. Because he held that 'the belief in magic was part of the constitutional foundation of sovereign power' in China, Weber says:

> Confucianism was helpless when confronted with the magic image of the world, however much it disdained Taoism. This helplessness prevented the Confucians from being internally capable of eradicating the fundamental, purely magical conceptions of the Taoists. To tackle magic always appeared dangerous for the Confucian's own power. (Weber 1964: 200, see also 194, 196)

Thus, orthodoxy and heterodoxy balance on the fulcrum of political power. But the toleration of Confucian orthodoxy toward magic compromises its rationalism with serious consequences for its 'economic mentality', which is of 'special interest' to Weber (1964: 177). So while there is a 'cleavage between the official institution of grace and non-classical popular religion' and while the latter is 'source of a methodical way of life differing from the official cult … which Confucianism … always treated as heterodox' (Weber 1964: 174–75), the 'relative toleration which was granted to heterodox cults for reasons of state' (Weber 1964: 217, see also 194), according to Weber, preserved China's political power structure but compromised its prospects for an economic revolution of the type experienced in Protestant Europe.

Weber's treatment of Confucian latitude toward heterodox religions and magic in terms of 'the disdainful "toleration" which is the natural attitude of every secular bureaucracy toward religion ... moderated only by the need for taming the masses' (Weber 1964: 217) is a generous lapse on his part. Only a sentence earlier, it is Confucian susceptibility to the persuasion of ghosts that is responsible. He says that 'according to de Groot's very plausible assumption, the *fēng shui* were decisive [in the retention of monasteries] for it was impossible to remove places once licensed for worship without incurring a perhaps dangerous excitement of the spirits' (Weber 1964: 217). In fact, temples and 'places of worship' were traditionally communal property in China, and it was not unusual for them to be put to nonreligious use as the need arose (Yang 1961: 326, 368). Weber is doing here what he does throughout, namely, sacralizing nonreligious phenomena—the concept of *dao*, which he says is accepted by both Confucianism and Daoism, refers to an 'unchangeable element' and therefore, an 'absolute value'; 'in short, it is the divine All-One of which one can partake' (Weber 1964: 181–82). Such spiritualization and attribution of divinity to the *dao* is explicitly rejected by Legge (1962: 65, 72), and none of the propositions Weber sets out here can be supported, not only relating to the supposed divinity of *dao* but also its supposed unchanging nature or abstract value, none of which either school accepts. Neither does Daoism promise a 'happy life in the world ... beyond', as Weber (1964: 204) supposes, although in this instance, he no doubt follows Legge (1962: 75–76) in a mistranslation of the *Laozi* (see Lynn 1999: 112 note 4; Chan 1963: 159).

The needs and exercise of political rule are important, as Weber says, for understanding the antagonistic differences between Confucianism and Daoism. But he is mistaken to hold that the approaches and practices he summarizes as orthodoxy and heterodoxy gravitate around questions of belief, not only religious belief, but belief at all, as we shall see. He says that:

> Ultimately, the substantive differences between orthodox and heterodox doctrines and practices ... had two sources ... [first] Confucianism was a status ethic of the bureaucracy educated in literature [and secondly] piety and especially ancestor-worship was retained as politically indispensable foundations for patrimonialism. Only when these interests appeared to be threatened did the instinct of self preservation in the ruling stratum react by attaching the stigma of heterodoxy. (Weber 1964: 213)

The correlative elements of Daoist heterodoxy which correspond to Confucian orthodoxy set out here are thus, first, that the 'mystics upheld the slogan: as little bureaucracy as possible' (Weber 1964: 184), and second, that the doctrine of 'little tranquility', that is 'the exclusive rule of individual interest', which Weber rightly sees as 'so irreconcilable with the filial piety basic to all Confucian ethics' is an 'anarchist social ideal' espoused as Daoist (Weber 1964: 212).

While Weber is here describing elements of beliefs associated with Chinese institutions as he sees them, his patterning framework is entirely European. For instance, he regards the Confucian inclination to leave 'the gods aside' to be analogous to 'Greek philosophical schools' which gave leeway to the 'old Hellenic deities' (Weber 1964: 175). This was a mirror of the Chinese situation because the 'cult of the heroic and folk deities of "Homeric" times was correspondingly developed as the official institution; but the teachings of the philosophers were the optional concerns of private citizens' (Weber 1964: 177). More pertinently, Weber regards the Chinese state as pursuing a dogma or doctrine, any contravention of which is a heresy to be challenged and removed:

> The Chinese state fought heresies, which in its view were hostile to the state, partly through indoctrination … and partly … through fire and sword, like the Catholic Church fighting the denial of sacramental grace and the Roman Empire fighting the rejection of the cult of the emperor. (Weber 1964: 214)

For these reasons, Weber says that 'the Chinese state approached a "denominational" state' which maintained its rule through 'the rejection of false doctrines' (Weber 1964: 215). But in making such a claim, Weber simply demonstrates that he fails to understand the basis on which Chinese imperial state power rested.

The situation he describes—of a state focused on the correctness of belief and therefore directed to discovering and exorcising heresy—closely follows developments in Christian Europe and has only ever been experienced once in China's long history and then more than half a century after Weber wrote *The Religion of China*, namely, during the Great Proletarian Cultural Revolution of 1966–1976 led by Chairman Mao. Only at this time was the question of an individual's beliefs of direct concern to a nationwide political organization that was in a position to propagate and manage a centrally controlled ideology and which had the means to administer and enforce it. The Party orthodoxy of being 'Red' did matter during this decade in the same way that appropriate belief mattered for the rule of European states in which the role of the Church in maintaining adherence to particular systems of belief was a core basis of upholding political order. Disagreements over religious belief were behind political changes and reconfigurations which repeatedly redrew the map of Europe from the sixteenth to the twentieth century. The entirely European view of culture and identity, as depending on the ideas a person believes, requires an encompassing apparatus—originally a dominant church organized as a national bureaucracy able to maintain control at the parish level—capable of generating and propagating to a subject population a single coherent belief system.

Chinese state adoption of Confucianism, unlike European state assertion of Christianity, served internal organizational purposes and did not entail enforced doctrinal adherence of state subjects. It is often noted that during the Han dynasty (206 BC to 220 AD) Confucianism was an 'official ideology' and therefore a state 'orthodoxy' (Balazs 1966: 18–19; Gernet 1996: 159–60). But the application of these English language terms to the Han court requires careful qualification, as indicated in Chap. 3. The regulation of both the court elite and state administration through Confucian humility, docility, submission, and seniority-hierarchy as well as inculcation of its doctrines, prescribing elite-group membership, did not preclude alternate currents in the broader society (Balazs 1966: 156–57) or threaten 'the eclectic character of intellectual life at the Han court' (Gernet 1996: 160). The Imperial civil service examination system, which came into regular use during the Song dynasty (Elvin 1973: 92), based on recitation of Confucian classics, was not to establish or maintain orthodoxy, according to Weber (1964: 121), but rather to promote a 'way of thought' that both preserved privilege and encouraged status group formation (Weber 1964: 46, 86, 117).

Chinese officials, with the singular exception noted earlier, have never been interested in the beliefs of the religions and movements they have opposed. It is only when such forces mobilize against the state or through their behavior, including expression of strong emotion or particularistic attachment or devotion, are seen as constituting a threat to public order that the state has attempted to control them: 'it was not philosophical or theological objection but practical political consideration that was the leading motivation for the traditional antagonism towards heterodoxy' (Yang 1961: 193). Indeed, the imperial state did not legislate for beliefs nor advocate doctrine. In matters of worship, Chinese state officials, as anthropologist James Watson puts it:

...were not concerned with ... mental constructs; what mattered was which deities people chose to worship, not what they believed about them. The state stressed form rather than content. There was never any attempt to foster a standardized set of beliefs in Chinese religion. (Watson 1993: 96)

The unity of the Chinese state was achieved not by orthodoxy, as Weber supposes, but orthopraxy; not rightness of belief, but of practice. Weber's concern with orthodoxy simply fails to understand the nature of Chinese culture and mentality as based on orthopraxy and its significance for political rule.

Watson reminds us that there are two modes of societal integration, one operates through a 'system of shared beliefs' and the other through a 'set of shared practices or rites' (Watson 1993: 83). In Imperial China, he goes on to say, 'orthopraxy (correct practice) reigned over orthodoxy (correct belief) as the principle means of attaining and maintaining cultural unity' (Watson 1993: 84). This is not to say that the Chinese lacked a set of shared beliefs, to which we shall return in the following section, but that the 'genius of the Chinese approach to cultural integration', as Watson puts it, is that 'the system allowed for a high degree of variation within an overarching structure of unity' which permitted China 'to attain a level of cultural unity that was never possible in other, large-scale agrarian societies' (Watson 1993: 89, 100). The Imperial Chinese state imposed a set of rites that regulated the life cycle and brought uniformity to the practices of everyday life. The rituals associated with birth, marriage, death, and relations with ancestors are remarkably similar throughout China and have continuity from earlier times to the present day. This is not to deny regional variation, but such variation is not disruptive of the commonality of practice and ritual which underlies the cultural unity of the Imperial Chinese state. The meaning of the associated symbols, however, yields to enormous variety.

Through orthopraxy, the same symbol may acquire a number of quite different meanings. In a study of the Empress of Heaven (*Tian Hou*) cult, Watson (1985) shows that the same single god has been given quite different meanings by different classes of people and by people in different regions and locations, all which share more or less the same ritual form and symbolic expression. A diversity of meaning in such a context has no significance for attribution of heterodoxy in itself. Indeed, such an arrangement is a significant feature of the structure of Chinese power in which central authority and local communities participated (Herrmann-Pillath 2000: 181–82).

Most Chinese religious observances require no clergy (Eastman 1988: 52–53), and in any event the clergy of Chinese religions has traditionally been small in number and poorly organized (Yang 1961: 307–27). This both reinforces the irrelevance of orthodoxy, through the relative absence of an apparatus of the mechanisms of uniform belief, and enhances the significance of orthopraxy as an alternative means of political order through shared practices or rites. Indeed, the relation between a political center and outlying local populations, which requires common symbols but permits diverse meanings, is a characteristic feature of Chinese political rule in which the relative autonomy of local communities in their relations with a remote central authority remains ordered and unified not in spite of but through local diversity (Watson 1993: 91). The expansion and maintenance of China's imperial political rule was achieved through a process of sinicization which 'involved no conversion to a received dogma, no professions of belief in a creed or set of ideas', but was realized 'by acting Chinese, by behaving ... Chinese' through the performance of key rituals (Watson 1993: 93; see also Herrmann-Pillath 2000: 184).

We have seen that Weber believes that Confucian tolerance of Daoist religious practices and principles constitutes a weakness of its orthodoxy. From the point of view of orthopraxy, however, such absorption of 'heterodoxy' is an abiding strength (Herrmann-Pillath 2000: 181–83). Indeed, in its doctrinal development and rectification Confucianism has drawn on Daoism during two significant periods of its long history—namely, during the post-Han *xuanxue* movement of the third century and in the construction of neo-Confucianism during the Tang and subsequent dynasties from the eighth century. As indicated in the previous chapter, the *xuanxue* movement was not designed to overthrow Confucius as the highest sage but to find a surer footing for Confucian rule in the previously marginalized texts of the *Laozi*, the *Zhuangzi*, and the *I Ching* (*Yijing*) (Chua 2010; Hon 2010). The availability of Daoist ideas to improve the basis and rationale of Confucian political order suggests not only the unsuitability of the concepts of orthodoxy and heterodoxy in understanding the cultural apparatus of the Imperial Chinese state, but also the transferable application of cultural elements that a Weberian approach will necessarily regard as problematic when ideas and values are ascribed elective affinities which are somehow inherent in the values themselves. This raises the question of what role ideas might be given in sociological explanation, and in the context of the discussion here, what role can be ascribed to the ideas associated with Daoist thought in particular.

ENTREPRENEURSHIP AND DAOISM

In reflecting on the forces which 'handicapped' the development of 'rational entrepreneurial capitalism' in China, Weber, as we have seen, mentions both institutional factors and also the 'lack of a particular mentality' which he locates in the orthodox 'Chinese "ethos" … peculiar to a stratum of officials and aspirants to office' (Weber 1964: 104). We have also seen that Weber (1964: 188) believes that Daoism, even more emphatically than Confucianism, lacks the basis of a 'vocational ethic'. It is of particularly interest, therefore, that Weber (1964: 188) also acknowledges what he teasingly calls 'Taoist "Manchesterism"' and a 'Taoist virtue of thriftiness'. These are immediately dismissed as efficacious, however, because by hypothesis they have a pedigree irrelevant for entrepreneurship in being 'contemplative' rather than 'asceticist' (Weber 1964: 188). Yet, Weber (1964: 183, 205) cannot help observing the worldly orientation of Daoism, and also its firm association with traders, merchants, and the propertied classes (Weber 1964: 186, 204, 224). This association is by no means accidental. The great Han Dynasty historian, Sima Qian (c.145–86 BC), anticipated Adam Smith by nearly 2000 years when he wrote:

> There must be farmers to produce food, men to extract the wealth of mountains and marshes, artisans to produce these things and merchants to circulate them. There is no need to wait for government orders: each man will play his part, doing his best to get what he desires…When all work willingly at their trades, just as water flows ceaselessly downhill day and night, things will appear unsought and people will produce them without being asked. For clearly this accords with the Way [*dao*] and is in keeping with nature. (Chien 1979: 411)

The root of laissez-faire in the concept of *wuwei*, which we saw earlier Weber regards as the basis of Daoist mysticism, is evident here not simply in the water metaphor, characteristic of *Laozi*, but especially in the idea that noninterference is naturalistic. Indeed, in the eighteenth century, François Quesnay developed his physiocratic theory of laissez-faire by borrowing the concept of *wuwei* to indicate the absence of state interference and regulation (Gerlach 2005; Hudson 1961, pp. 322–26; Reichwein 1968, pp. 99–110).

Weber would have been mistaken to believe that the traders, merchants, and members of propertied classes he perceives as having an association with Daoism (Weber 1964: 186, 204, 224) were predominantly Daoist devotees. Chinese devotional traditions do not operate in terms of followers of a faith or formations of congregations, but depending on the occasion, people would draw upon specialist services of Buddhist, Daoist, or some other type of practitioner or 'priest' (Granet 1975: 144). Indeed, there is a certain mobility of practices and the ideas associated with them, such that merchants in late Imperial China were likely to draw on Confucian self-cultivation practices, developed by scholars and literati, in orienting to commercial advantage (Lufrano 1997). Before reinterpreting Weber's observations concerning the apparent association of entrepreneurial groups and Daoist beliefs, it is first necessary to consider his classic claim regarding the association of the Protestant ethic with capitalistic orientation.

The data of Weber's well-known argument concerning the elective affinity of Protestantism and capitalism can be inserted into a different understanding of the relationship between ideas and outcomes than the one he proposes. It can be held that Protestantism contains or implies a particular cognitive apparatus in the sense that religious dissenters, as critics of an established order, may possess novel cognitive orientations or capacities. If such persons are business-orientated, then as a result of such cognitive dispositions, they may perceive opportunities for profit-making that might not otherwise be apparent. The difference between this argument and Weber's is that it is not principally that Protestantism leads to a capitalistic ethic, but that should a Protestant be capitalistically inclined, then their religion, not as a set of values but as an organizationally formed cognitive framework, may generate a perception of opportunity for profit, irrespective of whatever motive may direct them to profit-making.

The distinction drawn here is familiar as that between culture as the source of values which shape the ultimate ends of action, as in Weber's argument concerning elective affinities, and culture as a tool kit of habits or skills from which strategies of action can be constructed (Swidler 1986). The 'tool kit' model of culture emphasizes its framing, rather than its determinative capacities. The voluntaristic form of Swidler's argument, though, which supposes that culture comprises delinkable and variably available elements, consciously selected and strategically applied, fails to capture an aspect of systems of belief that includes an understanding of cognitive schemata which function as organizing principles that 'provide default assumptions about the characteristics, relationships and entailments' of objects and events (DiMaggio 1997: 269). This latter aspect of cultural apparatus inherent in belief systems is particularly relevant for perceiving opportunities for profit-making mentioned earlier, an 'ability to perceive new opportunities that cannot be proved at the moment at which action has to be taken' (Schumpeter 1991: 417). The opportunities relevant to entrepreneurs are thus prospective rather than given or material realities, and they become manifest only when they are taken. Effective opportunity structures therefore only exist as hypotheses or as discoverable possibilities dependent on conjectural perception.

The relationships that are important to enterprise in this sense are those of changing circumstances in which new opportunities for moneymaking can arise. In this context, the 'mentality' most likely to capitalize on such opportunities is consonant with the Daoist intellectual tradition that assumes unavoidable change and which has no conception of an idealized and enduring stability, as in Greek and also Christian thought. In this regard, Daoism is also set against Confucianism, which has a core understanding of the family as a source of assurance against external contingency. The *Laozi* and what might be called classical Daoism in general thus arguably presents characteristic cognitive schemata of acceptance of change and a direction of thought attuned to questions of how to deal with change and oriented to coping with it. This aspect of Chinese 'mentality' simply escapes Weber's attention. It is documented in empirical studies of Chinese subjects, compared with European and North American subjects, which reveal a propensity toward recognizing and accepting change (Ji et al. 2010; Nisbett 2003). In an ethnographic study of the Penang Chinese community, the anthropologist Jean DeBernardi (2006: 53–80) shows how these principles, practiced as 'improved luck' and 'good fate', emanate from Daoist notions encapsulated in Chinese popular religious culture. They provide the basis of a Chinese capitalist ethos absent in Weber's analysis (DeBernardi 2006: 53–54).

The cognitive formation indicated here as contributing to schemata of Chinese entrepreneurship is readily located in a number of texts associated with the Daoist tradition. Perhaps the most familiar idea of this sort today is the notion of strength in weakness, of advantage in threat or danger, which generate perceptions of opportunities in market engagements which might otherwise not be perceived; these are principles stated in the Daoist *Sunzi Bingfa* or *Art of War* (Tao 2000: 51, 52, 56, 62). A more general orientation to anticipation of and responding to change in this manner is found in the *Yijing* or *Book of Changes* (Lynn 1994: 51, 56, 64–65, 77). But the most detailed and thorough statement of this perspective is in the *Laozi*. Laozi's *dao* is paradoxically constant and continuous in its reversion and changeability; it holds that opposites are mutually productive of each other, that in order to achieve a purpose its obverse must be attempted, that a thing seems to be quite other than it is, and so on (Legge 1962: 47–48, 78, 84; Ames and Hall 2003: 80, 133, 140–41). Underlying these particular sets of relationships are the more general or abstract ideas that functionality derives from absence (Legge 1962: 54–55; Ames and Hall 2003: 91) and that a grasp of the imminent and the latent properties of things provides situational advantage (Legge 1962: 71, 106–7, 107–8; Ames and Hall 2003: 120–21, 175, 177–78). It is not assumed that these teachings have meaningful existence for persons through their participation in ritual practices. Rather, these schemata are 'diffused' in the sense that the outlook and concepts associated with them are insinuated in and dispersed through secular social institutions and practices, including Chinese language and popular culture (Yang 1961: 296–300).

Weber was prepared to acknowledge that the Chinese 'would be quite capable … of assimilating capitalism which has technically and economically been fully developed in the modern cultural area', and he suggests that this would be achieved through imitation (Weber 1964: 248, 242). But this is to ignore the success of overseas Chinese entrepreneurs in Southeast Asia who were establishing capitalistic businesses from the end of the nineteenth century. In his near-contemporary survey of foreign economic activity in the region, Helmut Callis wrote of the broad participation of overseas Chinese, typically manifest in the Netherlands Indies: 'The Chinese are the predominant factor in trade in almost every part of the country … [and] represented in almost every branch of agricultural and industrial endeavor' (Callis 1942: 35). Unlike earlier generations of traders involved in Chinese tributary relations with peripheral states who were under imperial supervision (Wang 1991; Reid 1996; Tagliacozzo and Chang 2011), these entrepreneurs were free of the constraining institutions Weber sees as inhibitory of capitalist development in China. Their ability to establish capitalist firms is not only testament to their appropriate 'mentality', but their doing so was at a time when Weber was penning his argument against such a possibility.

CONCLUSION

The discussion in this chapter is both deconstructive and constructive. In deconstructing Weber's treatment of Daoist ideas and texts, especially the *Laozi*, in terms both of his sources and more recent authorities, Weber's disjointed presentation is revealed to serve a purpose he brings to the analysis, and its limitations are exposed. Weber's appreciation of relations between religious belief and state power in European historical experience also is shown in the preceding discussion to be transposed onto his account of Chinese political rule through the framework of orthodoxy in tension with heterodoxy. This too has been shown to be a projection on the basis of European historical experience, rather than an accurate portrayal of Chinese institutions. An alternative understanding based on the notion of orthopraxy is presented in the discussion above. Finally, by briefly reconstructing Weber's treatment of the relationship between culture and economic practices, the signal role of Daoist thought in Chinese entrepreneurship has been seen to be more significant than would be expected on the basis of Weber's analysis.

The significance of Daoism to not only Chinese tradition but also for Chinese entrepreneurship is acknowledged by Weber, in a sense, even though the majority of his interpreters devote little attention to it. The present chapter deals not only with Weber's discussion of Daoism but also the treatment of Daoism in his sources, especially in de Groot and Legge. It has been shown that the conventional understanding of the *Laozi* as a site of advocacy for yogic breathing practices, which Weber accepts as confirmation of the idea that it is a mystic text, is not supported by the evidence. It is true that both de Groot and Legge indicate references to yogic breathing in the *Laozi* and that Legge, in particular, offers close textual analysis and commentary in support of the idea that breathing practices are of concern in this work, even though Norman Girardot (2002: 428) claims that Legge 'only very obliquely' considers these matters. It is shown in the discussion above that recent research concerning Chinese cosmology contemporary with the *Laozi*, however, suggests an entirely different approach to this aspect of the text.

Examination of Weber's discussion of Daoism and its leading literary source provides an opportunity to understand Weber's method or approach, his sources and how he uses them, and his apprehension of China through a lens of European history and its concerns. It also permits a reorientation of the understanding of the relationship between ideas and values on the one hand and economic entrepreneurship on the other that Weber developed from the *Protestant Ethic* and subsequent related works. Various aspects of these and cognate dimensions of Daoism and how they relate to Weber's exposition of Chinese institutions and thought traditions will be touched on further in the three following chapters, along with other matters that together provide a more complete appreciation of Weber's treatment of China and its traditions.

REFERENCES

Ames, Roger T. and Hall, David L. 2003. *Daodejing: A Philosophical Translation.* New York: Ballantine Books.

Balazs, Etienne. 1966. *Chinese Civilization and Bureaucracy.* New Haven: Yale University Press.

Barbalet, Jack. 2011. 'Market Relations as *Wuwei*: Daoist Concepts in Analysis of China's Post-1978 Market Economy'. *Asian Studies Review.* 35(3): 335–54.

Bendix, Reinhard. 1966. *Max Weber: An Intellectual Portrait.* London: Methuen.

Callis, Helmut G. 1942. *Foreign Capital in Southeast Asia.* New York: Institute of Pacific Relations.

Chan, Wing-Tsit. 1963. 'The Way of Lao Tzu: Introduction'. Pp. 3–93 in his *The Way of Lao Tzu: Tao-te ching.* London: Prentice-Hall.

Chien, Szuma. 1979. *Selections from Records of the Historian,* translated by Yang Hsien-yi and Gladys Yang. Peking: Foreign Languages Press.

Chua, Jude Soo-Meng. 2010. 'Tracing the Dao: Wang Bi's Theory of Names'. Pp. 53–70 in *Philosophy and Religion in Early Medieval China,* edited by Alan K.L. Chan and Yuet-Keung Lo. Albany: SUNY Press.

Creel, Herrlee G. 1977. 'What is Taoism?' Pp. 1–24 in his *What is Taoism? And Other Studies in Chinese Cultural History.* Chicago: University of Chicago Press.

Csikszentmihalyi, Mark. 1999. 'Mysticism and Apophatic Discourse in the *Laozi*'. Pp. 33–58 in *Religious and Philosophical Aspects of the Laozi,* edited by Mark Csikszentmihalyi and P.J. Ivanhoe. Albany: SUNY Press.

DeBernardi, Jean Elizabeth. 2006. *The Way that Lives in the Heart: Chinese Popular Religion and Spiritual Mediums in Penang, Malaysia.* Stanford: Stanford University Press.

de Groot, Jan Jakob Marie. 1910. *The Religion of the Chinese.* New York: Macmillan,

DiMaggio, Paul. 1997. 'Culture and Cognition'. *Annual Review of Sociology.* 23: 263–87.

Duyvendak, J.J.L. 1954. *Tao Te Ching: The Book of the Way and its Virtue.* London: John Murray.

Eastman, Lloyd E. 1988. *Family, Field, and Ancestors: Constancy and Change in China's Social and Economic History, 1550–1949.* New York: Oxford University Press.

Elvin, Mark. 1973. *The Patterns of the Chinese Past: A Social and Economic Interpretation.* Stanford: Stanford University Press.

Emerson, John. 1995. 'A Stratification of Lao Tzu'. *Journal of Chinese Religions.* 3: 1–27.

Erkes, Eduard. 1950. *Ho-shang-kung's Commentary on Lao-tse,* translated and annotated by Eduard Erkes. Ascona: Artibus Asiae.

Fung, Yu-lan. 1952. *A History of Chinese Philosophy*, volume 1. Princeton: Princeton University Press.

Gerlach, Christian. 2005. Wuwei *in Europe: A Study of Eurasian Economic Thought*. Working Paper No 12/05. Department of Economic History, London School of Economics.

Gernet, Jacques. 1996. *A History of Chinese Civilization*. Cambridge: Cambridge University Press.

Ghosh, Peter. 2008. 'Max Weber's Idea of "Puritanism": A Case Study in the Empirical Construction of the *Protestant Ethic*'. Pp. 5–49 in his *A Historian Reads Max Weber: Essays on the Protestant Ethic*. Wiesbaden: Harrassowitz.

Girardot, Norman J. 2002. *The Victorian Translation of China: James Legge's Oriental Pilgrimage*. Berkeley: University of California Press.

Granet, Marcel. 1975. *The Religion of the Chinese People*. Oxford: Basil Blackwell.

Hansen, Chad. 1992. *A Daoist Theory of Chinese Thought*. New York: Oxford University Press.

Herrmann-Pillath, Carsten. 2000. 'Strange Notes on Modern Statistics and Traditional Popular Religion in China: Further Reflections on the Importance of Sinology for Social Science as Applied to China'. Pp. 171–89 in *Opera Sinologica 11, Festschrift für Martin Gimm*, edited by Lutz Bieg, Erling von Mende and Martina Siebert. Weisbaden: Harrossowitz Verlag.

Hon, Tze-Ki. 2010. 'Hexagrams and Politics: Wang Bi's Political Philosophy in *Zhouyi zhu*'. Pp. 71–96 in *Philosophy and Religion in Early Medieval China*, edited by Alan K.L. Chan and Yuet-Keung Lo. Albany: SUNY Press.

Hudson, G.F. 1961. *Europe and China: A Survey of their Relations from the Earliest Times to 1800*. Boston: Beacon Press.

Ji, Li-Jun, Lee, Albert and Guo, Tieyuan. 2010. 'The Thinking Styles of Chinese People'. Pp. 155–67 in *The Oxford Handbook of Chinese Psychology*, edited by Michael Harris Bond. Oxford: Oxford University Press.

Kalberg, Stephen. 2012. *Max Weber's Comparative-Historical Sociology Today: Major Themes, Mode of Causal Analysis, and Applications*. London: Ashagate.

LaFargue, Michael. 1998. 'Recovering the *Tao-te-ching's* Original Meaning: Some Remarks on Historical Hermeneutics'. Pp. 255–75 in *Lao-tzu and the Tao-te-ching*, edited by Livia Kohn and Michael LaFargue. Albany: SUNY Press.

Lau, D.C. 1963. 'Introduction'. Pp. vii–xlv in *Lao Tzu: Tao Te Ching*, translated with an Introduction by D. C. Lau. London: Penguin.

Lau, D.C. 1979. *Confucius: The Analects*, translated with an Introduction by D. C. Lau. London: Penguin.

Lau, D.C. 2003. 'Introduction'. Pp. vii–xlviii in *Mencius*, translated with an Introduction by D. C. Lau. London: Penguin.

Legge, James. 1880. *The Religions of China: Confucianism and Taoism Described and Compared with Christianity*. London: Hodder and Stoughton.

Legge, James. 1962. *The Texts of Taoism: The Tao Te Ching of Lao Tzŭ; The Writings of Chung Tzŭ*. Part 1. New York: Dover Publications.

Lufrano, Richard John. 1997. *Honorable Merchants: Commerce and Self-Cultivation in Late Imperial China*. Honolulu: University of Hawai'i Press.

Lynn, Richard John. 1994. *The Classic of Changes. A New Translation of the I Ching as Interpreted by Wang Bi*. New York: Columbia University Press.

Lynn, Richard John. 1999. *The Classic of the Way and Virtue: A New Translation of the Tao-te ching of Laozi as Interpreted by Wang Bi*. New York: Columbia University Press.

Mote, Frederick W. 1989. *Intellectual Foundations of China*. New York: McGraw-Hill.

Needham, Joseph. 1956. *Science and Civilization in China. Volume 2, History of Scientific Thought*. Cambridge: Cambridge University Press.

Nisbett, Richard. 2003. *The Geography of Thought*. New York: The Free Press.

Reichwein, Adolf. 1968. *China and Europe: Intellectual and Artistic Contacts in the Eighteenth Century*. New York: Barnes and Noble.

Reid, Anthony (ed). 1996. *Sojourners and Settlers: Histories of Southeast Asia and the Chinese*. Sydney: Allen & Unwin.

Schluchter, Wolfgang. 1989. *Rationalism, Religion and Domination*. Berkeley: University of California Press.

Schumpeter, Joseph A. 1991. 'Comments on a Plan for the Study of Entrepreneurship'. Pp. 406–28 in *The Economics and Sociology of Capitalism*, edited by Richard Swedberg. New Brunswick: Transaction Publishers.

Schwartz, Benjamin I. 1985. *The World of Thought in Ancient China*. Cambridge, MA: Harvard University Press.

Slingerland, Edward. 2007. *Effortless Action: Wu-wei as Conceptual Metaphor and Spiritual Ideal in Early China*. Oxford: Oxford University Press.

Swidler, Ann. 1986. 'Culture in Action: Symbols and Strategies'. *American Sociological Review*. 51(2): 273–86.

Tagliacozzo, Eric and Chang, Wen-Chin. (eds). 2011. *Chinese Circulations: Capital, Commodities and Networks in Southeast Asia*. Durham: Duke University Press.

Tao, Hanzhang. 2000. *Sun Tzu's Art of War*. New York: Sterling Publishing Company.

Waley, Arthur. 1958. *The Way and Its Power: Lao Tzu's Tao Tê Ching and Its Place in Chinese Thought*. New York: Grove Press.

Wang, Gungwu. 1991. 'Merchants without Empires: The Hokkien Sojourning Communities'. Pp. 79–101 in his *China and the Chinese Overseas*. Singapore: Times Academic Press.

Watson, James L. 1985. 'Standardizing the Gods: The Promotion of T'ien Hou ("Empress of Heaven") Along the South China Coast, 960–1960'. Pp.

292–324 in *Popular Culture in Late Imperial China*, edited by David Johnson, Andrew Nathan and Evelyn Rawski. Berkeley: University of California Press.

Watson, James L. 1993. 'Rites or Beliefs? The Construction of a Unified Culture in Late Imperial China'. Pp. 80–103 in *China's Quest for National Identity*, edited by Lowell Dittmer and Samuel S. Kim. Ithaca: Cornell University Press.

Weber, Max. 1964. *The Religion of China: Confucianism and Taoism*, translated and edited by Hans H. Gerth, with an Introduction by C.K. Yang. New York: The Free Press.

Welch, Holmes. 2003. *Taoism: The Parting of the Way*. Boston: Beacon Press.

Yang, Ching Kun. 1961. *Religion in Chinese Society*. Berkley: University of California Press.

CHAPTER 5

Self-Interest

INTRODUCTION

The conception of the self that is commonplace in what might loosely be described as Western social contexts assumes clear boundaries between the self and others. Thus, the sense that an individual has of their own personal space, their private domain, their exclusive proprietorial rights over objects of their possession, and their self-selected and self-directed purposes, goals, or aspirations can be quite distinct and separate from those of others. It is frequently noted that such clear-cut boundaries between individual persons simply does not obtain in Chinese cultural areas. Whereas Western notions of the self may assume social distance between individuals, the Chinese notion assumes social intimacy; and whereas Western individuals ideally relate to each other on an assumption of horizontal equivalence, if not equality, Chinese relations assume hierarchy based on role differentiation of the type implicit in parent–child, teacher–student, ruler–ruled relationships. Indeed, it is arguable that such hierarchical role relations imply a dependency of one on the other, and therefore a particular sensitivity of one to the needs and purposes of the other.

The qualities of the Chinese conception of the self that is summarized here are captured in the notion of a 'relational-self', a concept developed by a number of Chinese social thinkers who draw upon and develop Confucian categories of thought (Fei 1992; Fung 1998; Hwang 2000; King 1985). A relational-self is an individual person who stands at the

© The Author(s) 2017
J. Barbalet, *Confucianism and the Chinese Self*,
https://doi.org/10.1007/978-981-10-6289-6_5

center of a number of relationships with others. While the boundaries between persons in such relationships are permeable to a degree and persons may influence the boundary of the relationships in which they are implicated, and in that sense the relational-self is 'egocentric', the relational-self is without the insularity and self-sufficiency associated with the Western ideal of individualism (Fei 1992: 65–70). To put this proposition another way, the idea of a relational-self may be seen as involving the subordination of an individual person's 'lesser self' (*xiao wo*) to a 'greater self' (*da wo*), which is constituted in the relationships in which the person participates. This is especially so for family relationships, but is not confined to family relationships. This notion, that the relationships in which an individual participates is the constitutive formation of not only their social being but their self-identity, indicates that the boundaries of self in this Chinese form extend to incorporate (relations with) significant others, and, as a consequence, that the behavior and interests of the individual self are determined in and through the relationships in which they participate. The ideas set out here correspond to various statements in key Confucian texts, which shall be described later. They are also seen as the basis of an indigenous Chinese social psychology (Bedford and Hwang 2003; Ho 1998; Ho and Chiu 1998; King 1991). And they are recognized by Weber (1964: 173, 182, 211–12) as distinctive of Chinese character and mentality.

While acknowledging the significance of the concept of the relational-self and the associated idea of a distinction between a greater self and a lesser self for an understanding of social relationships in Chinese cultural areas, this chapter will show that it is erroneous to assume that the interests of the single individual as a *xiao wo* or lesser self are not in fact directive of the behavior of participants in Chinese family relationships and in other types of relationships. The argument to be developed in this chapter is that even assuming a notion of self as an aggregation of role compliance, the interests related to advantage for discrete individual persons can be identified, which explain their direction of action and how they interpret the roles they perform. Subordination to a 'greater self' does not negate or nullify situated interests of individuals, as the traditional rationale for Chinese familism maintains, and as Weber supposes. Rather, it constitutes an arena in which self-interest is exercised. Any imputation, on the basis of a conception of the relational-self, that interests determinative of individual behavior are more or less exclusively those of the greater self, therefore confuses context and opportunity structure on the one hand with the actions that occur within that framework, on the other. This is not to say

that individuals are incapable of acting on behalf of collective or corporate entities. Nor is it to say that individuals do not act in a self-denying manner. Of course they may.

The claim to be developed here is directed against the assertion, that is widely seen to derive from the practice of Confucian ethics—namely, that self-interested action is absent from the organization of traditional Chinese society. This was the view expressed by Weber (1964: 173) when he wrote that in both the state and the family clan, 'individual interests per se remained out of the picture'. It will be shown in the present chapter, though, that self-interested action is indeed found in traditional Chinese families and also that the processes internal to such families are animated by this type of action. After briefly setting out the ideological and political basis of the notion of a greater self and the subordination of a lesser self to it in Confucian thought, the discussion shall consider the structure of the traditional Chinese family and demonstrate the operations of narrow self-interest within it in terms of the context of structural constraints and opportunities provided by the relations of filial piety (*xiao*). Finally, the discussion will turn to acknowledgement of self-interest in both Confucian and non-Confucian Chinese thought and it will be shown how the notion of the relational-self, when turned to the distinction between temporal phases of self—past, present, and future—relates to institutional selection of characterizations of self which not only situate the Confucian notion and, by implication, the Weberian understanding of the Chinese self, but also indicate the difference between distinctive Chinese notions of self, its interests, and how they might be achieved.

Confucian Selves

The notion of the relational-self in Chinese philosophy and sociology is derived from the Confucian ideal of familial role relations (parent–child, husband–wife, elder–younger sibling) and those relationships which are seen as morphologically similar to them in the political (ruler–ruled) and civic (patron–client) spheres of activity. The classical statement of this notion is the brief characterization of five human relationships (*wu lun*) set out in the classic Confucian text, the *Mencius*, in which it is contended that there should be: 'love between father and son, duty between ruler and subject, [role] distinction between husband and wife, precedence of the old over the young, and faith [or trust] between friends' (Mencius 2004: 60). It is less frequently noticed that the *Mencius* also indicates that it is a proper

function of state authority to inculcate and promote these relationships (Mencius 2004: 60). The summary distillation of human relationships into five affectively distinctive binary role sets is located in other Confucian classics, including the *Zhongyong* (Johnson and Wang 2012: 447), known in English as *The Doctrine of the Mean*, but more accurately translated as *Maintaining Perfect Balance* (Gardner 2007: 108–9; see also Johnson and Wang 2012: 181–85).

At the core of the five human relationships is the concept of filial piety (*xiao*). According to the *Zhongyong*, the quality of humanness (*ren*) is principally realized in 'devotion to one's family members', and in such devotion 'there is a hierarchy' (Johnson and Wang 2012: 447). Here are the joint elements of the relational-self mentioned above—namely, a combination of intimacy (rather than distance) and hierarchy. The fundamental idea, that one realizes one's being as a self through subordination in family relations, is expressed in the *Zhongyong* in a number of different ways. In Chap. 17, it is noted that filial piety leads to the attainment of more general social values—Shun's great filial piety 'inevitably gained his position ... his prosperity ... his reputation, and [his] longevity' (Johnson and Wang 2012: 439). While Shun's accomplishments seem to accrue to him in his own right, they are achieved by and reflect his filial piety through which a greater self is expressed. This idea, of the subordination if not submergence of the lesser self into a more dominant and causally prior greater self, through filial piety, is reinforced in a statement in Chap. 19 in which it is claimed that 'being filial was to skillfully perpetuate the purposes of others (i.e., their ancestors) and to skillfully carry on their undertakings' (Johnson and Wang 2012: 443). In Chap. 20, where the five human relationships are referred to, is the notion that self-cultivation counterintuitively requires subordination to family role requirements: '... the noble man cannot do otherwise than cultivate himself. If he intends to cultivate himself, he cannot do otherwise than serve his family members' (Johnson and Wang 2012: 447).

The subordination of the actions and interests of a single individual to the needs and imperatives of a family collective, which gives content to the distinction between the forms of self, the lesser and the greater, come out of a particular conception of the relation between the individual and their family. In Western societies, the family is predominantly seen as an institution within which the offspring of parents is nurtured and socialized in order for it to attain an independent existence, which is the hallmark of adulthood. In this sense, the family exists to support the individual for the limited period

CONFUCIAN SELVES 109

required to attain the capacities which would permit independence from it in attainment of adulthood. In traditional Chinese society, the relation between the individual and the family is the reverse of the one described here. The individual exists to serve the family and ensure its continuance. The traditional Chinese family functions in terms of a notion of a 'continuum of descent' in which any single living individual personifies all of his forebears or ancestors and also all of his descendants, both born and unborn. Indeed, the individual in a traditional Chinese family 'exists by virtue of his ancestors, and his descendants exist only through him' (Baker 1979: 26–27). This difference of family types is associated with another difference—in the conception of marriage. Marriage in traditional Chinese society is not a union of two individuals, as in Western society, but a union between two families; and the purpose of the union is not individual happiness, but the procreation of male descendants to ensure that ancestors might continue to receive ritual sacrifices (Liu 1999: 6–7). The traditional Chinese understanding of family is primarily in terms of the vertical consanguine and intergenerational relationship which is served by the horizontal conjugal relationship, the latter being subordinate to and in service of the former.

The characterization of the Chinese family in terms of a 'continuum of descent' indicates the burden of responsibility which falls on every living male person to both honor and support his predecessors, not only his living parents but also his dead ancestors, and to father sons through whom the family shall continue at least for the next generation, on to whom the responsibilities of the continuum of descent shall again assert themselves. In this sense, the Chinese family does not produce offspring who shall, on maturity, be independent of it, but rather produces offspring who, on maturity, are more firmly tied to the requirements of the maintenance of the family as a continuing entity. The institutional context in which this ideational formation operates is a family structure in which a number of functions are located, including a ceremonial function, through which ancestors are acknowledged and honored, and also a social function, which carries responsibilities of both caring for elderly parents and marrying in order to produce heirs. The economic function of the family is discharged by its member's activities, which contribute not to self-aggrandizement but to collective family fortunes. By custom and law, the traditional Chinese family is the locus of the control of property. This is not to say that property could not be held by individuals but that the traditional Chinese family owns property as a joint person (Freedman 1979: 257–58). More shall be said of this in the following section. The point to be made here, though, is that in discharging the economic function of the family an individual person's productive activity is necessarily directed toward maintaining and augmenting a collective family property. For an adult son this means contributing to the property of a family unit controlled by its head (*jia zhang*), who may be his father or grandfather and possibly his great-grandfather. This relationship, set out in Confucian principles, comprising a person's contribution to a collective wealth, is the material basis of a clear distinction between a lesser and a greater self, and of the subordination of one to the other.

The benefits to an individual of membership in a family formed by joint ownership of property controlled by a senior head are significant. As landed property is the dominant form of wealth in traditional China, a family in which the Confucian principle of filial piety is exercised and that encompasses more than two generations, possibly up to five, including senior parents, adult sons and their wives, their children and so on, would enjoy a number of obvious economic advantages. First, the available family-based workforce would be large enough to obviate the need to expend resources on the employment of outside labor. Second, an extended-family estate would provide savings in so far as a need for multiple dwellings and duplicate farming equipment is removed. Third, the surplus generated by an extended family is likely to provide opportunities for investment in additional land, and possibly in vertical enterprise integration through establishment of a factory or a retail outlet. Fourth, an extended surplus can also be deployed for investment in human capital, providing education to sons who, through success in the imperial examination, may join the civil service and thus link the family with political power.

There are also obvious political advantages that derive from large and extended families. These benefits accrue to both the individual and also to the political state. From the individual viewpoint, in addition to the indirect possibility of linking with political power through educational advancement and state employment, mentioned earlier, the benefit of simply being a member of a large family group is important in a society in which state regulation is pervasive, in which law offers little direct protection to business, and in which power is exercised in a particularistic fashion, at best, and frequently corruptly. From the point of view of the state, the extended family is a major source of social stability. Individuals subjected to the discipline of filial piety are not only rigorously regulated, but the means of regulation operate at no direct cost to the state as it is family members who police each other and have at their disposal the compelling ultimate sanc-

tion of expulsion from the family that provides to the individual person the economic and political security described earlier. It is little wonder, then, that the traditional Chinese state promoted Confucian filial piety. As the Confucian classic the *Daxue* (*The Great Learning*) indicates, in 'wishing to bring good order to their states [the ancients] first regulated their households' (Johnson and Wang 2012: 135).

THE TRADITIONAL CHINESE FAMILY

In the preceding discussion of the Confucian notion of filial piety and its expression in the extended or joint family (*jiating*), it has been shown that the well-being or interests of an individual person may be satisfied through their participation in the mutual responsibilities associated with collective family enterprise in terms of the principles of generational hierarchy and the subordination of individual self-interest that accompanies it. Confucian doctrine and cultural precepts understand the resulting arrangement to include the assimilation of the interests of the individual, characterized as the lesser self, into the interests of the collective entity arising from family relationships and the obligations that they entail, which can be seen to exist as a greater self. Indeed, through legal enforcement the traditional Chinese state, from the Han dynasty (206–220) to the end of the Qing dynasty (1644–1911), treated the family as a mutual responsibility group, so that the crime of one member may lead to punishment of all members. The state also gave force to the authority of the family head, both through his subjection to state-inflicted punishment for transgressions against filial piety and also legal impunity in his exertion of force in maintaining filiality on behalf of the family (Baker 1979: 113–15; Freedman 1979: 242). These threads come together in a state practice that is unyielding in defending filial piety:

In October 1865, Cheng Han-cheng's wife had the insolence to beat her mother-in-law. This was regarded as such a heinous crime that the following punishment was meted out. Cheng and his wife were both skinned alive, in front of the mother, their skin was displayed at city gates in various towns and their bones burned to ashes. Cheng's granduncle, the eldest of his close relatives, was beheaded; his uncle and two brothers, and the head of the Cheng clan, were hanged. The wife's mother, her face tattooed with the words 'neglecting the daughter's education', was paraded through seven provinces. Her father was beaten 80 strokes and banished to a distance of 3000 *li*. The

heads of family in the houses to the right and the left of the Cheng's were beaten 80 strokes and banished to Heilung-kiang. The educational officer in town was beaten 60 strokes and banished to a distance of 1000 *li*. Cheng's nine-month-old boy was given a new name and put in the county magistrate's care. Cheng's land was to be left in waste 'forever'. All this was recorded on a stone stele and rubbings of the inscriptions were distributed throughout the empire. (Hsu 1970–71: 31 quoted in Hamilton 1984: 417)

Against this background it is difficult to conceive that persons living under traditional Chinese conditions could be anything but self-abnegating, other-interested, and generally defined by the collective imperatives generated through the compelling relationships in which they were entwined and to which they were subordinated. Through close examination of the structure and processes of the traditional Chinese family it emerges, however, that self-interest is nevertheless central to the behavior of individuals in their negotiation of relationships with family members. The background and substance of an individual's social existence is indeed the family in which they have membership. This is the context in which is set the actions and strategies of individuals shaped by the constraints and opportunities of that context and which, at pivotal moments, is animated by an interest in realizing a self-directed purpose connected with those constraints and opportunities.

The social form of the family in traditional China, often described in terms of Confucian principles outlined earlier and summarized in the folk saying 'five generations under one roof', is an aspiration that in fact was seldom realized. It is estimated that at any one time, no more than 7 percent of Chinese families attained this ideal (Eastman 1988: 16). Indeed, the conjugal family form is the most common in traditional China, comprising at most two generations consisting of two parents and their unmarried children and typically made up of between three and six persons. Field studies conducted in the 1920s and 1930s found that the 'average size of the Chinese family is about five' (Hsu 1943: 555; Freedman 1979: 235). It is estimated that approximately 60 percent of families were of this type (Eastman 1988: 16). The prevalence of the conjugal family form in these circumstances derives from economic necessity resulting from the incapacity of family estates to support all of their members. Writing in the late 1930s of a village in the Yangtze Valley, the anthropologist Fei Xiaoyong (1962: 192) found that approximately 90 percent of the population in the village owned less that 10 *mow* or 1.5 acres, insufficient to support a family. In a slightly later study of a Yunnan village, it was found

that 'a minority of the population holds most of the land, and the majority is landless or has insufficient land for its support' (Fei and Chang 1948: 54). In both cases, families directly supported by tenancy and wage labor constitute the majority. When a family plot is too modest to sustain more than one adult son and his parents, then the other sons are compelled to leave the household. If the departed son is married then he, with his wife and children, will subsist as a conjugal family. The family that he leaves, in which the eldest adult son, possibly with a wife and children, remain with his parents, is a stem of the (potentially) extended family through which the Confucian ideal of extended joint family is achieved. The Confucian ethical norm which holds that adult sons are subordinate to and care for their parents within a single household can be achieved only on the basis of material sufficiency. As anthropologist Maurice Freedman (1979: 247) says, for the 'greater part of the population ... the unwieldy family suppressing individualism was ruled out by poverty and lack of power'. The interests of individuals facing the threat of poverty, if not poverty itself and hunger, will lead them to adopt relations with kin, including separation, which are the effective obverse of Confucian filiality.

The formation of conjugal families through the movement of adult sons out of joint families through self-interest arising from necessity, because of the limited economic capacities of the extended family unit, acknowledges declining family fortunes. Family fortunes may also rise. A feature of family life in traditional China is the possibility of changing fortune in either direction and the corresponding possibility of changing family size over the course of several generations (Baker 1979: 133; Eastman 1988: 16). A rhythmic pattern over historical time of wealth acquisition and loss of wealth, and a parallel movement in family size of increase or diminution, contributed to the political stability of Imperial China through the absence of a system of inherited class formations capable of challenging established political power (Baker 1979: 134–35). The mechanisms through which the possible augmentation or reduction of family size and subsequent changes in its form include the self-interested actions of individual family members, as indicated in the following discussion.

MEN AND THEIR INTERESTS

It has been noted above that the traditional Chinese family owns property jointly. While the collective family estate is managed by the family head (*jia zhang*), the eldest male of the most senior generation within the family, each male member of the family has a claim on it. The benefits to the individual family members of collective property were mentioned earlier. While the family property remains intact, then it is in the interests of each family member to maintain and augment the family estate. In doing so, there shall always be different capacities and inclinations between family members. Such differences, relating to the energy, foresightedness, and willingness of brothers to contribute to their collective property will be of relatively little importance while the eldest senior family member continues to live and oversee the estate. On his death, however, these latent differences are likely to become manifest, giving rise to disagreements and even conflicts about the management of and contribution to the joint family property to which the sons of the now deceased father each have a clearly individual claim. As the Confucian system is primarily generationally hierarchical, there is no compelling means of authoritatively resolving disagreements between sons or brothers in the absence of their father. It is at this time that the joint family is likely to divide (*fenjia*) into its stem components, each adult son taking his share of the family property and establishing a separate family unit.

It can be seen from the above that the self-interest of married sons in an extended family shall change with changes in the order of family supervision and that manifestations of their self-interest shall have different consequences during different phases of family circumstance. While the dominance continues of the senior father over both a joint family property and of the sons who have a share in it, then it is in the interest of each son to contribute to the family's composite wealth and suppress their rivalry. The father's management of the joint property and supervision of his son's behavior ideally contributes to the growth of the family estate which benefits all. Even at this stage of the cycle of the extended family, the different interests of the adult sons are expressed through the procreation of each of their wives and their wife's putative advocacy on her husband's behalf against the wives of his brothers (Freedman 1979: 272). Exposed against this background are the two opposing forces that structure traditional Chinese families—on the one hand, father–son relations underlying a consanguine form legitimated through Confucian norms, and on the other hand, husband–wife relations on which is based the conjugal family form.

It is in the interests of married sons in successful and wealthy joint families to suppress their differences and maintain consanguinity in order to better preserve and contribute to the family estate. On their father's death, however, and through disagreements about the best ways to manage their aggregated estate, adult sons at this time find it in their interest to follow the consequences of their manifest rivalry (Cohen 1976: 142–44, 195–96) and divide between them 'the partible estate … [with] the family segmenting into new units which are residentially … economically, and ritually distinct' (Freedman 1979: 304). Under a unifying managerial regime of the eldest senior male, the self-interest of each son is to contribute to, augment, and enjoy the benefits of a collective property. When the means of a unified family management are no longer available, and when the distinct and unequal contributions of each stem of the joint family are exposed with the absence of a hierarchical line of patrimonial command, then the self-interest of each adult son is to take his portion of the joint estate and establish his own independent family.

Up to this point, family members have been described in terms of blood relations and marriage. But the traditional Chinese household has a membership not confined to kin and spouses; it may also include non-kin members who provide labor of various kinds. Within this latter category are concubines (*qie*). In Chinese cultural areas, concubinage is so thoroughly understood to be an elemental aspect of traditional social arrangements that even though it ceased to exist in the People's Republic in 1949, it continued to enjoy legal status in British-administered Singapore until 1965 (Freedman 1979: 142) and in Hong Kong until 1971 (Liu 1999: 3). The ostensive customary reason to purchase a concubine is to provide reproductive services to a family in the provision of an heir. The sons of concubines are legitimate as their 'official' mother is the concubine's consort's wife (Freedman 1979: 260), but unlike wives, concubines themselves have no ritual relationship with their consort's ancestors and no independent property. However, concubines may be purchased not simply to produce heirs but to reflect the status of the household into which they are brought.

While the ideological legitimation of concubinage represents it as a means of overcoming the problem of a wife who fails to produce a son, as 'an institution to insure against the extinction of the male line of descent' (Freedman 1979: 99), in practice it is just as likely to symbolize the consort's social status. The incidence of households with concubines varies between regions and the wealth of the households in question, including the possibility of households in poor communities having a concubine, although concubines are most frequently found in households linked with wealth and power (Watson 2004: 176–77). In that sense, concubines may be purchased more out of self-interest than to serve the interests of the family as a unit through production of an heir. This possibility is emphasized further by the fact that a concubine will provide sexual intimacy to her consort. The social significance of this last point gains gravity when it is appreciated that in traditional Chinese society a man's wife is always chosen for him by his parents while he chooses his concubine himself, without regard to family connection or preference (Freedman 1979: 100). Not only are marriages arranged in traditional Chinese society, without consideration of the preferences of the individuals involved, but the organization of activities in traditional Chinese households generates not only an intense sexual division of labor, but also ensures a clear 'psychological' separation between spouses in which there is an 'obvious indifference between husband and wife' (Fei 1992: 85–86) and effectively social discouragement of sexual affection between them (Hsu 1943: 556). In this context, concubinage is an institution in which a man's self-interest is manifest—he could have 'as many concubines as he could afford, desire or tolerate, and he could choose them himself' (Baker 1979: 35). It is important not only to acknowledge the clearly self-interested aspect of a man's purchasing a concubine, but to contextualize it beyond the relationship a husband has with his wife, in which this expression of self-interest stands against the interest of conjugal union.

It was noted above that there are cross-cutting forces in traditional Chinese families—one being the consanguine relations in the Confucian ideal of a family as a continuously iterated intergenerational father–son connection and the other being a lateral conjugal relationship between husband and wife. Concubinage obviously provides opportunity for a man's self-interest in relation to his wife and his conjugal relationship with her. But any reduction of a man's interest in his wife, and therefore the conjugal axis of the traditional family, effectively provides support to the axis of consanguine relations—a man who finds 'other pleasures than his interest in his formal wife … is much less likely to side with [her] against his mother' (Hsu 1943: 561). In this sense, then, concubinage is functionally congruent with the joint family form. Indeed, as indicated above, in wealthy households ably managed by a family head, it is in an adult son's self-interest to support the joint family and contribute productively to its wealth.

The self-interest of an adult son in poor families is different than that of a rich family's son and it leads to different concerns and behavior. A wealthy family has no difficulty securing and replacing wives for its sons. This is not true for poor families. The loss of a wife and daughter-in-law is much more greatly felt in a poor family than in a wealthy family, and especially for a husband: 'It is therefore in the interest especially of the husband that he should side with his wife' (Hsu 1943: 561). There is another element to the difference between sons in rich and poor families. In the former, 'married brothers ... [stood] together, refusing to listen to their wives' complaints, ... because they were posed against their father ... whose power rested on the economic resources he controlled' (Freedman 1979: 246). In wealthy families, there is both encouragement of consanguinity and therefore interest formation, both positive and negative, on a father–son axis; there is a corresponding reduction of a husband's interest in conjugal relations and heightened interest in sibling relations. In poor families, Freedman (1979: 246) adds, the 'father's control was weak and the brothers highly individualized among themselves [with each] brother [standing] close to his wife'. This does not necessarily mean that there is greater affection between spouses in poorer families than in wealthier, but is does mean that it is in the interests of a husband not to alienate his wife in their relationship.

WOMEN AND THEIR INTERESTS

The position of family members changes over time through maturation, reproduction, and aging, and over time such changes are reflected in structural realignments within the family. In the Confucian scheme and in traditional Chinese families, the position of women, as both daughter and wife, is secondary to that of male family members. Daughters are temporary members of the family into which they are born. Through marriage, a woman enters another family in which her membership is consolidated by producing a son and heir. While a wife has ritual rights in relation to her husband's ancestors, her interests are not with this family and its male members as a whole but are only aligned with her husband's interests and his portion of the joint family wealth which shall eventually become available to her sons. Indeed, because the traditional Chinese family owns property as a joint person, in that sense, 'the family is composed only of males' (Freedman 1979: 258), and that 'by being born or adopted into a family a man is immediately endowed with a claim to its property'. A woman can have no direct claim to the property either of the family into which she was born or of the family into which she marries. A woman can only enjoy the material benefits of family indirectly through marriage and by producing a male heir. This does not mean, however, that women as wives are without property. On marriage, a woman is given a dowry and cash gifts that she alone possesses and controls, which constitutes her 'private money' (*sifang qian*)

(Baker 1979: 19–20; Cohen 1976: 164–91; Freedman 1979: 258; Watson 2004: 186). A wife may augment her *sifang qian* through paid employment or business. It follows, then, that 'since men are always in principal members of property-holding units, their earnings being absorbed into these groups, women are the only individual property owners in [traditional] Chinese society' (Freedman 1979: 259). As wives alone have private and personal means in the form of *sifang qian*, more directly than men, they are attributed with a singular material basis of self-interest.

The highly constrained dependent status of women in traditional Chinese households means that a wife's interests are aligned with those of her husband. While it is in their interests for brothers to suppress their rivalry while the household flourishes and its fortunes rises, wives' interests are competitively expressed against other wives in possibly quarrelsome advocacy of their husband's claims and in procreative activity. In this context, a wife is most likely to deploy her *sifang qian* in a manner that advantages her husband, and therefore, her own future situation. This is best achieved at the time of break-up of the joint family through the death of the *jia zhang* and when the collective property is shared among his sons. Subsequently, each son and his wife will form their own family unit and 'the wife is encouraged to part with her "private" wealth by the domestic climate preceding partition, which ... [is] characterized by the unity of husband and wife as they fight for their interests, and those of their children' (Baker 1979: 20). Apart from such pivotal events, a woman may continue to deploy her *sifang qian* independently of her husband in providing 'decided advantages for her children' (Watson 2004: 186), including the provision of education to a son, a dowry, and therefore, marriage to a daughter, and in other ways providing means to safeguard the economic interests of a son after his father's death. A wife's self-interests are refracted through and expressed in terms of her interest in her husband and children, especially in the ways in which she deploys her *sifang qian*. But this is not the only way in which a married woman may express self-interest in traditional Chinese society.

The domestic sphere in traditional Chinese society is an exclusively female domain, including not only wives and their children and older yet-to-be married daughters, but possibly also concubines (*qie*) and 'little maids' or 'menial women' (*ya huan*) who enter the household through purchase, debt, or wage employment. This sphere is subject to the authority of the oldest female member of the most senior generation. A newly-arrived daughter-in-law is an outsider in the household, and until she has given birth to a son and thus provides the family with an heir she will remain an unintegrated member of her husband's family. A newly-arrived daughter-in-law must learn new routines and the expectations of unfamiliar others. She will cook and perform other domestic tasks under the typically harsh discipline of her mother-in-law, who will see her as a rival in the cross-cutting loyalties of consanguinity and conjugality that characterize the traditional Chinese family structure. At this stage of her life, it will be most apparent to her that a woman is simply an item of property transferred from one family to another (Cheung 2005). It is in her interest to contribute to her husband's well-being by having a son as quickly as possible and otherwise engage in a strategy of long-term investment in their conjugal relations. But this is not the only formation of self-interest to which a newly married woman may commit; in a significant minority of cases she may feel that her hardships, which cannot be overexaggerated (Eastman 1988: 24–29; Fei 1962: 45–50), mean that her best interest is to exit the family of her marriage.

A relatively significant number of wives in traditional China depart their husband's families by means of suicide. A wife who feels that it is in her interest to remove herself from her mother-in-law's or husband's authority has few options. After marriage, her natal family becomes a 'foreign home' (Cheung 2005: 395–96) and returning to it is seldom possible. Relevant demographic data does not exist for Imperial China, but the sociocultural significance of suicide in China as an expressive form of protest or resistance is well documented (Ropp et al. 2001; Lee and Kleinman 2000). As well as being remarkably high, Chinese suicide rates in recent years manifest a comparative atypical pattern in which rural females of 15–25 years are approximately 2.5 times more likely to commit suicide than rural males and over 4 times more likely than urban males and females (Phillips et al. 1999). This pattern, of high suicide rates among young rural women, has been demonstrated for early twentieth-century (1905) Taiwan, a society in which traditional mores operated, against much lower contemporary international comparisons (Wolf 1975). In this context it is possible to understand suicide as a form of self-interested action. In Chinese society, suicide is an act of ultimate rebellion and possibly motivated by revenge against ill-treatment. After surveying a number of cases and considering the conditions leading to suicide in rural China, Wu (2011: 234) concludes that the majority of them 'are a form of resistance to family politics and domestic injustice'. Indeed, the cultural narrative in China of death by suicide is that it 'brings power' to the deceased as 'the means to punish her tormentors' (Wolf 1975: 114; see also Ji et al. 2001).

The power of the suicide is achieved through the agency of others as well as the actor's own culturally accepted 'capacities'. The suicide of a young wife is understood as a 'damning public accusation [a woman makes] of her mother-in-law, husband' and other family members (Wolf 1975: 112). In this way suicide as protest necessarily implicates others. The parents and especially the brothers of the suicide victim will seek redress from her husband's family, in law and through direct action, including possibly by 'destroying part' of their dwelling (Fei 1962: 49). A wife's kinship links are maintained through her brothers, who have a special role as 'protectors of their sisters and of the sons of their sisters' (Freedman 1979: 270; Watson 2004: 185). Indeed, maltreatment of a wife is taken by her brothers as an assault on their own honor. In the event of a wife's death, her brothers are required to visit their in-laws household not only 'to ensure that the obsequies are conducted on a scale commensurate with their own standing', but especially 'to see that death has not been the result of foul play or suicide' (Freedman 1979: 270–71). Other agents of the suicide's power include neighbors, who through gossip and ridicule shall cause the mother-in-law to suffer significant loss of face. The agency of the suicide herself is manifest in her continuing presence as 'a spirit' who is 'able to [take] revenge' against her mother-in-law and possibly other family members (Fei 1962: 49).

The power of the suicide to cause dissension within and disruption of the well-being of her husband's family and the self-interested motive of the suicide against the filial relations of the extended family she joined cannot be readily assimilated into the Durkheimian framework of suicide familiar to mainstream sociology. Durkheim's brief discussion of fatalistic suicide acknowledges it to be the opposite of anomic suicide, by which he means that it results from high, rather than low social regulation. But it is opposite in another sense he did not appreciate—whereas anomic suicide is seen to be structurally produced by the conditions with which it is associated and is therefore functionally emergent in them, as are egoistic and altruistic forms of suicide in Durkheim's schema, fatalistic suicide is described in a manner that suggests that it is a volitional reaction to 'excessive moral despotism' (Durkheim 1970: 276 note 25), although Durkheim does not make the point himself, and in any case such a suggestion violates his methodological functionalism. But it is possible to argue on the basis of Chinese cultural data that the agency of the persons who kill themselves under conditions of fatalistic suicide can be regarded as a factor in the explanation of the suicide event, in addition to the social structural conditions to which persons are subjected and which Durkheim focuses on. This is certainly a feature of the suicide of a Chinese wife.

The majority of women who join families through marriage do not kill themselves. It is in their interests to contribute to the family they have joined and become a confirmed member of it by giving birth to a son, and thereby contribute to her husband's engagement in the 'continuum of descent'. Through the birth of a son, a woman's status in the family changes—as a mother, her relationship with both her mother-in-law and husband will benefit from the provision to their family of an heir. In time, through her son's eventual marriage, she shall exercise over her son's bride the authority she was subjected to as a young wife. If she should outlive her in-laws, she may exercise effective control over an extended family, its members, and their joint property. Thus, changes in the relational position and status of an individual during the course of their life career will affect their interests and reflect changes in formal patterns of family structure and their changing position within it.

THE YIN AND YANG OF CONTEXT AND AGENT

In consideration of the traditional Chinese family, it has been shown that the self-interest of its individual members is significant at pivotal times in determining the course and direction of family life and family change. This is a prospect denied by Weber. The extended family is a context in which the self-interested actions of its individual members are directed to engagements with diverse others. As an individual's position in their family changes, through maturation, role change in marriage, death of the head of the family, childbirth and so on, so their interests also change. What does not change is the interaction between context and action through which the fortunes of both individuals and the family they inhabit lead to outcomes that affect the future direction and opportunities of both. The Confucian distinction between a greater self and a lesser self acknowledges this complex interplay of context and agent. At the same time, however, the doctrine of filial piety within Confucian thought denies the possibility that the self-interested actions of individual family members may routinely contribute to, if not generate, the dynamism of relations within a traditional household, within the parameters of the collective entity itself. This limitation of Confucian thought will be explored shortly. Before doing so, however, it is necessary to make some further general remarks.

Having argued for the importance of self-interested action in understanding the mechanisms of the traditional Chinese family structure, it is important to reiterate that self-interest, in this case, operates within the context of the traditional family and does not undermine it or serve to replace the associated kinship structure and the relations internal to it. While European social structure can be characterized as having a basis in non-kin cooperation and impersonal exchanges driven by the self-interest of the actors involved, in traditional Chinese society, on the other hand, kinship solidarity and intraclan enforcement of civic and commercial exchanges predominate. The argument here is that the predominance of kinship in traditional Chinese social organization and the associated role expectations internal to the patriarchal relations embodied in Confucian ethical precepts operate in terms of the agency of the individual actors. Such actors interpret their roles and animate them through an understanding of the advantages available to them in the circumstances in which they find themselves. The greater self of family membership develops through the actions of the lesser self of its individual members, directed to satisfaction of their interests within the situated relationships in which they are involved.

Through examination of a major institution of traditional Chinese society—namely, the traditional joint family—it has been shown that it is not contradictory to both acknowledge the operation of collective social forces to which individuals are subjected and to also accept that the mechanisms through which these forces lead to an unfolding and development of family life include the self-interested actions of particular family members. The examination earlier of the joint family in these terms has not been comprehensive but indicative; the role of self-interest in determining the actions of the family head (see Greenhalgh 1994), to mention only one omission, is not treated in the previous account. The self in traditional Chinese society is portrayed by Weber and other Western commentators—in line with Confucian self-portrayal—in terms of its subjection to collective imperatives, manifest in hierarchically structured binary role obligations within joint families, legitimated through the principle of filial piety. The tensions within such families, which arise from the contrasting axes of consanguinity on the one hand and its means of reproduction, conjugality, on the other, generate competing attachments and loyalties. The outcome of these tensions includes not only scope for but a necessity of self-interested action in directing the continuing relations of joint family life. The emergence of various particular manifestations of self-interested action in terms of the distinct phase of an individual's life cycle within sequential changes in the structural arrangement of family relationships has a number of implications. The self in traditional Chinese society is both subject to intimate collective forces and at the same time self-consciously aware not only of its role obligations, but also the choices available in managing them to the satisfaction of its personal individually defined purposes. The traditional Chinese self is therefore both alter-centrically role-obligated and also interested in realizing egocentric purposes. The traditional Chinese person's capacity to achieve the latter is significant in performance of the former.

SELF-INTEREST IN CHINESE TRADITIONS

While the dominant conventions of Confucian thought and practice diminish the role of self-interest in Chinese discourse and practice, indeed they exclude it from the Chinese view of desirable motivation, as Weber observes, it is important to acknowledge that there are other traditions of Chinese thought in which self-interest has a significant presence. It is also important to distinguish between the ideological representations of the conventions which exclude self-interest and the actual conduct of social relationships in traditional China. An appraisal of not only the family but also the Chinese imperial bureaucracy reveals the actual role of self-interest in its operation. What is indicated in the following discussion is that the Confucian construction of self-interest and selfishness, as the antithesis of filial piety, reveals a great deal about the limited nature of the Confucian conceptualization of self-interestedness, which in turn encourages a fuller account of not only self-interested action, but also the distinctive nature of different Chinese thought traditions. Weber's focus on the structure of Chinese thought as either Confucian or Daoist led him to neglect the broader spectrum of thought traditions in China.

The language of self-interest is pivotal in the utilitarian Legalist school (*fa-jia*) that flourished in early China. Lord Shang (Shang Yang), a fourth-century BC statesman and thinker, held that human nature leads people to strive for profit and comfort and avoid their obverse, so that it is necessary for rulers to 'give due consideration to what is profitable' because people will 'fear punishment and easily suffer hardship [in order to gain material advantage]' (Shang 2006: 121). In this way, the 'method by which a ruler of men prohibits and encourages is by means of rewards and penalties' (Shang 2006: 325). The idea, that self-interest underlies human nature and that behavior in livelihood, military affairs, and governance must operate in terms of it, is further developed in the third-century BC text *Hanfeizi* (Fung 1952: 327–28) and also in the slightly later and more benign *Huainanzi* (Ames 1983). Indeed, this approach of enticement and punishment assuming that 'people like personal profit and emoluments but dislike punishments and penalties' (*Hanfeizi* quoted in Ames 1983: 156) parallels the formation of self-interest as a vocabulary of motive in eighteenth-century Europe, where the promotion of self-interest functioned to curtail disruptive and destructive impulses (Hirschman 1997: 39–42).

An additional significant source in Chinese understandings of self-interest is the thought of Yang Tzu (Yang Zhu), who 'sought fulfillment of life not in its prolongation but its intensification' (Bauer 1976: 46). Nothing of Yang Zhu's writing survives although a chapter bearing his name in the *Liehzi* (Graham 1990: 135–57) is sufficient to indicate that his position is not the simplistic egoism which the principal interpreter of Confucius, Mencius, dismisses when he says: 'Even if [Yang Zhu] could benefit the Empire by pulling out one hair [of his head] he would not do it' (Mencius 2004: 151). The translator of *Liehzi* regards the Yang Zhu chapter as anomalous in this Daoist text, supposing its position to be merely 'hedonistic' (Graham 1990: 1). But others recognize that Yang Zhu's outlook, which holds that a person is responsible for their own well-being, is consonant with the tenets of philosophical Daoism as expressed in its principal texts, the *Daodejing* and the *Zhuangzi* (Fung 1952: 260–63), and, it can incidentally be added, anticipates the idea in Adam Smith (1979: 82–83) that 'every man is … first and principally recommended to his own care … [and] therefore is much more deeply interested in whatever immediately concerns himself than in what concerns any other man'. We shall return to aspects of this theme later.

It cannot reasonably be said, therefore, that the concept of self-interest is absent in traditional China. Indeed, the strong negative attention given to 'selfishness' in Confucian and Neo-Confucian writing indicates a concern with an ever-present 'problem' of self-interest. It has been suggested by Wang Bi, a third-century philosopher, that a system of moral virtue, such as Confucianism, may paradoxically promote practices of self-interest. The social and political preferment of moral conduct may lead one to 'cultivate that which can exalt him in hope of the praise involved and cultivate that which can lead to it in the expectation of the material advantage involved' (Wang 1999: 39). One may be moral because it is right, if others see that it is right, then it is in one's self-interest to behave morally: 'Because of hope for praise and expectation of material advantage, he will conduct himself with diligence, but the more splendid the praise, the more he will thrust sincerity away, and the greater his material advantage, the more contentious he will be inclined to be' (Wang 1999: 39). The point of this caution is not merely that Confucian admonishments against selfishness

SELF-INTEREST IN CHINESE TRADITIONS   125

may themselves promote self-interest but that proscription indicates the probable occurrence of what is opposed; there is no point prohibiting what is not likely to occur.

Confucian thought functions to provide organizing legitimacy to key aspects of Imperial Chinese society, not only the extended family but also the state bureaucracy. The norms of loyalty to emperor based on the analogue of filial piety within the family explicitly disqualify self-interest or 'selfishness' as an independent basis of motive. The practices of those operating within the imperial bureaucracy, however, were frequently marked by behaviors that may be seen as outcomes or machinations of self-interest—namely, corruption and bribery, underhand dealings, avoidance of responsibility and scapegoating, and unscrupulous ambition (Balazs 1964: 12, 18, 41–42). Indeed, the terminology of self-interest is required not only to characterize such improper selfishness but required also for an understanding of the optimal operations of imperial administration.

An official in China's imperial bureaucracy, according to the Chinese-American sociologist C.K. Yang (1959: 158), was subject to the 'continuous conflict between two incompatible organizational systems to … which he owed loyalty'. One was the imperial bureaucracy itself, in which the official's conduct of office required 'formalistic impersonality'; the other was the pressure of informal personal relationships, especially although not only those of kinship. The imperial system effectively generated this conflict by promoting kinship not only at the level of Confucian doctrine regarding the primacy of filiality but also in associated practices, encoded in formal rules, including the conferring of titles on the parents, wife, and sons of outstanding officials (Yang 1959: 159). A resolution at the individual level of the pressures of personal relationships on officials formally bound to execute the impersonal requirements of office is therefore made more difficult by these aspects of the operations of the imperial system itself.

Yang (1959: 158–59) describes a number of strategies engaged by individual bureaucrats, which in different ways acknowledge these competing influences and attempt to manage them. While Yang does not provide a sociological account of the resolution of such conflicts of value systems, which could not themselves arbitrate between the demands of impartiality of office and partiality of kinship, the mechanisms of their resolution must include a consideration of the individual official's own understanding of his best interests. Indeed, Yang (1959: 159) hints at such a necessity when he notes that in addition to temperament and social prestige, that enter 'into the functioning of [the official's] status with social approval, if not formal legitimacy', is his 'private material interests'.

SELF BEYOND THE CONFUCIAN MATRIX

Against the conventional denial of the possibility of self-interest in Chinese discourse and practice, its significance for any understanding of relationships within Chinese social institutions is difficult to avoid. It is necessary to begin with conceptions of selves that may have interests of their own. A number of writers have gone beyond the erroneous idea that the self is absent from the Confucian system and presented, instead, the notion of a relational-self that is characteristically Chinese, as we saw at the beginning of this chapter. An acknowledgement of the centrality of the family in traditional Chinese society and in its Confucian representation is fundamental to these discussions. Commentators note that the three familial elements of the five cardinal relations of Confucian ethics—namely, those of father and son, elder and younger brother, and husband and wife—are relations of discrete social roles. Indeed, the remaining two cardinal relations—of ruler and subject and of friendship—are conceived as analogues of these familial relationships. The practice of self-cultivation in the Confucian system is arguably designed to align an individual's self-identity with these roles. The leading Chinese philosopher of his generation, Fung Yu-Lan (Feng Youlan) claims on this basis that in traditional Chinese philosophy, 'the emphasis is upon the individual ... [in so far as it] is the individual who is a father or a son, a husband or a wife' (Fung 1998: 634). A person exists as an individual, in this sense, through their role compliance and performance. It is therefore 'quite wrong', Feng holds, 'that there was no place for the personality of the individual' in traditional Chinese society (Fung 1998: 636). Indeed, Feng adds a further dimension to his recognition of the significance of the individual self in Chinese society and thought when he says that 'according to traditional social theory every individual is the centre of a social circle which is constituted of various social relationships' (Fung 1998: 635). These relationships, according to Feng, radiate in both vertical and horizontal directions, and '[w]ithin the radius there are different degrees of greater and lesser affections and responsibilities' (Fung 1998: 635).

The idea, that the self may be located at the center of relationships, has been provided with sociological elaboration by Fei Xiaotong (1992) and also by the Hong Kong-based sociologist Ambrose King (1985), whose treatments of the relational-self will be outlined here. The relational, as opposed to the collective, nature of Chinese society has been strongly emphasized in an account provided by Fei (1992: 67) of the 'egocentric' rather than the group-centric nature of the self in Chinese traditions. That this egocentric self is at the center of 'elastic networks' rather than formal organizations, as in Western society, justifies for Fei (1992: 67) the claim that 'this notion of the self' does not amount, though, to 'individualism'. The difference between them is that egocentric selves operate in a system of qualitatively different categories, classifications, or roles, whereas individualistic selves are characterized by equivalence, equality, and therefore constitutionality, as found in the operations of formal organization (Fei 1992: 65–66). Confucian individuality thus emphasizes the uniqueness of each person in the performance of the roles they occupy, not their autonomy from prescribed positions in relationships (Hall and Ames 1998: 25–28; Hamilton 1990). Yet the networks resulting from the interactions of such selves are elastic because the context of action can be defined by the actor (Fei 1992: 69). This is a result of the fact that 'the self is an active entity capable of defining the roles for himself and others and, moreover, of defining the boundaries of groups of which the self is at the centre' (King 1985: 64).

The volitional and active imperative of Chinese selves acknowledged by both Fei and King is explained by them in terms of the ambiguities of the traditional roles of Chinese society (Fei 1992: 69–70; King 1985: 64–65). Such ambiguity and lack of clarity leaves room for individual discretion at the margins over who is and who is not a family or other group member (King 1985: 65). These ambiguities therefore require individual decision or 'egocentricism' in the determination of role behavior and network construction and maintenance. As King (1985: 60) implicitly acknowledges, however, when paraphrasing Dennis Wrong, that 'a human being is never merely a role player', this is a universal and not a Chinese feature of roles and of the actions required to animate them. Those accounts, which explain Chinese selves as 'a relational being endowed with a self-centred autonomy' (King 1985: 66), in terms of limitations of clarity in the Confucian system, require closer examination.

According to King (1985: 62), Confucian social ethics 'has failed to provide a "viable linkage" between the individual and the *ch'ün* [*qún*], the non-familistic group ... [The] boundary between the self and the group has not been conceptually articulated' (see also Fei 1992: 70). Indeed, the absence of this conceptual articulation is seen as the reason why 'all apparently group values and interests ... centre around the self' (King 1985: 62). The failure of Confucian clarity is thus seen as the basis of the egocentric relational self of Chinese society (Fei 1992: 69). Whether or not these characterizations of the limitations of Confucian theory are adequate, it is difficult to see how they could justify the causal supposition they propose—an absence is not a cause. King (1985: 61) relates that Confucians regard the human community as comprising three categories—the individual (*ji*), the family (*jia*), and the group (*qün*); the last of these, *qün*, lacks 'formal treatment' and even *jia* is 'conceptually unclear' in the Confucian system, according to King. While this may be true, it is unlikely to have the significance ascribed to it by these authors. It does, though, indicate something of importance for an understanding of self that King, Fei, and Feng do not discuss, to be developed later.

Before it is anything else, Confucianism is a system of moral governance focusing primarily on the maintenance of family order through filial piety (*xiao*) and political order through loyalty (*zhong*) to the sovereign. The relations between the three spheres of self, family, and group (or country) is set out in the *Daxue* (*Great Learning*), an early text elevated by the Neo-Confucian Zhu Xi:

> Wishing to order well their States [the ancients] first regulated their families. Wishing to regulate their families, they first cultivated their persons ... Their families being regulated, their States were rightly governed. Their States being rightly governed, the whole kingdom was made tranquil and happy. (Legge 1971: 357–59)

Such propositions concerning the centrality of the family in this scheme and the implied subordination of the individual to both *xiao* and *zhong* in order to bring about group harmony or peace require not conceptual clarity regarding the units of analysis, but that the statement as a whole is taken for what it is—namely, an injunction to accept the moral and political imperatives internal to it.

In a formalized system of instructions or edicts for proper behavior, conceptual boundaries do not require the type of clarification King and also Fei note are absent in the Confucian system. This is because the 'individual', 'family', and 'group' referred to in it are experiential or common-sense notions that are self-defined in the practices of *xiao* and *zhong*, rather than in a sociological theory about them. Relatedly, the concept of group or society in a sociological sense is redundant in the Confucian theory of social morality when governance through *xiao* and *zhong* is sufficient in understanding how 'peace in the world' might be achieved. The society to which these edicts are addressed is more or less composed of family, including clan structures, and the political state and its instrumentalities.

In such a world, in which there is an absence of the voluntary associations of autonomous individuals or formal organizations, which incidentally replaced the established forms of reciprocity and mutuality in Europe during the eighteenth century (in which the question of groups and society first arose in a sociological sense), only a morally infused political philosophy is possible. It is under conditions of the type found in eighteenth-century European developments mentioned here that political theory loses its monopoly of intellectual discourse, and sociological and economic theory gain ascendance over it.

What is described in the preceding paragraph, regarding a shift in eighteenth-century Europe toward a sociological sensibility concerning group formation, constitutes the conditions under which there was a transformation in the experience of self, in which a person possessing the 'faculty of forming a judgment of their own interests' indicates the historical move from a society in which self is based on 'status' to one in which it is based on 'contract' (Maine 1905: 150). The only point to take from this statement for the purposes of the present argument is that the particular notion of self which emerges historically, like the one that historically preceded it, is institutionally determined. Such a proposition seems to be absent in the account of the Chinese relational-self that is discussed in the preceding paragraphs and exemplified in the accounts of Fei and King. For both of these writers, the selves they described are free to interpret the roles they occupy and those to which they relate. While a lack of clarity in Confucian categories explains the relative freedom of relational-selves, the direction in which that capacity is exercised is simply taken for granted. While relational-selves function within networks or families, their volitional capacity to define these networks is conceived in terms of their 'ego-centrism'; why one form of association is chosen rather than another is not explained when it is assumed to operate in terms of an ambiguity-based freedom to choose; in that sense, it is without an institutional basis and the relational-self might in this case be described as pre-social.

THE INSTITUTIONAL CONTEXT OF SELVES AND THEIR INTERESTS

The idea in Fei and King of an active voluntaristic self at the center of flexible networks is not disputed here. The notion of a self that is interested in the roles it performs and how it performs them indicates an interest in the agent's own identity, a quality of the Chinese self for which there is literary evidence from at least the sixth century BC (Elvin 1985: 159). Self-interest in this sense has a necessary volitional and therefore self-determining dimension, which Fei and King recognize and which forms the basis of their conception of a relational-self. It is necessary to add, however, that this active capacity of self is practiced in not merely a social but especially an institutional context. Interactions between the self and the context it occupies contribute to the formation of the self, as we saw earlier in discussion of the traditional Chinese family and the self-interested actions of its members. This aspect of the argument is quite undeveloped in Fei and King. The social context mentioned here includes the gaze and evaluation of others. Face (*mainzi* and *lian*), in the Chinese cultural context, is made up of a projected self-image (Cheng 1986: 337–44), which is validated in public perception (Hwang 1987: 960–62). The interest social actors have in their 'face', including how face is perceived by others and the relations internal to it (Qi 2011, 2014: 143–64), is one mechanism regulating the egoistic selves at the center of the elastic networks (*guanxi wang*) Fei and King refer to.

There is a deeper level of determination of the self suggested by the brief reference earlier to eighteenth-century Europe and the historical nature of societies. Implicit in Maine's characterization of social change in terms of a move from a society in which status predominates to one in which contract principally operates is the idea that there are historically variable institutional selections of the form of self. This notion is developed in an evolutionary framework by the early twentieth-century American sociologist Thorstein Veblen. Veblen holds that within human nature there are a number of 'instincts', including the opposing instincts of 'workmanship' and 'predation'; which one of these predominates at any given time will be determined by habituation through institutionalization (Veblen 1946: 38–39). More generally:

> Social evolution is a process of selective adaptation of temperament and habits of thought under the stress of the circumstances of associated life. The adaptation of habits of thought is the growth of institutions. But along with the growth of institutions ... is a correlative change in human nature. (Veblen 1970: 145–46)

Veblen's characteristic account of social evolution refers to institutional selections of different forms of self.

Historicizing 'self' in terms of variable institutional selection of self-forms can be connected with the fact that the self also has an historical or at least a temporal dimension. Every person has a past and a future self as well as a present self, each with its own distinctive features and interests (Barbalet 2009, 2012). In the formation of the self and its interests, there are relations with other selves, including other temporal selves of the same person. The institutional patterns of self-formation which pay attention to the distinct temporal selves of a single person can be readily indicated (Pizzorno 1986: 370). The institutional form of the traditional family is one in which past selves command present selves. In this case, the 'past selves' include not only other selves of previous generations, in the form of ancestors, but also the past self of an individual person in so far as their birth, birth-order, and endowments of upbringing determine the decisions and especially the interests of their present self. The institutions of a market economy, on the other hand, tend to select future selves and their interests as crucial in self forma-tion, on the basis of past endowments of experience and skill and present opportunities. This is because economic ambition and striving for commer-cial or occupational success are necessarily future-orientated, and in attempt-ing to realize them, future selves effectively deploy resources generated by past and present selves. In this way, the institutional framework links persons not only horizontally, through relations of interpersonal connections with others, but also vertically in the form of intertemporal connections of the distinct selves of the same person.

Different societies will have different arrangements of institutions and different hierarchical relations between institutions with corresponding consequences for self-formation. A person's actions will be directed to the satisfaction of the interests of their past or future selves, depending on the institutional context within which the action occurs. Having now indi-cated the nature of institutional contexts of self-formation, left unclear by Fei and King, it is possible to appreciate the nature of classical Confucian concerns regarding 'selfishness' in terms of priorities of intertemporal selves and their interests. The family in the Confucian system can be thought of as an institution which constitutes a person in terms of priori-tizing the interests of the past self against the requirements of a present or future self. In this sense, Confucian admonishments against 'selfishness' are not prohibitions against self-interest so much as a formation of self-interest through an enforcement of the predominance of the interests of past selves against present and alternately-possible future selves. Thus admonishments against 'selfishness' are designed to limit actions directed to serve the interests of 'present' and 'future' selves against the interests of 'past' selves. More shall be made of this in the following section.

Like all institutional arrangements, conformity with the norms of the traditional family, the 'past' self, requires preparation and training, achieved through the Confucian practices of self-cultivation. It is of interest that self-cultivation implicitly acknowledges a distinction between the different temporal selves of an individual person in the sense that it seeks to achieve a future self with qualities, endowments, and orientations absent in a past or present self. Self-cultivation is a means of achieving an articulation of role requirements on the one hand, and role performance on the other. The requirements of roles in the Confucian system include the predominance of the interests of past selves in generation of present and future actions. But the general form of self-cultivation within the Confucian system, through which an individual develops their own powers of concentration, attention, and direction, can be removed from its original institutional context and transferred to nonfamilial applications.

SELF-CULTIVATION AND SELF-INTEREST

Traditional Chinese society was institutionally complex, comprising a national bureaucracy which was politically centralized but operationally dispersed, heterogeneous local communities in which kinship relations dominated, a national market economy without the benefit of comprehensive and centrally enforced property rights, and an ideological framework dominated by Confucian thought but in which Daoist and Buddhist reference points operated along with a great number of local symbols, meanings, and practices. Within this institutional matrix, self-interest necessarily took as many forms as the corresponding formations of selves were manifest. Commercialization of the Chinese economy, which began during the Song Dynasty in the tenth century, did not disrupt the agrarian nature of the society. This meant not that rural society escaped the influence of market relations, but rather, that peasant households were fully integrated in markets. The practices of everyday life were shaped by market institutions, so that not only was there 'respectability [in] the pursuit of riches', but also 'legitimacy of careful and interested financial dealings between neighbours and even close kinsmen' (Freedman 1979: 25–26).

A number of handbooks were published and circulated during the Qing dynasty (1644–1912) based on Confucian principles but directed to the guidance of merchants in pursuit of their pecuniary careers. In drawing on

Confucian self-cultivation practices, merchants advanced their future interests against the interests of their present selves, against 'selfishness'. This is not to say that Confucian values can consistently legitimize a profit motive and market activities. Such a 'rhetorical strategy' practiced during the sixteenth century, and at the present time, invites 'the opposite [Confucian] rhetoric of profit making as socially destabilizing' (Brook 1997: 38). To say that recruitment of a 'Confucian genealogy' in advocacy of market rationality is entirely 'forced' (Brook 1997: 41) does not deny, though, 'polarities in Confucian thought' (Schwartz 1959). But the sixteenth century texts:

> ...speak of commerce in the language of 'making' (*gong*), 'living' (*sheng*), and 'growing' (*zhi*). This language contrasts starkly with the anti-commercial vocabulary of conventional Confucianism, which expressed the essence of its Way in the language of 'reversion' (*fu*), 'preservation' (*shou*), and 'antiquity' (*gu*). (Brook 1997: 35)

These texts thus engage a temporal vocabulary of commercial future-orientation and a past-orientation of family-centric Confucian thought, mentioned earlier.

In his discussion of the merchant handbooks, historian Richard Lufrano (1997) shows how the traditional Confucian practices of self-cultivation were transferred from the institutions of kinship and state bureaucracy to those of the market. Whereas in their original context, these practices safeguarded past selves against the interests of present selves, in the market context, they safeguarded the interests of future selves against the desires of present selves. In each case, 'selfishness' is the problem dealt with. The 'inner mental attentiveness' (*jing*) central to Confucian self-cultivation functioned to first dispel or at least manage the external distractions which might lead 'honourable merchants' to errors of judgment in business, and second, to renounce the appeals of 'gambling, whoring and opium smoking' to which 'petty merchants were particularly attracted' (Lufrano 1997: 64), as we saw in an earlier chapter. The importance of self-control in suppressing selfish desires or the immediate interests of present selves in advancing economic success associated with the interests of future selves is explicit in these manuals (Lufrano 1997: 63–67).

The late Qing merchants who drew on Confucian self-cultivation principles in safeguarding the pecuniary interests of their future selves, against the 'selfish' satisfaction of sensual pleasures demanded by their present selves, enacted a self-regulation that is arguably a local variant of a more general phenomenon. Seventeenth-century European entrepreneurs found similar benefit in the guidance provided by Protestant tracts against 'spontaneous, impulsive enjoyment' which distracted from moneymaking, noted by Weber (1991: 119); contemporary manuals of emotions management performed the same function for early modern European capitalists, irrespective of their religious background (Barbalet 2008b: 85–102). Late modern corporate executives similarly employ forms of self-regulation to subordinate short-term interests in order to achieve more profitable long-term outcomes (Akerlof and Kranton 2010: 5).

The distinction between the interests of a present self and the interests of a future self, which underpin the discussion here, is acknowledged in different ways. The difference is understood psychologically as a distinction between short- and long-term interests, manifest as intrapersonal interests, about which there is intra-psychic bargaining (Ainslie 1986: 143–49). More abstractly, a difference is drawn between a 'present aim' theory of rationality and a 'self-interest' theory; the first referring to pursuit of aims formed at the 'moment of deliberation and action' and the second taking into account more long-term considerations of welfare (Frank 1988: 67–68). These are distinctions between immediate appetites and reflected considerations. The failure to make the distinction clear is not confined to Confucian treatments of 'selfishness' but has been a recurring problem in economics, to which Ainslie and also Frank, mentioned here, respond (see Knight 1971: 130–31).

The necessity of training, through Confucian self-cultivation or other means, to safeguard non-present-self-interests, either past or future, against the appetites of present selves derives from the quite different constitutions of these distinct temporal selves. Whereas present selves are experienced through sensory stimulation, past selves exist in a memory of such experiences. Future selves and their associated interests are paradoxically prior to experience of them and can only be known through the imagination (Barbalet 2009, 2012: 424–27). But this imagination may be more present to consciousness than sensation, especially in pursuit of (economic) ambitions (Knight 1971: 202). Indeed, memory relating to past selves also has a significant imaginative component. Thus, while pursuit of present interests requires no special preparation beyond the sensory apparatus which guides it, that humans have in common with other animal species, orientation to satisfaction of the interests of past and also future selves requires careful preparation assisted by manuals of self-cultivation, which frequently begin with admonishments against 'selfishness'. Confucian self-cultivation manuals and practices were not the only instruments of guidance in recognition of the interests of nonpresent selves in traditional China.

Self-cultivation practices serve all Chinese philosophical traditions. The principal text of Daoist thought, discussed extensively in the previous chapter, *Daodejing* or the *Laozi* (the two names refer to the same text), was written as a self-cultivation text for aspirants to state rule (LaFargue 1998: 263). *Daodejing* is known in sociology through Weber's (1964: 186) treatment of it as an exposition of 'contemplative mysticism'. Mysticism, involving self-surrender or self-transcendence, leaves self-interest without a subject. The supposed mystical elements of *Daodejing*, however, are 'misinterpretations' (Lau 1963: 38) and there is no evidence in the text of mystical practice or endorsement (Csikszentmihalyi 1999), as argued in the previous chapter. The widespread view that *Daodejing* advocates self-abnegation has textual support: '[the sage] benefits [others] yet exacts no gratitude; he accomplishes … task[s], yet lays claim to no merit' (Lau 1963: 6). But subordination of the actor's present purpose is to realize the full potential of events as they unfold, and the actor's apparent disengagement leads to satisfaction of their future interests: 'the sage puts his person last and it comes first … Is it not because he is without thought of self that he is able to accomplish his private ends?' (Lau 1963: 11). The institutional basis of orientation to future interests in this text is state leadership and administration, served by the sage who draws upon *Daodejing* (LaFargue 1994: 51–94). Thus, sacrificing present interests can serve to realize future interests. Indeed, this is the interpretation of Han Dynasty commentaries on *Daodejing* (Csikszentmihalyi 1999: 46–48). Approximately 30 percent of the chapters of *Daodejing* include reference to the realization of interests of future selves against the satisfaction of present self-interest. Indeed, the notion of the self in Daoist thought emphasizes the transition of self in process, as all things are in process (see Barbalet 2014). This contrasts with the notion of the self in Western thought traditions, in which the self is bounded and indivisible, and the Confucian self, as role determined. In the present account, then, is the idea that *Daodejing* presents an alternative to the Confucian focus on the interests of past selves through filial piety; more positively, *Daodejing* indicates the realization of the interests of future selves, and in this sense, at least shares with Confucianism a disdain for the satisfaction of present self-interest or 'selfishness'. This is a further dimension of the entrepreneurial potential inherent in Daoism, noted in the previous chapter.

CONCLUSION

Weber is not alone is regarding traditional Chinese state and clan formations as arenas of activity in which self-interest is simply absent. It has been
shown that the Confucian notion of self is characterized in terms of a distinction between a greater self and a lesser self, with the latter ethically
subordinate to the greater self through the imperatives of filial piety. But
this is an ideological representation which the economic reality for the
majority of families, of insufficient land to assure a material or resource
base sufficient to support a multigenerational family, and the authority of
the eldest male of the most senior generation, simply confounds. But even
in extended families, situated self-interest operates in the unfolding processes of family life even though, or rather, because of the constraining
context of familial relationships. Through a discussion of leading twentieth-
century Chinese social thinkers, Fei Xiaotong, Feng Youlan, and Ambrose
King, the Confucian notion of self has been further explored. In outlining
a critique of what might be called 'sociological Confucianism', a notion of
self has been outlined in which distinct temporal phases are acknowledged
as source to different types of self-interest connected with distinct forms of
institutional selection. The discussion here places the Chinese relational-
self in a context of institutional selection and a resolution of self-formation
into the generational capacity of relations between selves, including different temporal selves of the same person through which institutional arrangements operate, in the practical deployment of different self-interests.

One consequence of the characterization of self-interest in terms of the
different possible interests of distinct temporal phases of selves is a novel
characterization of two major strands of Chinese teachings, Confucianism
and Daoism, and their concerns. The depiction of the *Daodejing,* in particular, as a reference for the achievement of future-self-interests, challenges
most familiar interpretations of this text. It is shown here that a neglected
dimension of both Confucianism and philosophical Daoism—namely, their
respectively different conceptualizations of self-interest—clearly distinguishes them and is the fulcrum around which better known attributes of
each philosophy rotate. While the argument concerning the nature of self-
interest developed in this chapter operates in terms of Chinese subjects, the
analysis has broader application. The understanding of self which is outlined here, in terms of a differentiation of temporal phases of individual
selves, and the idea that each phase of self might have its own distinctive
type of self-interest, was originally presented by William Hazlitt (1969) in

the early nineteenth century and has more recently been given philosophical respectability (Parfit 1986: 199–306), although it remains neglected in sociology (Barbalet 2009), possibly because it goes against the widely accepted idea of a continuous self, supported by individual personal narratives and other cultural means that function in terms of psychological continuity or consciousness through time. By treating self-formation in terms of relationships between other selves, including other temporally-based selves of the same person, through institutional selection, then a sociological account of self-interest is possible that can uncover the operations of self-interest even when it is made obscure by prevailing doctrines, as in Confucianism, in which selfishness is admonished and the possibility of self-interest apparently denied.

It must be acknowledged that not only is there a Confucian antipathy to the notion of self-interest, but also a sociological unease with the concept. At some level, these are parallel concerns, arising in sociology from a perceived underlying assumption, in the notion of self-interest, of necessary orientation to utilitarian ends and calculative reasoning, even though these are not necessarily entailed in the concept (Barbalet 2012). Indeed, the development of sociology in antipathy to the utilitarian tradition is evident in Weber's augmentation of means-ends rationality with value rationality (Weber 1978: 24–25) and his addition of 'ideal' to 'material' interests, both subordinate to 'world images' or values (Weber 1970: 280). Durkheim's skepticism is more total, regarding self-interest as unavoidably egoistical, socially destructive, and fleetingly transitory (Durkheim 1964: 203–4). The pivotal distinction between self-interested and other-interested action, however, is not as sharp as the utilitarian purchase on 'self-interest' assumes (Barbalet 2009). Neither need it be held that the interests that selves pursue are necessarily material and pertain only to economic utilities or their equivalents. People have an interest in how they are seen by other, and also, an interest in maintaining a consistent value position, as well as an interest in effectively deploying limited means to achieve their goals or purposes (Barbalet 2008a: 804–7). Perhaps it is this sociological doubt regarding self-interest that led Weber to so readily accept the Confucian self-image in terms of which he wrote that 'individual interests per se remained out of the picture' (Weber 1964: 173). In this chapter, it has been shown why it is more useful to explore an alternate possibility, in which an appreciation of the nature and role of self-interest makes the picture itself larger and more detailed, and ultimately, more revealing of Chinese practices and thought traditions, especially Confucianism and Daoism.

REFERENCES

Ainslie, George. 1986. 'Beyond Microeconomics. Conflict among Interests in a Multiple Self as a Determinant of Value'. Pp. 133–75 in *The Multiple Self*, edited by Jon Elster. Cambridge: Cambridge University Press.

Akerlof, George A. and Kranton, Rachel E. 2010. *Identity Economics: How Our Identities Shape Our Work, Wages and Well-Being*. Princeton: Princeton University Press.

Ames, Roger T. 1983. *The Art of Rulership: A Study in Ancient Chinese Political Thought*. Honolulu: University of Hawaii Press.

Baker, Hugh D.R. 1979. *Chinese Family and Kinship*. New York: Columbia University Press.

Balazs, Etienne. 1964. *Chinese Civilization and Bureaucracy*. New Haven: Yale University Press.

Barbalet, Jack. 2008a. 'Pragmatism and Economics: William James' Contribution'. *Cambridge Journal of Economics*. 32(5): 797–810.

Barbalet, Jack. 2008b. *Weber, Passion and Profits: 'The Protestant Ethic and the Spirit of Capitalism' in Context*. Cambridge: Cambridge University Press.

Barbalet, Jack. 2009. 'Disinterestedness and Self Formation: Principles of Action in William Hazlitt'. *European Journal of Social Theory*. 12(2): 195–211.

Barbalet, Jack. 2012. 'Self Interest and the Theory of Action'. *British Journal of Sociology*. 63(3):412–29.

Barbalet, Jack. 2014. 'Laozi's *Daodejing*'. Pp. 17–31 in *The Oxford Handbook of Process Philosophy and Organization Studies*, edited by Jenny Helin, Tor Hernes, Daniel Hjorth and Robin Holt. Oxford: Oxford University Press.

Bauer, Wolfgang. 1976. *China and the Search for Happiness*. New York: Seabury Press.

Bedford, Olwen and Hwang, Kwang-kuo. 2003. 'Guilt and Shame in Chinese Culture: A Cross-cultural Framework from the Perspective of Morality and Identity'. *Journal for the Theory of Social Behaviour*. 33(2): 127–44.

Brook, Timothy. 1997. 'Profit and Righteousness in Chinese Economic Culture'. Pp. 27–44 in *Culture and Economy: The Shaping of Capitalism in Eastern Asia*, edited by Timothy Brook and Hy V. Luong. Ann Arbor: University of Michigan Press.

Cheng, Chung-ying. 1986. 'The Concept of Face and its Confucian Roots'. *Journal of Chinese Philosophy*. 13(3): 329–48.

Cheung, Steven N.S. 2005. 'The Enforcement of Property Rights in Children, and the Marriage Contract'. Pp. 389–43 in his *Economic Explanation: Selected Papers of Steven N.S. Cheung*. Hong Kong: Arcadia Press.

Cohen, Myron L. 1976. *House United, House Divided: The Chinese Family in Taiwan*. New York: Columbia University Press.

Csikszentmihalyi, Mark. 1999. 'Mysticism and Apophatic Discourse in the *Laozi*'. Pp. 33–58 in *Religious and Philosophical Aspects of the* Laozi, edited by Mark Csikszentmihalyi and Philip J. Ivanhoe. Albany: SUNY.

Durkheim, Emile. 1964. *The Division of Labor in Society*. New York: Free Press.

Durkheim, Emile. 1970. *Suicide: A Study in Sociology*. London: Routledge and Kegan Paul.

Eastman, Lloyd E. 1988. *Family, Fields and Ancestors: Constancy and Change in China's Social and Economic History, 1550–1949*. New York: Oxford University Press.

Elvin, Mark. 1985. 'Between the Earth and Heaven: Conceptions of the Self in China'. Pp. 156–89 in *The Category of the Person*, edited by Michael Carrithers, Steven Collins and Steven Lukes. Cambridge: Cambridge University Press.

Fei, Hsiao T'ung. 1962. *Peasant Life in China: A Field Study of Country Life in the Yangtze Valley*. London: Routledge and Kegan Paul.

Fei, Xiaotong. 1992. *From the Soil: The Foundations of Chinese Society*. Berkeley, CA: University of California Press.

Fei, Hsiao T'ung and Chang, Chih-I. 1948. *Earthbound China: A Study of Rural Economy in Yunnan*. London: Routledge and Kegan Paul.

Frank, Robert H. 1988. *Passion within Reason: The Strategic Role of the Emotions*. New York: Norton.

Freedman, Maurice. 1979. *The Study of Chinese Society: Essays by Maurice Freedman*, selected and Introduced by G. William Skinner. Stanford, CA: Stanford University Press.

Fung, Yu-Lan. 1952. *A History of Chinese Philosophy, Volume 1*. Princeton: Princeton: Princeton University Press.

Fung, Yu-Lan. 1998. 'The Philosophy at the Basis of Traditional Chinese Society'. Pp. 632–39 in his *Selected Philosophical Writings of Fung Yu-lan*. Beijing: Foreign Languages Press.

Gardner, Daniel K. 2007. *The Four Books: The Basic Teachings of the Later Confucian Tradition*. Indianapolis: Hackett Publishing.

Graham, A.C. 1990. *The Book of Lieh-tzŭ: A Classic of the Tao*. New York: Columbia University Press.

Greenhalgh, Susan. 1994. 'De-Orientalizing the Chinese Family Firm'. *American Ethnologist*. 21(4): 746–75.

Hall, David L. and Ames, Roger T. 1998. *Thinking from the Han: Self, Truth and Transcendence in Chinese and Western Culture*. Albany: SUNY Press.

Hamilton, Gary G. 1984. 'Patriarchalism in Imperial China and Western Europe: A Revision of Weber's Sociology of Domination'. *Theory and Society*. 13(3): 393–425.

Hamilton, Gary G. 1990. 'Patriarchy, Patrimonialism, and Filial Piety: A Comparison of China and Western Europe'. *British Journal of Sociology.* 41(1): 77–104.

Hazlitt, William. 1969. *An Essay on the Principles of Human Action.* Gainesville: Scholars' Facsimiles & Reprints.

Hirschman, Albert O. 1997. *The Passions and the Interests: Political Arguments for Capitalism before its Triumph.* Princeton: Princeton University Press.

Ho, D.Y.F. 1998. 'Interpersonal Relationships and Relational Dominance: An Analysis Based on Methodological Relationalism'. *Asian Journal of Social Psychology.* 1: 1–16.

Ho, D.Y.F. and Chiu, C.Y. 1998. 'Collective Representations as a Metaconstruct: An Analysis based on Methodological Relationalism'. *Culture and Psychology.* 4(3): 349–69.

Hsu, Dau-lin. 1970–71. 'The Myth of the "Five Human Relations" of Confucius'. *Monumenta Serica.* 29: 27–37.

Hsu, Francis Lang-Kwang. 1943. 'The Myth of Chinese Family Size'. *American Journal of Sociology.* 48(5): 555–62.

Hwang, Kwang-kuo. 1987. 'Face and Favor: The Chinese Power Game'. *American Journal of Sociology.* 92(4): 944–74.

Hwang, Kwang-kuo. 2000. 'Chinese Relationalism: Theoretical Construction and Methodological Considerations'. *Journal for the Theory of Social Behaviour.* 30(2): 155–78.

Ji, Jainlin, Kleinman, Arthur and Becker, Anne E. 2001. 'Suicide in Contemporary China: A Review of China's Distinctive Suicide Demographics in their Sociocultural Context'. *Harvard Review of Psychiatry.* 9(1): 1–12.

Johnson, Ian and Wang, Ping. 2012. *Daxue and Zhongyong: Bilingual Edition,* translated and annotated by Ian Johnson and Wang Ping. Hong Kong: Chinese University Press.

King, Ambrose Yeo-chi. 1985. 'The Individual and Group in Confucianism: A Relational Perspective'. Pp. 57–70 in *Individualism and Holism: Studies in Confucian and Taoist Values,* edited by Donald J. Munro. Ann Arbor: Center for Chinese Studies, The University of Michigan.

King, Ambrose Yeo-chi. 1991. 'Kuan-hsi and Network Building: A Sociological Interpretation'. *Daedalus.* 120(2): 63–84.

Knight, Frank H. 1971. *Risk, Uncertainty and Profit.* Chicago: University of Chicago Press.

LaFargue, Michael. 1994. *Tao and Method: A Reasoned Approach to Tao Te Ching.* Albany: SUNY.

LaFargue, Michael. 1998. 'Recovering the *Tao-te-ching's* Original Meaning: Some Remarks on Historical Hermeneutics'. Pp. 255–75 in *Lao-tzu and the Tao-te-ching,* edited by Livia Kohn and Michael LaFargue. Albany: SUNY.

Lau, D.C. 1963. *Lao Tzu: Tao Te Ching.* London: Penguin.

Legge, James. 1971. *Confucius: Confucian Analects, The Great Learning and The Doctrine of the Mean.* New York: Dover.

Lee, Sing and Kleinman, Arthur. 2000. 'Suicide as Resistance in Chinese Society'. Pp. 221–40 in *Chinese Society: Change, Conflict and Resistance,* edited by Elizabeth J. Perry and Mark Selden. London: Routledge.

Liu, Athena. 1999. *Family Law for the Hong Kong SAR.* Hong Kong: Hong Kong University Press.

Lufrano, Richard John. 1997. *Honorable Merchants: Commerce and Self-Cultivation in Late Imperial China.* Honolulu: University of Hawai'i Press.

Maine, Sir Henry Sumner. 1905. *Ancient Law: Its Connection with the Early History of Society and its Relation to Modern Ideas.* London: John Murray.

Mencius. 2004. *Mencius,* translated with an Introduction and Notes by D.C. Lau. Revised edition. London: Penguin.

Parfit, Derek. 1986. *Reasons and Persons.* Oxford: Oxford University Press.

Phillips, Michael R., Liu, Huaqing and Zhang, Yanping. 1999. 'Suicide and Social Change in China'. *Culture, Medicine and Psychiatry.* 23: 25–50.

Pizzorno, Alessandro. 1986. 'Some Other Kinds of Otherness: A Critique of "Rational Choice" Theories'. Pp. 355–73 in *Development, Democracy and the Art of Trespassing: Essays in Honor of Albert O. Hirschman,* edited by Alejandro Foxley, Michael S. McPherson and Guillermo O'Donnell. Notre Dame: University of Notre Dame Press.

Qi, Xiaoying. 2011. 'Face: A Chinese Concept in a Global Sociology'. *Journal of Sociology* 47(3): 279–96.

Qi, Xiaoying. 2014. *Globalized Knowledge Flows and Chinese Social Theory.* London: Routledge.

Ropp, Paul S., Zamperini, Paola and Zurndorfer, Harriet Thelma. 2001. *Passionate Women: Female Suicide in Late Imperial China.* Leiden: Brill.

Schwartz, Benjamin. 1959. 'Some Polarities in Confucian Thought'. Pp. 50–62 in *Confucianism in Action,* edited by David S. Nivison and Arthur F. Wright. Stanford: Stanford University Press.

Shang, Yang. 2006. *The Book of Lord Shang,* translated into English by J.J.L. Duyvendak and into Modern Chinese by Gao Heng. Beijing: Commercial Press.

Smith, Adam. 1979. *The Theory of Moral Sentiments,* edited by D.D. Raphael and A.L. Macfie. Oxford: Oxford University Press.

Veblen, Thorstein. 1946. *The Instinct of Workmanship and the State of the Industrial Arts.* New York: Viking Press.

Veblen, Thorstein. 1970. *The Theory of the Leisure Class: An Economic Study of Institutions.* London: Unwin.

Wang, Bi. 1999. 'Outline Introduction to the *Laozi* (*Laozi zhilue*)'. Pp. 30–47 in *The Classic of the Way and Virtue: A New Translation of the Tao-te ching of Loazi as Interpreted by Wang Bi*, translated by Richard John Lynn. New York: Columbia University Press.

Watson, Rubie S. 2004. 'Wives, Concubines and Maids: Servitude and Kinship in the Hong Kong Region, 1900–1940'. Pp. 169–98 in James L. Watson and Rubie S. Watson, *Village Life in Hong Kong: Politics, Gender and Ritual in the New Territories*. Hong Kong: The Chinese University Press.

Weber, Max. 1964. *The Religion of China: Confucianism and Taoism*, translated and edited by Hans H. Gerth, with an Introduction by C.K. Yang. New York: The Free Press.

Weber, Max. 1978. *Economy and Society: An Outline of Interpretive Sociology*, edited by Guenther Roth and Claus Wittich. Berkeley: University of California Press.

Weber, Max. 1970. 'The Social Psychology of World Religions'. Pp. 267–301 in *From Max Weber*, edited by H.H. Gerth and C. Wright Mills. London: Routledge.

Weber, Max. 1991. *The Protestant Ethic and the Spirit of Capitalism*, translated by Talcott Parsons. London: Harper Collins.

Wolf, Margery. 1975. 'Women and Suicide in China'. Pp. 111–41 in *Women in Chinese Society*, edited by Margery Wolf and Roxane Witke. Stanford, CA: Stanford University Press.

Wu, Fei. 2011. 'Suicide, A Modern Problem in China'. Pp. 213–36 in *Deep China: The Moral Life of the Person*, edited by Arthur Kleinman. Berkeley: University of California Press.

Yang, C.K. 1959. 'Some Characteristics of Chinese Bureaucratic Behavior'. Pp. 134–64 in *Confucianism in Action*, edited by David S. Nivison and Arthur F. Wright. Stanford: Stanford University Press.

CHAPTER 6

Magic

Introduction

In this chapter it is necessary first to step back from Weber's treatment of China and begin the discussion with his argument concerning the source of the capitalist spirit in the ethic of Protestantism as he originally conceived it in *The Protestant Ethic and the Spirit of Capitalism*. In this work, Weber outlines the origins in sixteenth- and seventeenth-century Europe of modern capitalist entrepreneurial orientations. The discussion of this account will set the stage for a more thorough investigation of the basis on which Weber distinguishes Protestantism from Confucianism. Through a close examination of Weber's argument it is shown that the pivot of what he regards as the major difference between these two ethical formations—namely, their respective relationship with magic—does not stand up to close scrutiny. His well-known characterization of Confucianism in *The Religion of China* as a creed unable to oppose magical practices and his treatment of Calvinism as the most thoroughly demagicalized and therefore rationalized religious formation are subject here to textual and historical consideration, leading to conclusions not found elsewhere in the literature.

The historical advent of the capitalist spirit, according to Max Weber's signature argument, occurs in a context of ethical innovation. The quest for profit as a virtue in and of itself is underpinned in its historically formative manifestation by a shift in religio-ethical principles—from Catholic to Protestant—which Weber (1991: 79) summarizes in the term 'calling

© The Author(s) 2017
J. Barbalet, *Confucianism and the Chinese Self*,
https://doi.org/10.1007/978-981-10-6289-6_6

(in the sense of a life-task, a definite field in which to work)'. It is important, however, to note that it is not Protestantism per se but rather Calvinism in particular that Weber believes provides what he regards as the facilitating affinity with the capitalist spirit. This is because the doctrine of predestination in Calvinism, the idea that God alone determines who is saved and who is damned, leads to an attitude of practical worldly engagement. Weber (1991: 113–14) says:

> The religious believer can make himself sure of his state of grace either in that he feels himself to be the vessel of the Holy Spirit or the tool of the divine will. In the former case his religious life tends to mysticism and emotionalism, in the latter to ascetic action; Luther stood close to the former type, Calvinism belonged definitely to the latter.

The Calvinist, then, was led to the rigors of 'a life of good works combined into a unified system' which are discharged not in a religious community (as with Catholicism) but in the flow of everyday practical engagements through which is realized the Calvinist ideal of 'proving one's faith in worldly activity' (Weber 1991: 117, 121). It is through this route that Weber links the Protestant ethic to the spirit of capitalism. It would follow, then, that in the absence of Calvinism the spirit of capitalism would fail to arise for want of a motivational basis. One consequence of this perspective that Weber went on to elaborate, as we shall see, is that through these historical contingencies the origins of capitalism are necessarily European.

A requirement of profit-seeking for its own sake, according to Weber (1991: 40, 75), includes 'economic rationalism' and a 'process of rationalization ... of technique and economic organization'. These are 'retarded', however, by 'anti-rational, emotional elements' that Weber (1991: 136–37) finds in non-Calvinist Protestantism, including Lutheranism, Methodism and Pietism, not to mention non-Protestant Catholicism. Indeed, a characteristic feature of Calvinism, according to Weber, is an anti-emotionalism that he associates with sponsorship of economic rationalism. The emotions-suppressive force of Calvinism, in Weber's estimation, combats the spontaneity and distraction from future prospects that would otherwise occur. He writes that 'Calvin viewed all pure feelings and emotions ... with suspicion' and that 'every rational type of asceticism ... enable[s] a man to ... act upon his constant motives ... against the emotions', thus encouraging the 'rational suppression of ... the whole emotional side of religion' (Weber 1991: 114, 119, 123; see also 105, 130–31).

The argument of *The Protestant Ethic and the Spirit of Capitalism*, then, is that the Calvinist suppression of emotions realizes an ethical rationalization that provides foundation to the capitalist spirit. *The Protestant Ethic* was originally published in 1905 and an augmented edition, along with other essays by Weber on the sociology of religion, was published in 1920. The argument that emotional suppression sponsors religious rationalization in Calvinism is present in both editions. But a new factor is introduced in the later edition. After describing the sense of inner loneliness inculcated by the doctrine of predestination the text of the 1905 edition immediately goes on to link this doctrine with 'the absolutely negative attitude of Puritanism toward all sensual and emotional elements ... because they were of no use for salvation' (Weber 2002: 74). In the 1920 edition, however, a new paragraph is inserted just prior to the one in which the above statement appears. It identifies a 'great historic process in the development of religions, [namely] the elimination of magic from the world which ... repudiated all magical means to salvation as superstition and sin' (Weber 1991: 105). The 1905 edition connects Puritan asceticism only with antihedonistic taste in art and leisure, while the 1920 text refers to the 'Puritan's ferocious hatred of ... all survivals of magical or sacramental salvation' (Weber 2002: 114; 1991: 168). References to magic in the second edition of the *Protestant Ethic* are not pervasive, however, and the original focus on emotional suppression as sponsoring religious rationalization in Calvinism is not displaced by it. But the references to magic signal a reconceptualization of Weber's research trajectory and the emergence of an interest in comparative studies of religions.

The significance of magic for an understanding of religion occurred to Weber when he began exploring non-European religions during the period 1910–1914. It was at this time that his vision was consolidated of a rationalizing Occident contrasted with an enchanted Orient, one giving rise to modern capitalism and the other where capitalism was autochthonously impossible. A major statement in which Weber develops these ideas is *The Sociology of Religion* (1963), a book-length treatment that became incorporated in his *Economy and Society* (1978: 399–634). *The Sociology of Religion* is a bricolage of summaries of and notes from countless sources that Weber fails to identify in the text. It constitutes Weber's overview and aggregation of historical, anthropological, folkloric, and allied knowledge of world religions. It is a work, uncharacteristically, in which ideal-type constructions are absent. *The Sociology of Religion* is a repository of information concerning various aspects of ancient and exotic religions organized in terms of Weber's preoccupation with social agents, what might be called 'interest-bearers', and processes of rationalization. It is 'a work that does not explain itself' (Whimster 2007: 166). It is noted that 'because the work has no footnotes, nor any kind of introductory literature review of current debates, it has been assumed that all the concepts were Weber's own [but] this is quite misleading' (Whimster 2007: 164). At a slightly later time, Weber reworks the ideas that he gleans from his extensive reading of diverse sources in a subsequent text discussed in previous chapters that will be considered again here, *The Religion of China*. In these works, Weber preserves in his own way a nineteenth-century approach to religion.

After reviewing Weber's account of magic in *The Sociology of Religion*, and especially its relationship with religion, the discussion below moves to consideration of his treatment in *The Religion of China* of magic in Imperial China and especially its relationship with Confucianism. Weber's purpose in his treatment of Confucianism as magic-tolerant and magically infused is to contrast it with Calvinism; this latter, he claims, has 'liquidated magic most completely' (Weber 1964: 226). It is on this basis that Weber is able to show in his own terms that not only did modern capitalism historically arise in the Occident, it also has no basis in China given the predominance of magic and the impossibility of a Confucian eradication of magic or sponsorship of rationalized religious and economic cultures. The problem with Weber's argument, to be discussed shortly, is that he is oblivious to the fact that Reformation Protestantism—and especially Calvinism—at a time it supposedly sponsors an unequivocal rationalization, was obsessed with demonic sorcery and the power of witches to control familiars, engage with the devil, and cause earthly chaos by magical means. This feature of historical Calvinism, ignored by Weber, undermines a key aspect of the contrast he draws between Calvinism and Confucianism. Calvinist prosecution of sorcery and witchcraft (like the Catholic before it), while arguably an eliminatory practice directed to sorcerers and witches, necessarily accepts the efficacy and power of the magical forces it opposes. The significance of this for Weber's argument concerning the differences between Calvinism and Confucianism is obvious; both reject magic for themselves but acknowledge its presence in the world as a real force; Calvinists opposed magic but did not eliminate it, their worldview requires it as a constitutive element, as we shall see. After considering these issues, the discussion goes on to briefly consider other bases of the rationalization of magic and religion during this period of capitalist development in Europe. Finally, Weber's treatment of Chinese magic is assessed. It is necessary, though, to first clarify Weber's statement regarding Calvinism's 'elimination of magic from the world' (Weber 1991: 105).

CALVINIST DEMAGICALIZATION IN WEBER

Weber's treatment of the Calvinist suppression of magic operates in terms of two distinct but connected claims. One of these—namely, that Calvinism contributes to the elimination of magic in the process of religious rational-ization—is entirely sociological insofar as it can be demonstrated in terms of the conduct of social actors and their orientation to the circumstances they encounter. This is the idea that there is an 'historic process in the development of religions, [namely] the elimination of magic from the world which had begun with the old Hebrew prophets and [continued in] Hellenistic scientific thought' (Weber 1991: 105). In this passage, Weber immediately goes on to make a second claim, that Calvinism 'repudiated all magical means to salvation as superstition and sin' (see also Weber 1963: 269 [1978: 630]; 1964: 226). This second claim, that Calvinism alone eliminates magical means to salvation, is theological rather than sociological insofar as it operates in terms of Calvinist critiques of Catholicism: 'the complete elimination of salvation through the Church and the sacraments ... was what formed the absolutely decisive difference from Catholicism' (Weber 1991: 105).

In *The Protestant Ethic and the Spirit of Capitalism* these propositions are conjoined so that they appear as a single proposition, not two separate propositions. But representation of Weber's claim as holding that Calvinism eliminates magic from the world only by repudiating magical means to salvation removes Calvinism from any contribution to the broader process of demagicalization, which Weber says began with the old Hebrew proph-ets and manifest in the development of scientific thought. Indeed, in *The Protestant Ethic* discussion of the development of the Puritan ethical ori-entation as an instance of rationalization implicitly supports what is described here as the sociological proposition. In his account of modern science, Weber (1970a: 139) defines intellectualization as rationalization in terms of the displacement of 'mysterious incalculable forces' with the instrument of 'calculation' so that there is no longer 'recourse to magical means'. The indirect 'influence' of Puritanism on the agents of this process is acknowledged by Weber (1970a: 142). This orientation of action and technique of conduct as general demagicalization is referred to again in the context of 'religiously qualified virtuosos' that Weber (1970b: 290) says fulfil two requirements of rationality. The first is effectively the same as what is described earlier—in this case, the separation of the practitioner from otherworldly, mystical, or ecstatic forces so that they primarily participate in an 'everyday life' in 'the real world'. Second, Weber (1970b: 290) says, they must give up 'the purely magical or sacramental character of the means of grace', for not doing so means that 'the decision about salvation' shall be linked to 'processes which are not of a rational everyday nature'. In this case, the second requirement, of repudiating magical means to salvation, is connected with the first, the rationalization of everyday life. In this characterization, avoidance of sacramental salvation is sociologically predicated on a prior elimination of magic from the world as rationalization.

In his account of Protestant, or more correctly, Calvinist repudiation of magical means to salvation, Weber (1963: 269 [1978: 630]; 1964: 226; 1991: 105, 168) asserts that this is exclusive to that particular denomination, a claim that is not sociological but theological. Weber's remarks in this context operate in terms of a religious doctrinal dispute between Calvinists and Catholics in which Weber effectively asserts his support for one side against the other without examination or justification. In referring to the fact that Calvinists repudiate magical means to salvation, Weber (1963: 25, 28 [1978: 422, 425]) claims that Catholics, on the other hand, embrace magic in their religious practices. A scholar best known for systematizing and promoting Weber's sociology of religion takes exception to Weber's description of the 'medieval Catholic priest as magician' and admonishes Weber by saying that 'Catholic sacramentalism must not be misinterpreted as mere magic' (Schluchter 1985: 168; see also Stark 1968: 204–5). In fact, Weber (1963: 25 [1978: 422]) does not refer to 'medieval' priests but to 'the Catholic priest who continues to practice' magic. Indeed, Weber's partisan Protestant orientation has not gone unnoticed in the literature (Aldenhoff 2010; Graf 1995; Honigsheim 1950; Swatos and Kivisto 1991), and although less frequently mentioned, his anti-Catholic prejudice has also drawn attention (Stark 1968).

The difference between Calvinist and Catholic understandings of the sacraments is in fact unclear. While Calvinist accusations of Catholic magic are well known, so is Catholic denial. Calvin (2002: 779) is forthright about his own commitment to sacraments as 'an external sign, by which the Lord seals on our consciences his promises of good-will toward us, in order to sustain the weakness of our faith, and we in our turn testify our piety towards him, both before himself, and before angels as well as men

... it [is] a testimony of the divine favour toward us, confirmed by an external sign, with a corresponding attestation of our faith towards Him'. This is not an unequivocal rejection of the sacraments as a means to salvation, as Weber (1991: 104–5) leads us to expect: 'the complete elimination of salvation through ... the sacraments' and 'no trust in the effects of ... sacramental forces in salvation'. As one literary scholar notes regarding the controversy between Protestant and Catholic views of the sacraments: 'the risk of oversimplification is great and the historian [or sociologist] is obliged to step warily' (Greene 2005: 32). It is shown by Greene that neither Catholic doctrine nor Protestant is homogenous, and also that Calvin's position is ambiguous in so far as he attempted 'to find a middle ground between competing doctrines' (Greene 2005: 33). From this perspective, Weber errs on the side of oversimplification.

Whereas Weber (1963: 25 [1978: 422]) regards the Catholic mass, in the transubstantiation of bread and wine into Christ's body and blood, as requiring the priest's magical power, Calvin (2002: 451), on the other hand, is not embarrassed to find a transposition to the sacraments in Christ's claim that he is 'living bread', that 'my flesh is meat indeed, and my blood is drink indeed (John 6:55)'. He goes on to say:

> The same doctrine is clearly seen in the sacraments; which, though they direct our faith to the whole, not to a part of Christ, yet, at the same time, declare that the materials of righteousness and salvation reside in his flesh ... Hence I often repeat, that Christ has been in a manner set before us as a fountain, whence we may draw what would otherwise lie without use in that deep and hidden abyss which streams forth to us in the person of the Mediator. (Calvin 2002: 451–52)

Calvin's objection to the Catholic mass is that those to whom it is directed may not themselves have faith in Christ, for as indicated above, Calvin regards the sacraments as an exchange, involving God's goodwill directed toward those who express piety toward him. In the case of the Catholic mass, then, it was deemed 'sufficient if the priest muttered the formula of consecration, while the people, without understanding, looked stupidly on' (Calvin 2002: 780). Instead of faith, there is here 'superstition' in the 'great profanation of the mystery', which 'was a kind of magical incantation' and has the 'same effect with them as magical incantation' (Calvin 2002: 780, 827 note 15, 836). Calvin seems here to be saying not that the Catholic mass is a magical sacrament or that Catholic priests practice magic, but that if the mass is addressed to people without prior faith, then it is simply superstition and has the appearance of a magical incantation. Again, this is rather removed from Weber's own perspective.

Calvin (2002: 884) accepts the sacraments as a 'seal' of salvation. His position is not the same as that of the Catholic Church but the two positions are on a common scale and not polar opposites. Calvin does object, though, to what he regards as 'fictitious sacraments' and the failure to distinguish 'between sacraments and other ceremonies' (Calvin 2002: 879). He finds these in the Catholic Church's 'five sacraments' (see Calvin 2002: 877–97), one of which is marriage:

> ...which, while all admit it to be an institution of God, no man ever saw to be a sacrament, until the time of Gregory, [even though it] is a good and holy ordinance of God ... For in a sacrament, the thing required is not only that it be a work of God, but that it be an external ceremony appointed by God to confirm a promise. That there is nothing of the kind in marriage, even children can judge. But it is a sign, they say, of a sacred thing, that is, of the spiritual union of Christ with the Church. (Calvin 2002: 895)

The allegation raised by Calvin here could be described as a claim of Catholic overreach, but not one of magical invocation on the part of priests. Indeed, Calvin's argument that the Catholic Church is excessive in claiming nonsacramental ceremonies as sacraments operates in terms of Calvin's defense of the significance of sacraments for the faithful and for their salvation.

Weber's insistence that only Calvinists effectively repudiate magical means to salvation, and also his claim that sacramental salvation is rejected by Calvinists are unproven assertions, if not errors. His insistence that sacramental salvation is equivalent to magical invocation is also an exaggeration not accepted by Calvin. Weber's own position on these matters is difficult to distinguish from partisan theological commitment. Weber's claim that Calvinism alone repudiated sacramental salvation sits uncomfortably with his claim in *The Sociology of Religion*, that the rationalization of religion is achieved with the formation of a professionally trained priesthood and that this is the means by which religion transcends magic, when faith substitutes for magical powers (Weber 1963: 31, 195 [1978: 426–27, 567]). In this latter case, not only Calvinism in particular but Christianity in general, including Catholicism, arguably represents a repudiation of magic in salvation. But to accept such a determination risks jeopardizing the Protestant ethic thesis itself. In the following section, Weber's account of the disengagement of magic in religious rationalization is considered. Later in the chapter the compromise of Reformation Calvinist rationalization through opposition to satanic witchcraft is discussed. While Calvinist prosecution of sorcery and witchcraft (like the Catholic before it) is arguably an eliminatory practice directed to sorcerers and witches, it necessarily accepts the efficacy and power of the magical forces it opposes. This is an opposition to magic, certainly, but cannot be an elimination of it as magic in this case is a constitutive element of a worldview, a component part of everyday life in the real world.

MAGIC IN RELIGION

In his 'discovery' of magic, reported in *The Sociology of Religion*, Weber inextricably connects magic with religion, as the latter's primitive or original form. Magic is an object that may be constrained, opposed, rejected, and ultimately displaced in the process of rationalization, exemplified religiously in Calvinism and intellectually in modern science (Weber 1970a: 139; 1970b: 275, 282). In *The Sociology of Religion*, Weber (1963: 27, 31, 210 [1978: 424, 427, 579]) goes so far as to indicate that through an evolutionary process, the significance of magic in religion diminishes over the course of historical time. To put it this way is simply to acknowledge Weber's own usage, which corresponds with his discussion elsewhere of 'social selection' (Weber 1978: 38–39; 2014: 319–20) even though commentary on Weber's thought typically insists that he has an antiselectionist orientation (see Mommsen 1989: 158–61). The point, though, is that for Weber, magic and rationality are on an historical continuum, with original religion and Calvinism standing as polar opposites. Only with Calvin's religious rationalization through demagicalization is the spirit of capitalism possible, according to Weber.

Weber opens his discussion in *The Sociology of Religion* by saying that it is not possible to begin with a definition of religion but insists that magic is integral to religion in the most elemental way. The two are brought into alignment from the very first page, where Weber (1963: 1 [1978: 399–400]) writes of 'religious or magical factors', 'religiously or magically motivated behaviour', 'religious and magical actions'. Weber goes on to claim that while magic and religion are originally inextricable, when religion takes an ethical form—which occurs when priests predominate over magicians (Weber 1963: 30 [1978: 426])—then the magical element is diminished and in the unique case of ascetic Protestantism magic is 'completely eliminated' (Weber 1963: 269 [1978: 630]). Magic is understood by Weber to exist in at least three distinct forms, depending on how practitioners relate to it. In its historically earliest manifestation, magic has a practical purpose and in that sense it is rational in so far as it 'follows rules of experience', even though magically motivated action is not necessarily 'in accordance with a means end schema' (Weber 1963: 1 [1978: 400]). Second, magic is 'transformed from a direct manipulation of forces into a symbolic activity' (Weber 1963: 6 [1978: 403]). The trend of Weber's discussion here suggests that as religious consciousness develops, and as the gods become of increased significance, then prayer and sacrifice become more important than magic (Weber 1963: 26–27 [1978: 422–23]). At this stage, magic is used to coerce the gods, as distinct from worshiping them. Weber notes that such coercive elements of religious practice are 'universally diffused' and 'even the Catholic priest continues to practice something of this magical power in executing the miracle of the mass' (Weber 1963: 25 [1978: 422]). The third manifestation of magic in religion is in aesthetic expression, in the form of art and also in the activity of craft in the artisan, even though the artisan's *modus operandi* is rational calculation (Weber 1963: 8, 97–98 [1978: 405, 483]). In what follows only the first and second forms of magic are discussed.

Given the progressive though qualified separation of magic from religion, relative to their original integration, as postulated by Weber, a question arises concerning what factors promote such a development. Weber's discussion is tentative and conditional, with acknowledgement of a number of courses that contribute to the process of differentiation. One possible factor, although Weber is less than explicit about it, is the emergence of a distinction between gods and spirits, with the latter maintaining a direct link with magic. As the importance of gods increases, Weber (1963: 20 [1978: 415–16]) claims, so the significance of spirits diminishes. Worship of gods, what Weber calls 'divine worship', has two elements: prayer and sacrifice (Weber 1963: 26–27 [1978: 422–23]). These latter, he says, permit or constitute 'departures from magic' (Weber 1963: 27 [1978: 423]). While Weber regards such developments as part of 'a special evolutionary process' (Weber 1963: 27 [1978: 423]), the separation is not complete because the 'boundary' between prayer and 'magical formula ... remains fluid' (Weber 1963: 26 [1978: 422]).

Weber goes on to propose, although with continuing irresolution, another possible way of separating religion from magic, in the distinction between religion and sorcery:

The relationships of men to supernatural forces which take the forms of prayer, sacrifice and worship may be termed 'cult' and 'religion', as distinguished from 'sorcery', which is magical coercion. Correspondingly, those beings that are worshiped and entreated religiously may be termed 'gods', in contrast to 'demons' which are magically coerced and charmed. (Weber 1963: 28 [1978: 424])

This distinction, however, with gods pertaining to religion and demons to magic, cannot be sustained because 'practically everywhere … numerous magical components' persist in religion (Weber 1963: 28 [1978: 424]). Even more telling, in the elaboration of religious creed and practice, and in the succession of religious forms, as well as in the context of religious war and contestation, strict differentiation between religion and magic in terms of the difference between gods and demons is confounded 'when a secular or priestly power suppressed a cult in favour of a new religion, with the older gods continuing to live on as demons' (Weber 1963: 28 [1978: 424]).

Given Weber's failure in these prior considerations to provide a clear substantive distinction between religion and magic, a 'sociological aspect of the differentiation' is invoked, referring to the social or more properly organizational distinction between the 'priesthood' and 'practitioners of magic' (Weber 1963: 28 [1978: 424–25]). Again, Weber acknowledges that this distinction is 'fluid'; while priests 'influence the gods by means of worship' and magicians 'coerce demons by magical means', the distinction is not watertight because in 'many great religions, including Christianity, the concept of the priest includes … a magical qualification' (Weber 1963: 28 [1978: 424]). Indeed, Jesus himself is distinguished by 'his magical power to work miracles' (Weber 1963: 271 [1978: 631]). Weber's 'sociological' distinction, on the other hand, points to the fact that priests are 'employees or organs operating in the interests of the organization's members' (Weber 1963: 28 [1978: 425]) whereas magicians 'are self-employed' (Weber 1963: 29 [1978: 425]). But this distinction also is incomplete. While employment status may 'conceptually' distinguish priests and magicians, it is 'fluid in actuality' as a 'sorcerer is not infrequently a member of an organized guild' (Weber 1963: 29 [1978: 425]).

Weber goes on to mention another distinction which, again, is inadequate to completely separate priests from magicians, as priests are held to possess a 'professional equipment of special knowledge, fixed doctrine, and vocational qualifications' while magicians 'exert their influence by virtue of personal gifts (charisma) made manifest in miracle' (Weber 1963:

29 [1978: 425]). This distinction is porous because 'the sorcerer may sometimes be very learned, while deep learning may not characterize working priests' (Weber 1963: 29 [1978: 425]). A related but clearer distinction between religion and magic, Weber holds, is not in the fact of specialist learning per se, but in its nature, with priests having a 'rational training and discipline' while the training of magicians draws on 'irrational means and aiming at rebirth and proceeds in part as a training in purely empirical lore' (Weber 1963: 29 [1978: 425]). 'But in this case also', Weber (1963: 29 [1978: 425]) says, 'the two contrasted types flow into one another'.

Weber arrives at greater clarity in the distinction between religion and magic when he considers not merely the organizational nature of the priesthood or its specialist training, but rather, the formation of a defining interest that derives from the particular organizational role of priests. Weber says that 'the crucial feature of the priesthood [is] the specialization of a particular group of persons in the continuous operation of a cultic enterprise, permanently associated with particular norms, places and times, and related to specific social groups' (Weber 1963: 30 [1978: 426]). He goes on to say:

> The full development of both a metaphysical rationalization and a religious ethic requires an independent and professionally trained priesthood, permanently occupied with the cult and with the practical problems involved in the cure of souls ... [The] rationalization of religious life was fragmentary or entirely missing wherever the priesthood failed to achieve independent class status. (Weber 1963: 30 [1978: 426])

Only in this way, through the agency of a priesthood with interests formed in and expressive of a permanent cult, can religion 'transcend the stages of magic', according to Weber (1963: 31 [1978: 427]). The complete realization of this prospect, Weber holds, is achieved with Protestantism: 'Only ascetic Protestantism completely eliminated magic and the supernatural quest for salvation' (Weber 1963: 269 [1978: 630]).

This trend 'of religious evolution ... set in motion by the existence of vested interests of a priesthood in a cult' (Weber 1963: 31 [1978: 427]) operates through a number of mechanisms that can be summarized in terms of an emergent dominance of faith over magic:

> By virtue of [a] charismatic confidence in god's support, the spiritual representative and leader of the congregation, as a virtuoso of faith, may act

differently from the layman in practical situations and bring about different results, far surpassing normal human capacity. In the context of practical action, faith can provide a substitute for magical powers. (Weber 1963: 195 [1978: 567])

Weber's iterated, hesitant, and possibly tedious quest for a basis on which religion and magic can be clearly distinguished reflects both the nature of his literary exercise in *The Sociology of Religion*, of attempting to find a way through and order the content of numerous texts, and also confirmation of his opening hypothesis concerning the magical origins of religion. The importance of this hypothesis for Weber's broader argument is that it permits his particular claims concerning the rationalization of the Protestant ethic to now have a world historical context, rather than the more human developmental context of impulse control and emotions management that it had in 1905 with the first publication of *The Protestant Ethic and the Spirit of Capitalism*.

In setting out his argument concerning the original magical nature of religion and the sequential decommissioning of different aspects of magic in the development of religion, reaching a culmination of rationalization and demagicalization in Protestantism, and especially Calvinism, Weber is in a position to contrast a number of distinct cases. One which recurs in *The Sociology of Religion* is that of China, in which there is 'a cult without a specialized priesthood' in the form of Confucianism so that 'ethics developed into something quite different from a metaphysically rationalized religion' (Weber 1963: 30 [1978: 426]). Indeed, according to Weber, China is one place where a separation of religion from magic was never achieved, with significant negative consequences for the prospects of a native capitalist development.

CHINA AS A MAGIC GARDEN

Weber's most detailed discussion of Confucianism, *The Religion of China*, develops an account set out earlier in *The Sociology of Religion* which understands Confucianism as the ideology of the Chinese bureaucratic caste (Weber 1963: 90, 120, 124 [1978: 476–77, 502, 506]). This approach is continued in what in effect is Weber's first concentrated historical sociology of comparative religion, although to describe *The Religion of China* in this way captures but a portion of its content. Weber revised *The Religion of China* and two other works published soon after it, *The*

Religion of India and *Ancient Judaism*, as well as the much earlier *The Protestant Ethic and the Spirit of Capitalism*, for publication in 1920, along with a handful of essays, as a three-volume *Collected Essays in the Sociology of Religion*. This publication realized a substantial part of his project concerning the *Economic Ethics of the World Religions*, the first fruit of which is summarized in *The Sociology of Religion*.

Weber's project mentioned here was designed to demonstrate that a rational form of capitalism arose exclusively in Europe because only with the advent of the Puritan creed was the ethical basis of profit-making for its own sake possible. No other religion, in Weber's estimation, possesses the capacity for ethical rationalization generative of modern capitalism. In *The Religion of China*, Weber (1964: 248) argues that while Confucianism developed a rational ethos, it failed to engender a 'rational mastery of the world' because 'Confucian rationalism means rational adjustment to the world'. The world-accommodating ethos of Confucianism failed, therefore, to realize the potential in the Imperial Chinese economy for the development of modern capitalism, a potential which Weber (1964: 100, 104) acknowledges. Being complicit with traditional cosmology, Confucianism instead effectively 'transformed the world into a magic garden' (Weber 1964: 200).

Weber (1964: 155) does acknowledge that Confucians 'in principle doubted the reality of magic' because they were 'only interested in the affairs of this world such as it happened to be'. Indeed, he notes the 'profound internal antagonism of Confucianism toward all emotional religiosity and toward magic' (1964: 203). These apparently definitive statements are not without qualification, however. Weber's reference to an 'in principle' opposition to magic in Confucianism and a merely 'internal antagonism' toward magic are amplified in his argument that Confucianism has an accommodating relationship with the acceptance and practice of magic by Daoists and others. Further, not only do Confucians typically fail to confront magic when it is practiced by non-Confucians, Weber goes on to argue, but there is in many Confucian beliefs and practices, in spite of stated principles to the contrary, acceptance of elements of magic. These two compromises of Confucian opposition to magic detected by Weber will be dealt with in turn.

Weber in effect argues that irrespective of the marked philosophical differences between Confucianism and Daoism it is difficult to maintain a firm distinction between them with regard to magic. He says that the Confucian literati 'treated with tolerant disdain' the magic of Daoist priests because they regarded it 'as a diet suitable for the masses' (Weber 1964: 204). Indeed, in China 'belief in magic was part of the constitutional foundation of sovereign power', according to Weber (1964: 200), so that:

> Confucianism was helpless when confronted with the magic image of the world, however much it disdained Taoism. This helplessness prevented the Confucians from being internally capable of eradicating the fundamental, purely magical conceptions of the Taoists. To tackle magic always appeared dangerous for the Confucian's own power. (1964: 200; see also 194, 196; 1963: 90 [1978: 476–77])

Confucian toleration of magic compromises its rationalism, so while there is a 'cleavage between the official institution of grace and non-classical popular religion' and while the latter is 'source of a methodical way of life differing from the official cult … which Confucianism … always treated as heterodox' (1964: 174–75), the 'relative toleration which was granted to heterodox cults for reasons of state' (1964: 217; see also 194), according to Weber, preserved China's political power structure while at the same time, compromised its prospects for an economic revolution of the type experienced in Protestant Europe.

Rather than simply notice Confucian tolerance of magic initiated by others, Weber claims also that Confucian literati practices entail a direct engagement with magic. First, Weber suggests that the charismatic possibilities of office derive from magical qualification. In *The Sociology of Religion*, Weber (1963: 2 [1978: 400]) notes that charisma has two forms—one a consequence of a person employing extraordinary means while the other inheres 'simply by virtue of natural endowment', although the term 'natural' here is misleading as Weber (1963: 2–3, 29 [1978: 401, 425]) means that such charismatic powers are experienced as magical. In *The Religion of China*, Weber (1964: 135) writes that officeholders, especially those qualified by examination, possess a 'magical charisma' that leads to their advice being sought 'in all important affairs' and that 'High mandarins were considered magically qualified'. This is not strictly evidence of magical practice, however, as the conception of 'magical-charismatic … qualification for office as tested by examination' and the idea of the 'magical significance of written work and of documents' are respectively 'popular' and 'primeval', according to Weber (1964: 135), and not of the Confucian official's own making. Weber does say, though, that there is additionally a direct Confucian acceptance and practice of magic in the imperial court rituals officiated by literati, and third, in the worship of ancestors.

The 'educated Confucian', according to Weber (1964: 229), 'adhered to magical conceptions with ... skepticism while occasionally submitting to demonology'. This equivocal lapse, however, is not merely a matter of individual disposition or choice, according to Weber, but structurally required. This is because 'the cardinal virtue and goal in self-perfection [of the Confucian] meant ceremonial and ritualist propriety in all circumstances of life' (Weber 1964: 228). Weber argues that the commitment to traditionally based and stable social conventions means that Confucian 'salvation' is achieved, not by being free of sin in the Christian sense, but rather by avoiding 'offences against traditional authorities, parents, ancestors, and superiors in the hierarchy of office' (Weber 1964: 229):

> The right path to salvation consisted in adjustment to the eternal and supra-divine orders of the world, Tao, and hence to the requirements of social life, which followed from cosmic harmony ... This ethic of unconditional affirmation of and adjustment to the world presupposed the unbroken and continued existence of purely magical religion. (Weber 1964: 228–29)

The link between adhering to ceremonial and conventional expectations on the one hand and 'purely magical religion' on the other is in the idea that any contravention of social conventions will violate cosmic harmony; fulfilling traditional obligations therefore placates 'purely magically-conceived spirits' (Weber 1964: 228). Imperial court rituals and the role of Confucian literati in magically-infused ceremonials (Weber 1964: 109–11) are designed, according to this account, to preserve cosmic harmony.

A particular case of this general phenomenon, according to Weber, is filial piety as ancestor worship. Filial piety, in Weber's terms, has the function in patrimonial states of providing the generic form of subordination (Weber 1963: 90 [1978: 476]; 1964: 158, 213). He says that 'the most important status obligation of bureaucracy' is 'adherence to unconditional discipline', and this is achieved through and demonstrated by filial piety (Weber 1964: 158). Although ancestor worship and filial piety are not strictly equivalent, they are inevitably connected because filial or family piety rests on 'the belief in spirits' (Weber 1964: 236) or 'magic' (Weber 1963: 210 [1978: 579]). This is because the notion that the well-being of persons in the present generation is contingent on the satisfaction of the spirits of their predecessors or ancestors. The means by which the favor of ancestral spirits is secured is the ritual provision of sacrifices (Weber 1964: 87). One consequence of this dimension of Confucianism includes a strong sense of personalist association and cohesion. To the extent that sacrifice to ancestral spirits is a 'religious duty', says Weber (1964: 236), then 'the pious Chinese ... develop[s] himself within the organically given, personal relations'. This contrasts with the Puritan's sense of 'religious duty toward the hidden and supra-mundane God', through which the Puritan regards all human relations, including family relations, as 'mere means and expression of a mentality reaching beyond the organic relations of life' (Weber 1964: 236).

Weber's account of ancestor worship as a religious duty misunderstands its nature and purpose. There is no assumption in Confucian filial piety of the divinity of ancestors. Sacrifice to spirits of ancestors in not an acknowledgement of anything sacred or holy in a person's forebears, but rather consists of practices designed to maintain a consciousness of the connection between intergenerational transmission and personal responsibility. There is no assumption concerning the immortality of ancestors' souls and no expectation that ancestor worship shall contribute to the worshiper's own salvation or in any way affect their own spiritual being. Rather, filial piety and ancestor 'worship' relate to respect and reverence and are associated with development in a person of the qualities of benevolence and righteousness. These are moral virtues rather than religious beliefs and practices, properly understood, that function in terms of the priority of family relations over all others. Weber's observation regarding the political consequence of filial piety as general subordination, mentioned above, is accurate; it is indicated in the *Analects* (I, 2) that a filial son will not offend or transgress against his superiors. The development of self within the 'organically given, personal relations', as Weber describes filiality, does not come out of a 'religions duty', however, but from an acknowledgement that a single person is a point on a 'continuum of descent' in which any single living individual personifies his ancestors and his descendants, both born and unborn (Baker 1979: 26–27). In this sense, the individual exists to serve his family, a notion in sharp contrast with the Puritan's qualified regard for family relations, as Weber indicates, mentioned earlier.

A further and associated consequence of what Weber understands as worship of ancestral spirits, then, is the rejection in Confucianism of asceticism and escape from the world. Weber says that this leads to Confucian persecution and eradication of all 'forms of congregational and redemptory religiosity' and to 'completely suppress all independent ecclesiastical development and all congregational religion' (Weber 1964: 229; 1963: 90 [1978: 476–77]). These claims—that Confucian rejection of asceticism leads to the persecution of religions with ascetic practices and congregational forms—are not supported with evidence by Weber. Certainly, the imperial state's suppression of the Taiping Rebellion, a movement which Weber (1964: 219) describes as subject to 'the influence of Protestant missionaries and the Bible' and based on an ethos that 'radically and puritanically rebuked every belief in spirits, magic, and idolatry' and possessing a 'half ascetic' ethic, was not motivated by an assessment of these religious factors, but rather, by the Taiping's endeavor to overthrow the imperial state. Nevertheless, the personalism of the Confucian ethic means, for Weber, that it has no place for a Puritan form of asceticism.

While both Confucian and Puritan ethics are rational and both tend toward utilitarian possibilities, by which Weber means that neither is mystical, they nevertheless are fundamentally different in one major regard, according to Weber. He says that Confucians lack what Puritans possess—namely, 'rational matter-of-factness, impersonal rationalism, and the nature of an abstract, impersonal, purposive association' (Weber 1964: 241). He continues:

> Whereas Puritanism objectified everything and transformed it into rational enterprise, dissolved everything into the pure business relation, and substituted rational law and agreement for tradition, in China, the pervasive factors were tradition, local custom, and the concrete personal favour of the official. (Weber 1964: 241; see also 229–30)

As Weber indicates a number of times, religious rationalization means at least divestment of magic. We have seen Weber argue that while Confucianism is rational, its rationality is qualified from the point of view of a comparison with Puritan rationality in being world-accommodating and also in its various concessions to magic. Protestantism, on the other hand, Weber (1964: 226) says, has 'liquidated magic most completely' and nowhere 'has the complete disenchantment [demagicalization] of the world been carried through with greater consistency'.

Puritan 'liquidation' of magic does not mean, Weber acknowledges, that it was not free 'from what we nowadays customarily regard as "superstition" [as evidenced by the] Witch trials [that] flourished in New England' (Weber 1964: 226; see also 155). This qualification, of lingering superstition evidenced by witch trials, deserves scrutiny, given that the hallmark distinction between Calvinism and Confucianism is the discharge of magic from one and its continued acceptance by the other. By their nature. witch trials spring from much more than mere superstition as they are conducted to eradicate magical practices believed by those involved to be real and efficacious. If Weber's claims regarding Puritan rationalization through demagicalization are an exaggeration, then his insistent claims concerning the distance between Confucian rationality and Puritan rationality will lose their credibility.

DEMONIC MAGIC IN REFORMATION PROTESTANTISM

Weber's acknowledgement of Puritan 'superstition' is curious not only in its qualification with quotation marks, but more seriously in the fact that the Salem witch trials in colonial Massachusetts between February 1692 and May 1693, which he refers to, were minor events compared with the witch hunts that occupied Calvinist Geneva from 1537 to 1662—which Calvin personally supervised during the period 1541–1543—and in Calvinist Scotland from 1563 to 1736, both of which Weber fails to mention. Indeed, the Protestant 'obsession' with demonology and witchcraft during this period (Scribner 2001: 357), shared by both Luther and Calvin, led to witch hunts also in Brandenburg, Württemberg, Baden, Bavaria, Mecklenburg, Denmark, and Transylvania (Trevor-Roper 1978: 64–65). That Weber fails to mention these events or is unaware of them calls into question his judgment that Protestantism 'liquidated magic most completely'. Indeed, any understanding of Reformation Protestantism, including Calvinism, which fails to appreciate how thoroughly saturated it was with concerns of sorcery and witchcraft and how it accepted that magic had the capacity to affect human well-being, fails to grasp the continuity in this regard of the theology of medieval Europe and Reformation Protestantism.

In the *Protestant Ethic*, Weber (1991: 111–12) writes:

So far as predestination was not reinterpreted, toned down, or fundamentally abandoned, two principal, mutually connected, types of pastoral advice appear. On the one hand it is held to be an absolute duty to consider oneself chosen, and to combat all doubts as *temptations of the devil*, since lack of self-confidence is the result of insufficient faith, hence of imperfect grace. The exhortation of the apostle to make fast one's own call is here interpreted as a duty to attain certainty of one's own election and justification in the daily struggle of life ... On the other hand, in order to attain that self-confidence *intense worldly activity* is recommended as the most suitable means. It and it alone disperses religious doubts and gives the certainty of grace. (emphasis added)

Weber takes from this the idea of 'calling', in which practical worldly activity is routinized or rationalized into 'a life of good works combined into a unified system' (Weber 1991: 117). What Weber fails to grasp, however, for his account of Protestant disenchantment, is the nature, force, and significance of both the 'temptations of the devil' and the materiality of demons and sorcery experienced by Reformation Protestants.

The 'daily struggle of life' that Weber refers to in the quotation above includes, for Reformation Protestants, not merely mundane and pedestrian pursuits, as he suggests. Underlying these and other concerns is a profound sense of human sin and also risk of being subject to the 'temptations of the devil', as Weber acknowledges. The power and consequence of temptation were not merely psychological or personal, however, but operated in a force field subject to both God's will and the agency of Satan:

> Temptation was central to Protestant demonism because it could be understood experientially in a way that far less common physical manifestations could not ... [The Devil] could introduce sinful thoughts into the mind, or take hold on man's corrupted will and turn him to sin. This understanding was intended to allow Satan's power to be felt within the life of every Christian, and demanded an empathic engagement with the experience of 'sin', rather than a separation from it ... Thus Protestant demonism was predicated on a satanic reality that was experiential rather than contingent. (Johnstone 2004: 177–78)

The notion of demonic agency was not a fanciful construct for Reformation Protestants, but experienced as a daily occurrence that occupied their 'intense worldly activity', and that was therefore as much an element in the structure of a 'life of good works' as civic and commercial relations. As Johnstone (2004: 188) goes on to say:

> Anger, envy, the desire to eat, to have sex, to dance, to give church a miss in favor of the alehouse—these were within the experience of all men and women. If a blanket interpretation of diabolism could be placed upon them, Satan could be brought convincingly into the most intimate aspects of people's lives, and the norm of his agency could be made insidious through the sheer banality of the sinful thoughts he was credited with introducing into the mind.

Demonic meddling in human affairs was for both Luther and Calvin, and for Reformation Protestants in general, a prospect with many manifestations that included the prevalence of magic and witchcraft. Weber's recognition,

that 'Puritanism came to consider all magic as devilish' and that it 'repudiated all magical means to salvation' (Weber 1964: 227; 1991: 105), is not
sufficient to affirm demagicalization. This is because while salvation may
require rejection of the devil, so long as it is believed that satanic magic is a
real force to be avoided, then rationalization and demagicalization are
incomplete.

In Reformation Europe, the Devil, as the source of demonic personae
and currents, was not merely acknowledged by Calvin but formed the
basis of his understanding of the human condition. In the *Institutes of the
Christian Religion*, Calvin (2002: 115) refutes those 'who foolishly allege
that devils are nothing but bad affections or perturbations suggested by
our carnal nature' and therefore subjective or emotional attributions of
afflicted persons; rather, they 'are not motions or affections of the mind,
but truly, as they are called, minds or spirits endued with sense and intel-
lect'. This is to say that Calvin believes that devils are agents in their own
right. His knowledge of the fact comes from what is for him the highest
authority; they are 'found in passages of Scripture on this subject, passages
neither few nor obscure' (Calvin 2002: 115). Indeed, the Protestant
Reformation was not merely an affirmation of biblical authority, but also
an assertion of the accessibility of the Word of God to the entirety of the
faithful. Each believer know directly God's nature and commandments
through reading the Bible, extensive distribution of which was achieved
through the printing revolution begun in 1440. Protestant knowledge of
Satan, and of witchcraft and sorcery, was provided from this source. The
biblical injunction 'You shall not permit a sorceress to live' (Exodus 22:18,
New King James Version—used throughout) legitimated the execution of
witches in early modern Europe. Explicit statements of the reality of
magic, as a domain of human practice, and of the efficacy of magic as a
material and not simply ethereal force, are emphatically provided in the
Bible that is the script for if not the motive of the extensive witch hunts
that occupied Reformation Europe.

Perhaps the best known testimony of the reality of magical power is in
the Old Testament book of Exodus (7:10–12), which reports that the
magicians of the Egyptian Pharaoh were pitted against Moses and Aaron,
who also engaged magical powers. Both sides demonstrated their magical
capacity by transforming a staff into a serpent. The serpent that was
Aaron's staff, however, devoured the serpents conjured by the Egyptian
magicians, thus demonstrating the superiority of his magic. The success of
Aaron's magic (see also Exodus 8:16–18), according to this text, resulted

from the fact that he was God's foil. The more powerful magic of the Jewish God, against Pharaoh's magicians, places it on a higher plane as a 'miracle'. Weber (1967: 222) notes this distinction and claims that the 'miracle is more rational than magic' because it is aggregated to a central-izing force—in governing the world, a providential God commands the future, something unknowable to humans. Human uses of magical power, then, not only disregard God's authority but challenge it by posing an alternative instrument of control. For this reason the Jewish God of the Old Testament forbids 'one who practices witchcraft, or a soothsayer, or one who interprets omens, or a sorcerer, or one who conjures spells, or a medium, or a spiritist, or one who calls up the dead'; these are 'an abomi-nation to the Lord' (Deuteronomy 18:10–12). God is so concerned to prevent the possibility that any of his people might practice magic, possi-bly but not necessarily against him, that an attempt to do so requires their death (Exodus 22:18; Leviticus 20:27). This last point is demonstrated in another instance of the power of magic reported in the Bible and well understood by Reformation Protestants.

The Old Testament recounts King Saul's recruitment of a medium to call up the dead Samuel. Saul wishes to seek Samuel's advice concerning an impending battle with the Philistines (1 Samuel 28:7–14). Saul had previously expelled mediums and spiritualists from his realm and the medium he recruits therefore assumes entrapment. She is reassured and proceeds to bring Samuel from the dead. In the subsequently battle, Saul's army is defeated, and rather than face capture and suffer humiliation Saul falls on his own sword (1 Samuel 31:4). It is explained elsewhere, how-ever, that 'Saul died for his unfaithfulness which he had committed against the Lord ... because he consulted a medium for guidance' (1 Chronicles 10:13). This account reiterates the points made above—that magic is a real force in the world, and that the Jewish God denies his subjects access to it because he aggregates magical power to himself. This last point has additional force in so far as the Old Testament prohibition against magic applies only to God's Jews; He acknowledges magic practiced by other peoples but they are not his concern (2 Kings 17:17; 21:6; 2 Chronicles 33:6). A third feature of Old Testament discussion of magic, in service to the second point above, is its degradation by association. Magicians and sorcerers are grouped with adulterers, perjurers, and exploiters of poor workers, widows, and orphans (e.g., Ezekiel 22: 28–29; Malachi 3:5). Denigration of magic by association is extended in the New Testament, where sorcery is similarly described as unclean and included with adultery, harlotry, theft, and so on (Galatians 5:19–21; Ephesians 5:11; Revelation 9:21; 21:8; 22:15). The New Testament acknowledges, though, an additional dimension of magic.

Magic is not merely oppositional to God according to the New Testament, but false in itself. The prohibition on magic is, with this claim, universal and not confined to a limited population of God's chosen people. The claim that magic is 'false' is not a denial of the reality and potency of magic; magic is false in the sense that it is a major countervailing power against the true faith of Christ as God, specifically in the form of the Devil or Satan. Jesus warns against 'false christs and false prophets [who] will rise and show great signs and wonders to deceive' (Matthew 24:24) and Paul describes a sorcerer as a 'son of the devil' (Acts 13:10), as indeed does Jesus (John 8:44). Satan has no presence in the Old Testament, even though the New King James Version and similar translations inserts him there (Job 1:6–13; 2:1–7). A correct rendering of Devil or Satan in these translations is the much more ambiguous Adversary (see *Tanakh* 1985: 1339–40). The construction of magic, including witchcraft, as the work of the Devil, initiated in the New Testament, has particular significance for Protestant demonology, and for the witch obsession of sixteenth- and seventeenth-century Calvinism.

For Calvin, the power of Satan is contingently equal to that of all-powerful God. He goes so far as to argue that the Catholic Church itself is an agent of Satan: its 'prohibition of marriage [of priests] is a doctrine of devils' (Calvin 2002: 762). He regards 'the Roman Pontiff as the leader and standard-bearer of that wicked and abominable kingdom' of Satan as the Antichrist because he has 'impudently transferred to himself the most peculiar properties of God and Christ' (Calvin 2002: 647, 700). In the everyday world that Calvin and his followers inhabit, the threats of Satan are pervasive: 'The tendency of all that Scripture teaches concerning devils is to put us on our guard against their wiles and machinations' (Calvin 2002: 111). In this context, it is readily understood that a 'Witches Sabbath' involved worship of and copulation with the devil as well as sundry performances of sorcery, including communication with familiars and flying (Trevor-Roper 1978: 16–17). These were only the most extreme forms of magic the Reformation opposed, others include divination, astrology, mediumship, magical healing practices, and similar 'arts' biblically proscribed (Scribner 2001: 351).

The opposition to sorcery and witchcraft proclaimed by Reformation Protestantism was, then, not a disengagement from these forms of magic but an assertion of their power. The witch hunts prosecuted by Puritan and Calvinist churches, rather than a suppression of magic, were a sacramental engagement with it. The burning and drowning of individual witches were practical confirmations of the presence of magical and demonic forces. And the principal safeguard against Satan and his agents recommended by Calvin (2002: 561–62) and the Reformation—prayer— also borders on magical practice in so far as it is a spiritual invocation of an unseen power as a means to influence events (Calvin 2002: 524, 538, 545–46; see also James 2002: 359–60; Johnstone 2004: 193–94; Scribner 2001: 352–53, 357–58, 360).

Weber's conception of Reformation Protestantism, as having 'liqui- dated magic most completely', simply fails to engage with the object of his enquiry and reflects, rather, the self-image of late nineteenth- and early twentieth-century Protestantism rather than accurately representing the sixteenth- and seventeenth-century religious forms he claims to describe. He does concede, however, that spirits and demons may become decisive 'regardless of the official god-concept of the ostensibly rationalized reli- gion', and that in the Reformation, 'at least in theory', such subordination was claimed (Weber 1963: 20 [1978: 416]). The idea of the Reformation as initiating a process of religious rationalization, which has become iden- tified with the thought of Max Weber, derives from his creative application of notions current at the time of his writing, including the concept of 'charisma' developed by the church historian Rudolph Sohm (Haley 1980; Smith 1998), a debt Weber (1978: 216, 1112) acknowledges, and Schiller's poetic phrase 'disenchantment of the world' (Angus 1983; Lyons 2014). These are then projected backward without the benefit of proper investigation or apparent awareness of major currents of the Reformation, including the witch hunts in those areas where Calvinism was dominant. It is necessary, then, to consider other sources of rational- ization through which magic atrophied as a meaningful presence in Protestant Europe by the end of the nineteenth century.

One element of rationalization in this context would presumably be the end of the obsession with witchcraft as a demonic manifestation, evidenced by cessation of the prosecution of witches. The end of the witch trials in Protestant Europe by the eighteenth century, however, was more a result of the removal of clergy from juridical power than an end to their concern with sorcery as demonic power (Trevor-Roper 1978: 98). Indeed, when the Scottish Witchcraft Acts were finally repealed in 1736, reaction from the Calvinist pulpit was loud and hostile (Maxwell-Stuart 2004: 81, 92).

The clerical loss of power over the course of the seventeenth and eighteenth centuries is no doubt a potent factor in the incremental rationalization of both the religious and secular worlds. This process can be explained in a number of ways, including the idea of the 'death of God', popularized by Nietzsche to indicate the declining relevance of religion as a source of moral guidance. More comprehensive is the idea of a shift in effective authority from institutional religion to the secular political state. This is an idea crystalized in Machiavelli's *The Prince* and realized in a long and slow process of development in Europe from the early sixteenth century, which was still incomplete in Weber's Germany (Clark 2008; see also Berghahn 2005), and elsewhere in Europe, up to the beginning of the First World War. This is an important factor in its own right, with a number of cognate aspects that promote rationalization, including the growth of bureaucratic administration, about which Weber (1978: 956–1005) has much to say, as well as taxation and fiscal regulation (Glete 2002).

There is another dimension of order, no doubt associated with the growth of the state and the rationalizing consequences of secular political order, but which can be seen as a separate factor. This is a decline in the religious hostilities that traversed Europe from the sixteenth century until the end of the eighteenth century, although in many jurisdictions these continue to the present day. Commentaries observe the coincidence of witch hunts and sectarian hostilities (Monter 1971; Trevor-Roper 1978). Indeed, the outrage against the repeal of the Scottish Witchcraft Acts from the clergy coincided with their anxiety concerning the growth of evangelical movements inspired by Wesley's Methodism encroaching from England, just as the installation of the Acts a century earlier was arguably provoked by a perceived threat from the barbaric Highlands (Maxwell-Stuart 2004: 92). The notion, that 'when a secular or priestly power suppressed a cult in favour of a new religion, [then] the older gods continuing to live on as demons' (Weber 1963: 28 [1978: 424]), applies in such cases. A decline of interest in miracles and magic, that is source to a process of rationalization, is reported to occur in seventeenth-century Europe as religious disquiet and disputation gives way to tranquility (Daston 1991: 118). While ecclesiastical conflict may not entirely decline in these circumstances, its relevance is displaced in an emergent political space in which the actors in religious dramas are disempowered (Daston 1991: 123).

There is much evidence that a significant portion of what might be called 'popular magic', which flourished in Europe from the earliest times up to the end of the nineteenth century, was associated with what can loosely be called 'healing' (Thomas 1997: 177–211). Given the entirely reasonable interest persons have in their health and well-being and that of their kin, and given the relative effectiveness of almost any intervention through the 'placebo effect' (Coe 1997; Moerman 2002), it is not surprising to find that magic, as Weber (1963: 1 [1978: 400]) indicates, is rational in the sense that it 'follows rules of experience'. Rationalization as a decline in popular magic can therefore be attributed to the way in which folk healing practices were rendered unnecessary and therefore became less prevalent through such things as sanitation and deep drainage and in improvements in diet from the mid-nineteenth century. This process was more or less completed with the development and growing availability of scientific medicine from the late nineteenth century.

The last point above, that magic may be directed to physical well-being rather than religious concerns, raises a matter fundamental to the understanding Weber has of not only religious rationalization in Calvinism, but the very idea of an integral association of magic and religion, set out in *The Sociology of Religion* and applied to the discussion of Confucianism in *The Religion of China*. Certainly, in the history of Christianity, and Abrahamic faiths more generally, magic is necessarily a matter of religious consideration. But this is because in these traditions, magic is conceived as a challenge to the authority of a providential God, as shown earlier. It is only in the context of a belief that nature is created by God (Genesis 1:1–31) that an attempt to manipulate it through sorcery becomes a matter of religious concern. Indeed, in this tradition nature is not an independent system but, given God's proprietorship over it (see Leviticus 25:23), a moral system. In principle, then, any interference with nature may be subject in these traditions to religious sanction although scientific understanding of nature has at times received clerical approval. Given Weber's opening observation in *The Sociology of Religion*, that magic is originally practical in its application even though not necessarily efficient (Weber 1963: 1 [1978: 400]), the conception of a necessary link between magic and religion is not justified.

Another approach, emergent at the time Weber wrote and which broke with the nineteenth-century view of magic as primitive religion that he captures and borrows from in his survey of writings brought together in *The Sociology of Religion*, holds that 'magic seem[s] to have preceded inward [religious] piety historically … [so that] the whole system of thought which leads to magic, fetishism, and the lower superstitions may just as well be called primitive science as called primitive religion' (James 2002: 29; see also Thorndike 1923), a perspective that continues to draw attention

(Styers 2004; Tambiah 1990). There is another possibility, however, to be explored in the following section of the present discussion, which takes up neither of these characterizations. Because magic is an applied and instrumental practice, it has a purpose unlike that of science, which is deductive and speculative (in the sense of 'blue sky' research). In this sense, magic need not be seen as a progenitor of science. More important for our purposes here, though, is that magic in societies untouched by Abrahamic religious principles need not be considered to be in competition with nor allied to religion at all.

MAGIC IN CHINA

It is necessary to critically examine Weber's treatment of Chinese magic, outlined earlier, as it has been to reconsider his account of Calvinist divestment of magic. It is frequently acknowledged that Weber's discussion of China is limited by the sources he draws on. It has to be accepted, however, that the sources he uses were not the only ones available to him. In commenting on Weber's (1964: 154) assessment of Confucian science, historian Nathan Sivin (1985: 38) observes that 'Every sentence in this passage is incorrect ... [but] could have been corrected from sources available' to Weber at the time. The 'problem', Sivan (1984: 48 n.5) goes on to explain, 'was not one of accessibility, but was rather due to Weber's preference for the writings of Protestant over Catholic missionaries'. It will be suggested here that Weber's discussion of Chinese magic as expressive of Chinese religion is shaped by Christian concepts and frameworks and by missionary concerns of the day. The concept of religion itself was unknown to Chinese culture and thought until it was introduced at the very end of the nineteenth century, from the Japanese language, and sinicized as *zongjiao*. An earlier Chinese term, *sanjiao*, used from the ninth century to refer to Buddhism, Daoism, and Confucianism collectively, means not 'three religions' but 'three teachings' (Sun 2005: 232–33; see also Ashiwa and Wank 2009: 9). Before these considerations are taken up, however, it is necessary to begin with another. The idea that China was a rich and fertile source of magic, a 'magic garden' (Weber 1964: 200), should not lead to neglect of those Chinese traditions and sources which Weber ignores that opposed the notion of a supernatural realm dominated by sorcery and charms.

It was noted earlier that Weber acknowledges Confucian indifference to magic, and at the same time, insists that this indifference is compromised.

This is not the only qualification of his general claim that magic was pervasive in Imperial China. In this context, he acknowledges that the Daoist source text, *Daodejing*, did not fully develop a 'doctrine of immortality' (Weber 1964: 182), associated with alchemic practices, and he concedes that the '*Tao Teh Ching* [*Daodejing*] was apparently largely free of magic' even though its doctrine, he paradoxically claims, has a 'purely magical aspect' (Weber 1964: 185, 192). Weber (1964: 191) says that there is a 'general tendency in the Chinese value scheme', coterminous with 'Lao-tzu's teachings', which holds that 'death is an absolute evil ... [that] should be avoided for a truly perfect man'. It is true that avoidance of death was addressed by Chinese alchemy, a subject to be taken up below. At this point, it can be indicated that Weber simply ignores the discussion in Daoist classics of the folly of the impossible quest for immortality. Although he fails to take heed of the fact, one of Weber's sources notes that a projection of Laozi's infrequent remarks on long life to the 'later Tâoist dreams about the elixir vitae' is an 'abuse of [this] and other passages' of the text (Legge 1962a: 103). Other Daoist sources, also in response to purveyors of elixirs for longevity and immortality, ridicule such alchemic quests. The *Zhuangzi*, a text from approximately 300 BC, mocks the idea of immortality and confirms the naturalness of death (Legge 1962b: 241–43) as does the much later (fourth century) *Liezi* (Graham 1990: 17–31). In both of these works, magical performances are lampooned, and explained in naturalistic terms, an approach that cuts across Weber's generalized view of China as a 'magic garden'.

Extended philosophical discussions of the supernatural in Chinese sources similarly indicate that it is erroneous to assume an undifferentiated acceptance of magic. The essay by the fourth-century BC anti-Confucian logician Mozi, 'Percipient Ghosts' (Johnston 2010: 279–305), takes the form of a discussion between a ghost-skeptic and Mozi, who advocates acceptance of belief in ghosts. The nature of evidence for ghosts and the social function of ghost-belief are central to the narrative. The essay opens with the claim that the state is poorly governed, society is disjointed and the people are debauched and dishonest. This is because 'everyone is doubtful ... [about] whether ghosts and spirits exist ... and do not clearly understand that ghosts and spirits are able to reward the worthy and punish the wicked' (Johnston 2010: 279). The skeptic responds to this account by claiming that the evidence for the existence of ghosts is not credible; Mozi counters by recourse to the numbers of witness accounts of ghost sightings and the social standing of witnesses and adds, for good measure, the authority of historical documents that report incidents relating to ghosts. The argument then changes ground and the skeptic doubts that belief in ghosts can benefit parents and enhance filiality (Johnston 2010: 303). Mozi concedes that if ghosts do not exist, sacrifice to them 'might seem like a waste of materials' (Johnston 2010: 305). Nevertheless:

> Within the family members and without ... all get what is provided and drink and eat it, so, although ghosts and spirits may not truly exist, this still means that large numbers can meet together for enjoyment and this fosters a closeness among the people of the district and village. (Johnston 2010: 305)

After acknowledging the social solidarity consequences of ghost rituals, the essay concludes with the claim that if kings, nobles, and administrators wish to 'promote the benefits of the world and eliminate its harms', then they should 'accept the existence of ghosts and spirits', and at the same time 'honour them as all-seeing' (Johnston 2010: 305). The idea that ghosts perform a positive moral role, then, is primary in justifying belief in them according to Mozi, even though 'ghosts and spirits may not truly exist'.

Indeed, the idea that ghost belief has a consequence of moral rectitude is enduring in Imperial China, if the popularity of Ji Xiaolan's stories, from the early Qing during the eighteenth century, of ghosts who punish the wicked and support the righteous (Pollard 2014) and similar accounts are accepted as evidence. This literature cuts against the view expressed by Weber (1963: 92 [1978: 478]; 1964: 200) that in China magic is devoid of ethical content. The question of evidence, remains, however, and as we have seen in Mozi's account, it is something about which dispute is always possible. Against this background it is difficult to insist that there was a Chinese cultural predisposition concerning belief in ghosts and spirits, even in the face of the idea that ghost belief may have a moral value. The view expressed by the third-century BC Confucian thinker Xunzi, that 'when men think that there are ghosts, the confirmation of it is certain to be an occasion when they are startled or confused' (Knoblock 1999b: 697–99), may coexist with a notion of the ethical functionality of ghost belief. Xunzi, however, dismisses this latter notion as well.

The opening passage of Xunzi's 'Discourse on Nature' indicates that the underlying forces of nature cannot be influenced by the actions of persons, and that to ignore the regularities of nature is to 'behave with foolish recklessness' (Knoblock 1999b: 533). Indeed, Xunzi argues that 'We do not perceive the process [of nature], but we perceive the result—this indeed is why we call it "divine"' (Knoblock 1999b: 535). The suggestion here is that non-naturalistic thinking is simply ignorant of the basic operations of nature. Xunxi goes on to insist that the human domain is not influenced by natural events, such as 'revolutions of the sun and moon and the stars' or 'the seasons' (Knoblock 1999b: 539–41). He proceeds to argue that such things as 'the sun and moon being eclipsed' and similar 'unusual events' are simply things 'We may marvel at … but we should not fear' (Knoblock 1999b: 543); these are natural events that cannot meaningfully be read as forebodings and need not be managed by priests.

If practices, including rituals, are designed to intervene in the natural order, they will simply be ineffective and necessarily fail, according to Xunzi: 'If you pray for rain and there is rain, what of that? I say there is no special relationship—as when you do not pray for rain and there is rain' (Knoblock 1999b: 547). Xunzi's discussion is not intended to be an argument against ritual, however. According to Xunzi, rituals should be seen as commemorations of 'meritorious accomplishments' and as 'markers' that permit people to appreciate and acknowledge principles of social and political order (Knoblock 1999b: 549, 551). For Xunzi, then, rituals are not a supernatural or magical intervention into the natural order, but rather, relate to an ordering of the human world through being means or instruments of a politico-moral construction. This is not only an argument against superstition and magic, then, but indicates that ritual in China was understood to have a social psychological, and institutional rationale and not necessarily a religious magical one, as Weber (1964: 109–11, 228–29) holds. The discussion of ghosts, spirits, and ritual, in Mozi and Xunzi, provides a perspective on Chinese 'magic' rather different from the one presented by Weber. Xunzi's work was not available at the time that Weber wrote, with the exception of a single chapter on human nature, included by Legge (1895) in his introduction to the works of Mencius. The writings of Mozi, on the other hand, were more fully available (Faber 1877; David-Neel 1907) as indeed were the Daoist classics through Legge's translation, which Weber selectively draws on.

In *The Religion of China*, Weber (1964: 199) refers to a 'superstructure of magically "rational" science' that operated in China. One such 'science' is alchemy, and consideration of Chinese alchemy provides an opportunity to identify aspects of the framework of Chinese thought that are relevant for understanding so-called Chinese magic in general. Alchemy may be regarded as a proto-science in the sense that it is not only historically prior to modern chemistry, but also bears an underlying basis for its early development. The idea of a coexistence of alchemy with modern science is possibly reinforced by acknowledgement of Isaac Newton's responsibility for major scientific discoveries in the seventeenth century and his concurrent preoccupation with alchemy (White 1999). While this association may run counter to Weber's general expectation that science supersedes magic as an antagonistic mode of thought (Weber 1970a: 139), the other aspect of Newton's alchemical interests, that they were expressive of his religious convictions (Figala 2004: 375), does not. The present argument, however, proposes continuity neither with alchemy and modern natural science, nor with Chinese alchemy and religion.

The alchemist's quest, not only in China but wherever alchemy was practiced, is to achieve perfection by manipulation of nature. Material perfection is exemplified in gold, a metal immune to decay; by analogy, human perfection is achieved with immortality. Chinese alchemists were less interested in gold than cinnabar (mercury sulfide) as they believed that various elixirs could be distilled from it (Sivin 1976: 515–56). Knowledge of the chemical processes that Chinese alchemists employed was borrowed from artisans who produced metals from ore. The purpose of the alchemists was not merely chemical metamorphosis, however, and their intellectual apparatus had a much broader reach than what was required for the extraction of metals. The Chinese conception of the universe that informed their practices, unlike the European, was organic rather than mechanical. It accepted no principal or first cause and no supreme creator: 'Chinese ideals involved neither God nor Law ... the mechanical and the quantitative, the forced and the externally imposed, were all absent' (Needham 1956: 290; see also 287). The underlying organic principle of development in Chinese cosmology, including the life cycle phases of birth, growth, maturity, decay, and death, was seen to apply not only to animals and plants but also to minerals.

What are often referred to as the Five Elements (wood, fire, earth, metal, water) of Chinese cosmology, which derive from its organic conceptualization, are better described as Five Phases (*wu xing*) of organic cycles. These operate with the other foundational principle of the Chinese conception of the universe, yin and yang:

> The phases Fire and Wood, for instance, made possible a finer analysis of the yang, or active, aspect of change. Wood is the name of the phase of growth and increase, and Fire is the maximal flourishing phase of activity, when the yang is about to begin declining and yin must once again reassert itself. (Sivin 1976: 515)

The organic cycles involving the Five Phases necessarily operate through time. The alchemist's discovery, according to Sivin (1976: 522), was that 'the life courses of minerals could be accelerated by man ... [Rather than] wait 4320 years to experience nature's production of an elixir ... an alchemist who set out to fabricate an elixir ... was creating an opportunity to witness the cyclical sweep of universal change'. The alchemic performance, then, was to manipulate or compress time.

The universal temporal order was accessible to alchemic intervention only if the related practices were conducted in a manner that was properly aligned with the spatial order of the universe. The alchemist's laboratory therefore 'was oriented to the cardinal points of the compass, the furnace centred on it, and the reaction vessel centered in the furnace to make it the axial point of change' (Sivin 1976: 521). This relates to another form of Chinese 'magic', *feng shui*, not temporal but spatial manipulation and concentration. The purpose of alchemy is the production of elixirs that would enhance health, material prosperity, and possibly achieve an ideal of immortality. In addition to the chemical processes, the alchemist was required to perform detailed rituals in order to manipulate the organic universal processes in condensing time. The rituals were not religious in any meaningful sense, but devised to concentrate the heart-mind (*xin*), the alchemist's cognitive and affective or emotional state (Qi 2014: 172–76), in order to achieve comprehension of nature and its processes.

That alchemists may have believed that their rituals provided access to the 'spirit' of the order their practices manipulated does not imply a religious element. They did not address a God who is author of the domain they relate to, either in worship or coercion; neither did they invoke demons or spirits to do their bidding. The alchemic art is to manipulate the cosmos for practical and earthy purposes; the means are physical or chemical, and also ritual, with the ritual involving mental and performative concentration involving what the alchemist saw as natural and organic, rather than supernatural forces. Alchemic searches for immortality, as we have seen, were not unquestioned in China and neither was the Five Phases theory it was based on universally accepted; indeed, Xunzi explicitly rejects it (Knoblock 1999a: 127–29). These disputes, though, related to the realms of what is naturally possible, and it is therefore unnecessary to assimilate Chinese alchemic magic into a religious framework. Weber's discussion of Chinese magic, his particular characterization of magic, and his assimilation of magic with religion, all operate in terms that are artificially brought to bear on the Chinese material he discusses and which he fails to properly understand.

It is important to appreciate that Weber came to his study of China with the idea that religious rationalization in Calvinism permitted the emergence of a motivational form coterminous with the capitalist spirit. It was required therefore, by hypothesis, to examine what he saw as strictures of economic development in China in terms of limitations in the rationalization process of religion. He found in Confucianism a rational ethic that, in some ways, parallels Calvinist rationality, but as we have seen, he also found in it a tolerance for magic. While Weber accepts that Confucianism is not a religion, its alleged magical elements bring it into the realm of religion because of his prior understanding of the essentially religious nature of magic, first set out in *The Sociology of Religion*. But again, this is a proposition imported into the analysis by hypothesis and, as we have seen, need not be accepted.

The idea that magic has a necessary connection with religion, expounded by Weber not only in *The Sociology of Religion* but also in *The Religion of China*, derives its sense and meaning from the Christian, and more broadly the Abrahamic religious traditions in which a providential God aggregates magical powers in the form of miracles and opposes the exercise of magic on the part of His subjects with the penalty of death. Chinese traditional cosmology, on the other hand, has no notion of supreme agency or ultimate cause; it viewed the world as an organic field or domain in which covariation and mutual interactivity prevailed. Those things that Weber describes as Chinese magic, therefore, have no meaningful religious connotation or value. Such engagements primarily related to affecting practical outcomes rather than religious purposes. Indeed, the notion of religion in the sense that Weber uses the term was introduced into China by Christian missionaries during the nineteenth century under the cover of military might and the opium trade. In reaction to this Western incursion the Qing court, among other things, augmented in 1898 a Hundred Days Reform (*Wuxu Bianfa*). At this time, the Confucian reformer Kang Youwei introduced for the first time the notion *zongjiao* (religion) as representing the spiritual force and organizational form of Western strength that had reduced China to its suppliant state. This notion of religion stood in contrast to another, *mixin* (superstition), which was seen at the time as a summary of Daoist, Buddhist, and local cults that the Chinese population related to in various ways. In this sense, then, China had no religion, only superstitions.

For these reasons, it is necessary to say that Weber's account of Chinese magic is misleading in so far as it operates in a quite different universe than one formed through the image of Christian faith founded on an all-powerful God. At the same time, Weber's account of magic in China ignores the counternarratives of skeptical appraisal. Not only does Weber tend to exaggerate the acceptance of magic in Chinese society, he also exaggerates its effects. He claims, for instance, that the 'magic stereotyping of technology and economics ... completely precluded the advent of indigenous modern enterprises in communication and industry' (Weber 1964: 199). He goes on to say that when rail was introduced it was by foreign capitalists who had to struggle against the influence of 'geomancy' (Weber 1964: 199; see also 1981: 361). It is true that foreigners in China were confronted by geomancy or *feng shui* during the nineteenth century. As the British anthropologist Maurice Freedman (1979: 315) put it, 'sinologues, missionaries, Western administrators' and others 'were put on to geomancy by its emergence as a political force in the encounter between China and the West'. He goes on to say:

> The building of churches and European-style houses, the laying down of roads and railways, the digging of mines, and so on, were likely to be attended by Chinese protests that the *feng-shui* of villages, towns, or districts was being ruined. Sometimes the reactions blocked a proposed development; often they allowed projects to go forward in exchange of monetary compensation. (Freedman 1979: 315; see also 317)

Rather than being simply a backward-looking religiously-based orientation, as de Groot (1910: 74–76) describes it and Weber accepts, the nature of *fung shui* has a specific context. At the time of Weber's writing and of his sources, *fung shui* was a means of frictional cultural resistance in the context of political contestation in which China's subordination to foreign domination is primary.

Weber is correct to notice, as indicated earlier, that rail was first introduced to China by foreign capitalists. But it was not 'magic stereotyping of technology', as Weber claims, that 'precluded the advent of indigenous modern enterprises in communication and industry'. Rather, 'when the time came for railways to be built ... the financial institutions were not in place to handle the gathering and transfer of funds on the scale required' (Faure 2006: 25). It was not *fung shui* that prevented Chinese investment in rail but problems attending capital accumulation, as we shall see in the following chapter. In 1876, a British merchant company built China's first rail line, and they did so without Chinese official approval. It was this latter fact that first provoked local opposition, which was only increased when a Chinese pedestrian was struck and killed by the train (Kent 1907: 10–13).

Chinese attitudes at this time to the possible introduction of rail were mixed. Opposition was focused on two major concerns that Weber fails to mention. One was related to political stability. It was believed that the introduction of rail would force large numbers of traditional transport workers into unemployment, generating discontent and civic disruption, as had occurred with the Taiping Rebellion and similar uprisings during this period. Second, after defeat in the Opium Wars, which ended in 1860, there was concern that rail would be used by foreign powers for troop movement (Huenemann 1984: 39–40). Among ordinary people, opposition to European-built rail was expressed as concern that rail would disturb *feng shui*, the balance of geomantic forces (Huenemann 1984: 40–41), that is, as resistance to foreign interference expressed in terms of a traditional trope. While *fung shui* was the factor most frequently emphasized by foreign commentators at the time (Kent 1907: 9–10), it was the least significant. When the advantage of rail became obvious to the Qing court, after China's defeat in the Sino-Japanese war in 1895, rail grew rapidly, from an average of 18 miles per year between 1881 and 1895 to approximately 345 miles per year from 1895 to 1911 (Huenemann 1984: 75).

CONCLUSION

Religion in the sense employed by Weber and his sources was simply absent from the Chinese society he discusses. The intention of achieving Chinese conversion to Christianity led missionaries to an inclination to find, in Chinese thought and practice, religious elements amenable to missionary purposes, whether they were understood by the Chinese in these terms or not (Clark 2014; Girardot 2002). The intellectual formations that derived from these engagements became current in sinological writings up to the early decades of the twentieth century, which are Weber's sources. Chinese traditions of temples, ritual practices, and ceremonial practitioners relate to local communities and the rhythms of their needs in multifunctional spaces in which liturgy and clerics in the Christian sense are unknown and performative elements prevail. This distinction was effectively irrelevant to Weber because of his acceptance of the idea that religion and magic coexist on an evolutionary continuum. But the ambiguity of this position regarding what might be meant by religion, inherent in Weber's account, is apparently resolved by acknowledging a more restricted understanding of religion as 'cult' or a system of belief carried by a congregation organized by a professional clergy, as against something that is not religion, in this narrow sense, that is 'superstition' (see Ashiwa and Wank 2009: 9–12). In Weber's discussion, Chinese practices are forced into one of these two categories, and sometimes both. But Weber's treatment of so-called Chinese religion and superstition, including magic, is to make a point about Calvinism and its contrast with Confucianism in terms of the former's rationalization as demagicalization. This too, we have seen, is a construction of Weber's own efforts that bears only the most distant relationship with historical reality.

REFERENCES

Aldenhoff, Rita. 2010. 'Max Weber and the Evangelical-Social Congress'. Pp. 193–202 in *Max Weber and his Contemporaries*, edited by Wolfgang J. Mommsen and Jürgen Osterhammel. London: Routledge.

Angus, Ian H. 1983. 'Disenchantment and Modernity'. *Human Studies.* 6(2): 141–66.

Ashiwa, Yoshiko and Wank, David L. 2009. 'Making Religion, Making the State in Modern China'. pp. 1–21 in *Making Religion, Making the State: The Politics of Religion in Modern China*, edited by Yoshiko Ashiwa and David L. Wank. Stanford: Stanford University Press.

Baker, Hugh D.R. 1979. *Chinese Family and Kinship*. New York: Columbia University Press.

Berghahn, Volker. 2005. *Imperial Germany 1871–1918: Economy, Society, Culture and Politics.* New York: Berghahn Books.

Calvin, John. 2002. *Institutes of the Christian Religion*, translated by Henry Beveridge. Grand Rapids: Christian Classics Ethereal Library.

Clark, Anthony E. (ed). 2014. *A Voluntary Exile: Chinese Christianity and Cultural Confluence since 1552.* Bethlehem: Lehigh University Press.

Clark, Christopher. 2008. 'Religion and Confessional Conflict'. Pp. 83–105 in *Imperial Germany 1871–1918*, edited by James Retallack. Oxford: Oxford University Press.

Coe, Rodney M. 1997. 'The Magic of Science and the Science of Magic: An Essay on the Process of Healing'. *Journal of Health and Social Behavior.* 38(1): 1–8.

Daston, Lorraine. 1991. 'Marvelous Facts and Miraculous Evidence in Early Modern Europe'. *Critical Inquiry.* 18(1): 93–124.

David-Neel, Alexandra. 1907. *Socialisme Chinois: Le Philosophe Meh-Ti et l'Idée de Solidarité.* London: Luzac and Co.

de Groot, Jan Jakob Marie. 1910. *The Religion of the Chinese.* New York: Macmillan.

Faber, Ernst. 1877. *Die Grundgedanken des alten chinesischen Socialismus oder die Lehre des Philosophen Micius*. Elberfeld: Friderichs.

Faure, David. 2006. *China and Capitalism: A History of Business Enterprise in Modern China*. Hong Kong: Hong Kong University Press.

Figala, Karin. 2004. 'Newton's Alchemy'. Pp. 370–86 in *The Cambridge Companion to Newton*, edited by I. Bernard Cohen and George Edwin Smith. Cambridge: Cambridge University Press.

Freedman, Maurice. 1979. 'Geomancy'. Pp. 313–33 in his *The Study of Chinese Society: Essays by Maurice Freedman*, edited by G. William Skinner. Stanford, CA: Stanford University Press.

Girardot, Norman J. 2002. *The Victorian Translation of China: James Legge's Oriental Pilgrimage*. Berkeley: University of California Press.

Glete, Jan. 2002. *War and the State in Early Modern Europe: Spain, the Dutch Republic and Sweden as Fiscal-Military States, 1500–1660*. London: Routledge.

Graf, Friedrich Wilhelm. 1995. 'The German Theological Sources and Protestant Church Politics'. Pp. 34–41 in *Weber's Protestant Ethic: Origins, Evidence, Contexts*, edited by Lehmann Karl and Guenther Roth. Cambridge: Cambridge University Press.

Graham, A.C. 1990. *The Book of Lieh-tzŭ: A Classic of Tao*. New York: Columbia University Press.

Greene, Thomas M. 2005. 'Language, Signs and Magic'. Pp. 29–42 in his *Poetry, Signs and Magic*. Newark: University of Delaware Press.

Haley, Peter. 1980. 'Rudolph Sohm on Charisma'. *The Journal of Religion*. 60(2): 185–97.

Honigsheim, Paul. 1950. 'Max Weber: His Religious and Ethical Background and Development'. *Church History*. 19(4): 219–39.

Huenemann, Ralph William. 1984. *The Dragon and the Iron Horse: The Economics of Railroads in China, 1876–1937*. Cambridge: Harvard University Press.

James, William. 2002. *The Varieties of Religious Experience*, Centenary Edition. London: Routledge.

Johnston, Ian (translator). 2010. *The Mozi: A Complete Translation*. Hong Kong: The Chinese University Press.

Johnstone, Nathan. 2004. 'The Protestant Devil: The Experience of Temptation in Early Modern England'. *Journal of British Studies*. 43(2): 173–205.

Kent, Percy Horace. 1907. *Railway Enterprise in China: An Account of its Origin and Development*. London: Edward Arnold.

Knoblock, John (translator). 1999a. *Xunzi. Volume 1 (Library of Chinese Classics: Chinese-English)*. Hunan: Human People's Publishing House.

Knoblock, John (translator). 1999b. *Xunzi. Volume 2. (Library of Chinese Classics: Chinese-English)*. Hunan: Human People's Publishing House.

Legge, James. 1895. 'That the Nature is Evil by the philosopher Hsün'. Pp. 79–88 in his *The Chinese Classics: Volume II, The Works of Mencius*. Oxford: The Clarendon Press.

Legge, James. 1962a. 'The Tâo te King'. Pp. 45–124 in *The Texts of Taoism*, Volume 1. New York: Dover.

Legge, James. 1962b. 'The Writings of Chuang Tzŭ: Part 1'. Pp. 127–309 in *The Texts of Taoism*, Volume 1. New York: Dover.

Lyons, Sara N. 2014. 'The Disenchantment/Re-enchantment of the World: Aesthetics, Secularisation, and the Gods of Greece from Friedrich Schiller to Walter Pater'. *Modern Language Review*. 109(4): 873–95.

Maxwell-Stuart, Peter. 2004. 'Witchcraft and Magic in Eighteenth-Century Scotland'. Pp. 81–99 in *Beyond the Witch Trials: Witchcraft and Magic in Enlightenment Europe*, edited by Owen Davies and Willem de Blécourt. Manchester: Manchester University Press.

Moerman, Daniel E. 2002. *Meaning, Medicine and the 'Placebo Effect'*. Cambridge: Cambridge University Press.

Mommsen, Wolfgang J. 1989. *The Political and Social Theory of Max Weber*. Cambridge: Polity Press.

Monter, E. William. 1971. 'Witchcraft in Geneva, 1537–1662'. *Journal of Modern History*. 43(2): 179–204.

Needham, Joseph. 1956. *Science and Civilization in China. Volume 2, History of Scientific Thought*. Cambridge: Cambridge University Press.

Pollard, David E. (translator). 2014. *Real Life in China at the Height of Empire: Revealed by the Ghosts of Ji Xiaolan*. Hong Hong: The Chinese University Press.

Qi, Xiaoying. 2014. *Globalized Knowledge Flows and Chinese Social Theory*. New York: Routledge.

Schluchter, Wolfgang. 1985. *The Rise of Western Rationalism: Max Weber's Developmental History*, translated, with an introduction, by Guenther Roth. Berkeley: University of California Press.

Scribner, R.W. 2001. 'The Reformation, Popular Magic, and the 'Disenchantment of the World'. Pp. 346–65 in his *Religion and Culture in Germany (1400–1800)*. Leiden: Brill.

Sivin, Nathan. 1976. 'Chinese Alchemy and the Manipulation of Time'. *Isis*. 67(4): 513–26.

Sivin, Nathan. 1985. 'Max Weber, Joseph Needham, Benjamin Nelson: The Question of Chinese Science'. Pp. 37–49 in *Civilizations East and West: A Memorial Volume for Benjamin Nelson*, edited by E.V. Walter, Vytautas Kavolis, Edmund Leites and Marie Coleman Nelson. Atlantic Highlands: Humanities Press.

Smith, David Norman. 1998. 'Faith, Reason, and Charisma: Rudolph Sohm, Max Weber and the Theology of Grace'. *Sociological Inquiry*. 68(1): 32–60.

Stark, Werner. 1968. 'The Place of Catholicism in Max Weber's Sociology of Religion'. *Sociological Analysis*. 29(4): 202–10.

Styers, Randall. 2004. *Making Magic: Religion, Magic, and Science in the Modern World*. Oxford: Oxford University Press.

Sun, Anna Xiao Dong. 2005. 'The Fate of Confucianism as Religion in Socialist China: Controversies and Paradoxes'. Pp. 229–53 in *State, Market, and Religions in Chinese Societies*, edited by Fenggang Yang and Joseph B. Tamney. Leiden: Brill.

Swatos, William H. and Kivisto, Peter. 1991. 'Max Weber as "Christian Sociologist"'. *Journal for the Scientific Study of Religion*. 30(4): 347–62.

Tambiah, Stanley J. 1990. *Magic, Science and Religion and the Scope of Rationality*. Cambridge: Cambridge University Press.

Tanakh. 1985. *Tanakh: The Holy Scriptures*. Philadelphia: The Jewish Publication Society.

Thomas, Keith. 1997. *Religion and the Decline of Magic: Studies in Popular Beliefs in Sixteenth and Seventeenth Century England*. New York: Oxford University Press.

Thorndike, Lynn. 1923. *A History of Magic and Experimental Science*. Volume 1. New York: Columbia University Press.

Trevor-Roper, Hugh. 1978. *The European Witch-craze of the 16th and 17th Centuries*. Harmondsworth: Penguin.

Weber, Max. 1963. *The Sociology of Religion*, translated by Ephraim Fischoff. Boston: Beacon Press.

Weber, Max. 1964. *The Religion of China: Confucianism and Taoism*, translated and edited by Hans H. Gerth, with an Introduction by C.K. Yang. New York: The Free Press.

Weber, Max. 1967. *Ancient Judaism*, translated and edited by Hans H. Gerth and Don Martindale. New York: The Free Press.

Weber, Max. 1970a. 'Science as a Vocation'. Pp. 129–56 in *From Max Weber: Essays in Sociology*, edited by H.H. Gerth and C. Wright Mills. London: Routledge.

Weber, Max. 1970b. 'The Social Psychology of World Religions'. Pp. 267–301 in *From Max Weber: Essays in Sociology*, edited by H.H. Gerth and C. Wright Mills. London: Routledge and Kegan Paul.

Weber, Max. 1978. *Economy and Society: An Outline of Interpretive Sociology*, edited by Guenther Roth and Claus Wittich. Berkeley: University of California Press.

Weber, Max. 1981. *General Economic History*, translated by Frank Knight. New Brunswick: Transaction Books.

Weber, Max. 1991. *The Protestant Ethic and the Spirit of Capitalism*, translated by Talcott Parsons. London: Harper Collins.

Weber, Max. 2002. 'The Protestant Ethic and the "Spirit" of Capitalism (1905)'. Pp. 1–202 in *Max Weber: The Protestant Ethic and the "Spirit" of Capitalism and Other Writings*, edited and translated by Peter Baehr and Gordon C. Wells. London: Penguin.

Weber, Max. 2014. 'The Meaning of "Value Freedom" in the Sociological Economic Sciences'. Pp. 304–34 in *Max Weber: Collected Methodological Writings*, edited by Hans Henrik Bruun and Sam Whimster. London: Routledge.

Whimster, Sam. 2007. *Understanding Weber*. London: Routledge.

White, Michael. 1999. *Isaac Newton: The Last Sorcerer*. Reading: Helix Books.

CHAPTER 7

Capitalism

INTRODUCTION

Weber's purpose in writing *The Religion of China* was to demonstrate that capitalism could not develop in China on the basis of indigenous elements. The counterfactual form of his investigation invites its own difficulties (Hamilton 2006). Independently of that consideration Weber's argument concerning why capitalism could not originate in China, taken at face value, requires three qualifications. First, Weber does not deny the existence of commercial petty commodity and other types of pre-modern capitalism in Imperial China; rather, he is concerned to show why modern industrial capitalism did not arise from such beginnings. Second, Weber does not deny that modern capitalism could operate in China if it were transplanted from a European source. Finally, as indicated in the first qualification above, the China that Weber refers to is pre-1912 China, China before the first modernizing revolution overseen by Sun Yat-sen and the republican movement. There is no suggestion that Weber's account of Chinese society and economy developed in *The Religion of China* could be applied to China today, which most commentators agree has a market economy of a possibly capitalist form.

In light of these considerations some interesting questions arise. First, given Weber's characterization of Chinese institutions and mentality, how would a transplanted capitalism in China differ from the original or source variety of capitalism? Second, does the ideal-type presentation of modern

© The Author(s) 2017

J. Barbalet, *Confucianism and the Chinese Self*,
https://doi.org/10.1007/978-981-10-6289-6_7

industrial capitalism that Weber sketches in *The Religion of China* and that he outlines more thoroughly in *Economy and Society*, and again, in the *General Economic History*, help us understand the present-day Chinese economy? In this final chapter, these and related issues shall be considered. Discussion begins with aspects of China's economy, which Weber suggests resembles, but do not constitute, modern capitalist attributes. Then Weber's ideal-type concept of modern capitalism is signified. The transition of China's economy from the collectivist socialism of the Mao era to the 'reformed' market economy developed under the sponsorship of Deng Xiaoping is briefly outlined in order to consider how the economy of China today might be characterized. Over the course of this discussion the question is posed of how the process of capital accumulation might be fitted into Weber's ideal type of modern capitalism.

FORMS OF CAPITALISM IN WEBER'S CHINA

Weber (1964: 242) acknowledges that under 'foreign influence and the incessant advance [in China] of occidental capitalism' the Chinese could learn the 'methodical business conceptions which are rational in nature and are presupposed by modern capitalism'. Indeed, he says that this occurs at the time of his writing in Canton (Guangzhou), where foreign influence is longstanding. He reiterates the point again a few pages later:

> The Chinese in all probability would be quite capable, probably more capable than the Japanese, of assimilating capitalism which has technically and economically been fully developed in the modern culture area. It is obviously not a question of deeming the Chinese 'naturally ungifted' for the demands of capitalism. But compared to the occident, the varied conditions which externally favoured the origin of capitalism in China did not suffice to create it. (Weber 1964: 248)

Here again is the suggestion that while the primary origins of capitalism are external to China, an introduced capitalism could be assimilated in or diffused to Chinese conditions. The assessment here, that the Chinese are in all likelihood better able to assimilate capitalism than the Japanese, is reversed a short time later when in *The Religion of India*, first published in 1916, Weber (1960: 275) writes:

> [The Japanese] feudal relationships making for recallable, contractually-fixed, legal relationships offered a basis much more favourable to 'individualism' in

the occidental sense of the word, than did Chinese theocracy. With relative ease Japan was able to take over capitalism as an artifact from the outside, though it could not create capitalism out of its own spirit.

Leaving aside Weber's apparent change of mind concerning national inclinations to capitalist adaptation, it should be noted that the above passage refers to one element of a prerequisite or condition for the development of modern capitalism—namely, rational law. This is not the only one he insists on.

Weber frequently advances arguments in terms of what he calls 'ideal types', namely, intellectually constructed concepts in which aspects of social phenomena are identified and delineated in order to facilitate research (Weber 1949: 90–102). The function of ideal-type representations, Weber says, is to offer 'guidance to the construction of hypotheses', and to 'give unambiguous means of expression' to descriptions of reality, and 'to make clearly explicit ... the unique individual character of cultural phenomena' (Weber 1949: 90, 101). In terms of this approach, the 'most general presupposition for the existence of present-day capitalism', Weber (1981: 276) says, is 'rational capital accounting as the norm for all large industrial undertakings which are concerned with provision for everyday wants'. The components of rational capital accounting therefore form the elements of an ideal-type conceptualization of modern industrial capitalism, as distinct from other forms of capitalism in which rational accounting is either absent or underdeveloped. As Weber (1981: 276) acknowledges, 'capitalism of various forms is met with in all periods of history, [but] the provision of the everyday wants by capitalistic methods is characteristic of the occident alone and even here has been the inevitable method only since the middle of the nineteenth century'. Other forms of capitalism that he mentions include 'illegal, political, colonial, booty, and monopoly types of capitalism' (Weber 1964: 247).

It was noted above that Weber thought that nineteenth-century Japan may be ripe for modern capitalism because the element of rational law was incipient in its earlier regulatory relations. In China, on the other hand, Weber (1964: 243) sees 'only beginnings of legal institutions ... characterized essentially by their technical imperfection'. The importance of formally rational administration and law, apart from its provision of a favourable basis of 'individualism' as Weber claims in the passage quoted, is that it is 'calculable' (Weber 1978: 162; 1981: 277), that a quest for profit can be based on knowing that contracts are secure and guaranteed in law. This is a situation in which political authority secures the conditions of law through which contracts are subject to 'reliable purely formal guarantee' (Weber 1978: 162). The point here is that political authority supports and maintains the rule of law; whereas law imposes a regime of order that provides stable and continuing conditions of regulation, political authority in the absence of law, however, threatens only arbitrariness. This is the difference between rational capitalism and what Weber (1964: 242, 247; 1978: 166) calls 'political capitalism'. The latter is not rational but takes opportunities for profit-making from 'extortionist practices of office' (Weber 1964: 242). Thus, Weber insists on calculable law as one of the elements in the ideal-type conception of modern rational capitalism. The additional elements will be outlined shortly, but first it is necessary to say more about the character of calculability and Weber's estimation of the form it takes in Imperial China.

Weber (1964: 242) acknowledges the 'calculating mentality' of 'the Chinese'; he goes on to say, however, that:

> The Chinese shopkeeper haggled for and reckoned with every penny, and he daily counted over his cash receipts ... [Out] of this unceasing and intensive economic ado and the much bewailed crass 'materialism' of the Chinese, there failed to originate on the economic plane those great and methodical business conceptions which are rational in nature and are presupposed by modern capitalism. Such conceptions have remained alien to China.

The reason for this state of affairs, according to Weber (1964: 242–43), is that there were 'no rational forms of industry ... no rational method of organized enterprise in the European fashion'. He then goes on to say what such a method would consist of, in terms of its absence in China; these include 'no truly rational organization of commercial news service, no rational money system ... only beginnings of legal institutions ... technical inventions were little used for economic purposes [and f]inally, there was no genuine, technically valuable system of commercial correspondence, accounting or bookkeeping' (Weber 1964: 243). This rudimentary checklist of components of an ideal-type conception of modern capitalism, expressed in the negative form of absence, is not a complete statement of Weber's ideal type, as we shall see below. Whether this statement is an accurate depiction of Chinese inadequacy is a separate issue from how Weber accounts for this state of affairs. He does so in terms that we have seen in earlier chapters. He writes that the 'Chinese lacked the central, religiously determined, and rational method of life which came from within and which was characteristic of the classical Puritan'; the Chinese instead measured business success or failure in terms of external factors, namely, 'magically and ceremonially significant merit or offense' (Weber 1964: 243). Similarly, whereas the Puritan is able to suppress 'petty acquisitiveness', which, Weber (1964: 244) says, 'destroys all rational, methodical enterprise', the 'repression of natural impulses' was 'alien' to the Confucian. Weber's rendering of the European capitalist as a religious Puritan, and the Chinese shopkeeper a Confucian literati, simply conflates roles and backgrounds. Because these issues have been discussed in earlier chapters there is no need to pursue them again here.

Weber's depiction of what the Chinese lacked from the point of view of rational capitalist accounting invites reflection. For instance, the claim that China had 'no rational money system', noted earlier, is not supported even by Weber's own discussion in *The Religion of China* and elsewhere. Weber (1964: 53) notes an 'increasing general drift toward [a] money economy'. This assessment is consistent with Weber's observation of medieval innovation, in the development in China of paper money and bills of exchange (Weber 1964: 7–11; 1978: 1104), and his observations regarding the *banco*-money policy of the Chinese guilds which, Weber (1978: 160–61) holds, 'formed the model for the Hamburg banco mark, [and which] came up to modern standards of rationality'. Three problems attend Weber's discussion here. In the closing pages of *The Religion of China*, Weber's rhetorical style leads to overreach in his insistence that China was devoid of any form of rationality that might support capitalistic economic formations. Second, Weber's sources are inadequate. Historian Mark Elvin's comment is relevant:

> Weber's range of reading was extraordinary, but his failure to use some of the major French sources on the Chinese economy was an avoidable weakness. Had he consulted, for example, the eighteenth-century *Mémoires concernant les Chinois*, he would have been aware of interesting phenomena such as Chinese macro-economic theory, which had a rationality of its own, but different from that of Europe. (Elvin 1984: 385)

Finally, irrespective of his sources, scholarship since Weber's time has added important insight on Imperial China's economy and the practices of those involved in it. Weber's comment regarding the absence of bookkeeping in China is a case in point. Weber's reference to bookkeeping does raise questions concerning the adequacy of his own understanding of its origins and function (Aho 2005: 4–5, 9–11, 25; Barbalet 2008: 155–58); but more pertinent to the present discussion is the advance in our knowledge of Chinese bookkeeping since Weber wrote (Lin 1992; Yuan et al. 2015). It is now accepted that from the late fifteenth century, Chinese merchants and bankers developed various forms of double-entry bookkeeping, reflecting developments in markets, business, and production: 'As the volume and complexity of the commercial and industrial activities grew, double-entry bookkeeping became a necessary device to keep track of the expanded business transactions' (Lin 1992: 120). Lin goes on to write that the 'lack of large-scale commercial and industrial productions before the nineteenth century ... hampered the further progress of Chinese double-entry bookkeeping', suggesting that accounting techniques are not necessarily causal in capitalist development but interactive with it.

THE IDEAL-TYPE CONCEPTION OF MODERN CAPITALISM

Weber's discussion of the Chinese economy and its development is all too frequently conducted in *The Religion of China* without regard to the specific period or region to which the facts he relates connect, as a number of commentators have observed, making many of his statements regarding the character of the Imperial Chinese economy both confused and difficult to assess. It is now known that Chinese business affairs and social relations in general were structured by a culture of contract that was fully established as early as the fourteenth century (Hansen 1995). This comes close to Weber's requirement for capitalist accounting such that the instrument of contract influenced the regulation of 'consumption, production and prices', what he calls 'substantive freedom of contract' (Weber 1978: 162). With regard to access to the market, it is now established that hereditary occupational classifications had been completely eliminated by the Qing dynasty and that geographic mobility was unhindered so that freedom to participate in market activities and to establish business enterprises was, by this period, unfettered (Zelin 2004). Thus, another element of the ideal type of rational capitalism set out by Weber (1981: 276), 'freedom of the market', is satisfied. In different specific accounts of it, Weber offers different but overlapping statements of the ideal-type conceptualization of modern rational capitalism, identifying eight elements in *Economy and Society* (Weber 1978: 161–62) and six in *General Economic History* (Weber 1981: 276–78). Behind all of them is the idea that capitalism requires economic enterprise to be orientated to optimal market outcomes for the enterprise itself, unencumbered by familial or political prerogatives, and that those who operate the enterprise are able to form a view of the financial costs involved, and therefore, able to anticipate their profits, or at least appreciate that their activities would lead to profit, even though the prospective magnitude of profit could not necessarily be specified.

There is now a large and compelling literature on Chinese economic development which shows that by the eighth century intense commercial activity had transformed rural society and towns, and that during the period of the sixteenth to the eighteenth century, China enjoyed an inflow of silver supported by sophisticated production and commerce that included exports to Europe of silk, porcelain, tea, and other goods. The quality of Chinese exports was superior to anything that could have been produced in Europe at that time and they generated a fascination with Chinoiserie, noted in Chap. 2 above. China's internal trade at this time continued to expand, based on high productivity and generation of abundance. Indeed, the evidence suggests that the expansion of the Chinese economy, based on sophisticated organization of commercial enterprise, continued into the nineteenth century (Elvin 1973; Huang 1990; Pomeranz 2000; Rowe 1998). The argument here is not that through these developments China manifested a modern capitalist economy and therefore Weber was mistaken about the impossibility of an indigenous Chinese capitalism. For reasons that we shall see later, an economic structure that paralleled European capitalism was not able to develop in Imperial China. But Weber's approach to the problem of defining capitalism and his comparison of Chinese and European developments cannot avoid drawing critical commentary.

Weber's ideal-type conception of modern capitalism was formed on the basis of the experience and character of European and American economies of the late nineteenth and early twentieth centuries (Weber 1981: 276; 1991: 52). The empirical complexion of these economies, individualistic, competitive, and world-dominant, is reflected in Weber's ideal-type concept of modern capitalism. One question that might be asked is whether Weber's ideal type is completely meaningful today, when corporations dominate all economies and arguably remove the individualistic and competitive elements of markets that Weber regards as necessary (Wilks 2013). It might be added that Weber's idea of 'freedom of the market' in any event misunderstands the institutional nature of markets in their necessary subjection to legal, political, and conventional or moral constraints

(Schultz 2001; Schumpeter 1966: 417–18). The global financial crisis that peaked in 2008 provides further evidence of the possible unsuitability of Weber's ideal type for understanding the nature of modern capitalism in so far as this crisis demonstrated the way in which regulation, rather than 'complete absence of formal appropriation of rights to managerial functions' (Weber 1978: 162), can better secure the future of modern capitalism. Finally, under conditions of globalization, capitalism in regional or national jurisdictions requires participation in intergovernmental organizations such as the World Trade Organization (Hoekman and Mavroidis 2015). In a similar vein, given what is agreed about the nature of the Chinese economy from the sixteenth to the eighteenth century, an ideal-type conception based on European capitalism during, say, the eighteenth century would have resulted in a very different assessment of Chinese 'capitalism' at that time (see Pomeranz 2000). All of this tells us something about ideal-type conceptions rather than about capitalism.

Weber's argument concerning the origins of capitalism in Europe and the absence of a native capitalism in China does not only commit the fallacy of counterfactual argument but effectively compares unlike phenomena. Every school child knows not to compare apples with oranges. We are reminded that Karl Marx avoided this temptation by acknowledging that whereas European societies may have historically transitioned from 'feudalism' to 'capitalism', an understanding of other societies, including the Chinese, required a distinctive characterization 'which [Marx] called "Asiatic society", and for the time being left it alongside the other stages, not yet having decided where it belonged in the progressive evolutionary series' (Balazs 1964: 36–37). A major problem with Weber's ideal-type method is that by design it disregards differences between cases. Writers entirely sympathetic with Weber have shown exasperation regarding his use of the ideal-type method. The economist and sociologist Joseph Schumpeter, who was a coworker with Weber on the *Verein für Sozialpolitik* (Krüger 2010), refers to the distortion of historical representation through the method of ideal-type analysis, the 'habit' in Weber of 'painting unrealistic pictures' (Schumpeter 2008: 191). The American sociologist, Talcott Parsons, who translated Weber's *Protestant Ethic* into English, refers to the 'hypostatization of ideal types' in which 'the organic unity both of concrete historical individuals and of the historic process' is broken up (Parsons 1968: 607).

In fact, Weber acknowledges the problem of distortion, indicated above, but is focused on a higher or at least a different goal. When referring to the Continental textile industry in *The Protestant Ethic and the Spirit of Capitalism* (Weber 1991: 66), presented 'for purposes of illustration' as an ideal type drawn from different branches of the industry in different places, it is therefore 'of course of no consequence that the process has not in any one of the examples we have in mind taken place in precisely the manner we have described' (Weber 1991: 200 note 25). Weber acknowledges the same problem, of method exaggerating 'characteristic differences' that does 'violence to historical reality', in order to make an argument against the evidence, namely, to make relative differences between Catholic and Protestant doctrine appear absolute (Weber 1991: 233–34 note 68). The question must be asked, then, of how well Weber's ideal-type conception of capitalism can characterize actual capitalism in any given economic system, and also, of what it could possibly reveal of the Chinese case.

The provision of a checklist of attributes of 'rational accounting in production enterprises' (Weber 1978: 161; 1981: 276) as a characterization of modern industrial capitalism operates in terms of Weber's larger argument concerning rationalization as a societal variable, differences in the extent and form of which are held to distinguish historically different societies and social entities, including organizations, religions, music, and so on. A problem, however, as indicated earlier, is not only the inconclusive nature of ideal-type conceptions, but also that they do not discriminate between or are insensitive to historical and other particular characteristics of the things to which they are applied. Karl Marx was mentioned above as being aware of the need for historical specificity in the characterization of economic systems. Marx, of course, has a distinctive approach to the notion of capitalism that contrasts with Weber's. Whereas Weber focuses on the capitalist's instruments for determining the measurement of the profit of the enterprise—namely, the basis and means of rational accounting—Marx focuses on the relations of production through which profit is generated. Weber and Marx agree that the relations of the market place underpin what each conceptualizes as primary. But by focusing on the relations of production, Marx accentuates an aspect of capitalism that is not highlighted by Weber's approach.

Weber (1964: 244–47; 1991: 51–54) regards capitalist moneymaking as an end in itself. Marx, on the other hand, appreciates that in the competition between units of capital, a requirement of capitalist production is investment of profit in the enterprise, and therefore that a necessary feature of a continuing or viable capitalist economy is the accumulation of capital.

As Marx (1976: 741–42) notes, 'although the expenditure of the capitalist … is always restrained by the sordid avarice and anxious calculation lurking in the background, this expenditure nevertheless grows with his accumulation, without the one necessarily restricting the other … Accumulate, accumulate! That is Moses and the prophets!' Weber (1964: 247) does mention accumulation, as 'an ascetic compulsion to save' (see also Weber 1991: 51). But for Weber, then, accumulation refers only to an increase of personal wealth through a psychological disposition. In a modern capitalist economy, the capitalist's moneymaking cannot be an end in itself, for Marx, but must serve the accumulation process, and if it does not do so, the capitalist will fail against competitors and suffer bankruptcy. On this basis, it is possible to consider again features of the Chinese economy that Weber investigated and notice aspects of it that Weber failed to appreciate.

The Chinese economy that Weber discusses included significant involvement of the imperial household and state, principally in mining and salt monopolies. But rather than prevent private ownership and enterprise, this state involvement generally encouraged the economic activity of merchants and non-state manufacturers. It has to be noted, though, that in the context of the Chinese economy, private ownership was not individual ownership but household ownership and also lineage or clan ownership. One of the stipulations for modern capitalist accounting identified by Weber (1978: 162) is 'the most complex separation possible of the enterprise and its conditions of success and failure from the household or private budgetary unit and its property interests'. But household and clan ownership did not prevent capitalistic enterprise in China for at least two reasons, as indicated in Chap. 2. First, Weber's assumption that the 'personalist principle was … a barrier to impersonal rationalization' (Weber 1964: 236) is false, both with regard to Chinese enterprise (Peng 2005: 338–39, 347–49) and in general (Selznick 1948). Second, clan managers were innovative in developing financial devises that provided rational protection to clan investment folios (Zelin 2009). The issue is rather more complicated than Weber indicates.

Weber (1978: 162; 1981: 277) refers to the importance of formally rational or calculable law as underpinning modern capitalism. He acknowledges the 'beginnings of legal institutions' in China, but holds that they suffer 'technical imperfection' (Weber 1964: 243). But rather than the structure of law, rational or otherwise, it is enforcement that determines the efficacy of law and Weber's account does not direct our attention to that dimension of the issue. This is particularly important in the case of Weber's China because a characteristic of law in Imperial China was that in the relationship between legal instruments on the one hand, and merchants and manufacturers on the other, the latter were largely indifferent in drawing upon or utilizing the former. Law existed, certainly, but rather than use law in protection of property rights or in resolution of disputes, people in business would in all likelihood rely on private compulsion, patronage, and favor, or some other unofficial means of arbitration or enforcement in preference to legal sanction. Protection of capital and of opportunities to increase wealth were typically left to the private connections that business people had with the bureaucracy and its officials than to legal procedure. Again, there are a number of reasons why this is so; the most obvious, though, include the high social status of Imperial Chinese officials and the strategy of successful families, in business or agriculture, to invest in the education of their children with a view to the child's success in the imperial examination leading to official bureaucratic appointment, thus providing the family with a link to officialdom which would both enhance the family's social standing and provide it with a source of protection against the arbitrariness of the state and competition from other families and their businesses.

Weber (1964: 158–59) makes much of the denigration of business and commerce, of 'thrift' and 'profitable enterprise', in Confucian ideology, and he holds it to be partly responsible for the lack of success of capitalism in China. The Confucian relegation of trade to a subordinate position in Imperial Chinese society was irrelevant to the fortunes of commercial families in terms of economic success, however, and the strict divide between officials on the one hand, and businesses on the other is not empirically sustainable (Elvin 1973: 291–93). The significance of the high status of officials relative to merchants or entrepreneurs, for the development of capitalism, lies in another direction. The profits of enterprise in Imperial China were less directed to capital accumulation and more directed to noncapitalistic investment, including the allocation of resources for education and recruitment of family members to the state bureaucracy. In addition, successful commercial families were inclined to invest the profit of their enterprises in land; although returns from rent were low, investment in land attracted very little economic risk and, importantly, brought high prestige (Balazs 1964: 52). In Imperial China, then, capitalistically generated wealth was not significantly channeled into capital accumulation. Investment in enterprise was necessary for economic success but protection of that success required investment in public office and links with officialdom. A major consequence of this for the process of capital accumulation was not only the constrained reinvestment in commerce and industry, which affected the scale of enterprise directly, but also the failure to develop financial instruments able to support investment in large-scale industry. Thus, even assuming that in late Imperial China there was sufficient capital to achieve industrialization, 'the mechanism for focusing enough of it on industrial enterprises' was absent (Faure 2006: 12).

At the time that Weber first published *The Religion of China* in 1915, and certainly by the time of the augmented edition in 1920, the Chinese economy was more thoroughly capitalist than could be imagined on the basis of his discussion. After the collapse of the imperial dynasty in 1912, financial institutions quickly developed in Republican China, which encouraged significant capital accumulation (Cheng 2003), and while the established institutions of the economy remained in place, industrialization and capitalist development proceeded significantly even though the world economy suffered a major depression and political development in China during the period was turbulent (Richardson 1999; Rawski 1989). The revolutionary transformation of China was not concluded with the overthrow of the Qing dynasty in 1912 and the formation of the Republican regime, however, and in 1949 the Chinese Communist Party founded the People's Republic of China. Private business continued after the communist victory until 1956, when socialization of the private economy was more or less complete (Kraus 1991: 49–58). The period of socialist transformation of China was itself relatively brief, at least in the economic sphere, as the death of Chairman Mao Zedong in 1976 preceded another turning point in China's economic development. While the Mao era was one of collectivization and anticapitalist agitation, the period from 1978 introduced market reforms that quickly saw China, under the leadership of the Communist Party, join capitalist globalization and a further major transformation of China's economy took place. After indicating the nature of the present-day Chinese economy, it can be asked what Weber's approach to economic sociology offers an understanding of China today.

DENG XIAOPING'S CAT: CHARACTERIZATIONS OF CHINA'S POST-1978 ECONOMY

The architect of China's post-Mao economy is Deng Xiaoping, who from 1978 had the title paramount leader of the People's Republic of China. Deng was a lifelong associate of Mao who long argued for the prospects of a socialist China benefitting from market reform (Vogel 2011). Deng famously said: 'It doesn't matter whether the cat is black or white, as long as it catches mice'. This statement is generally taken to mean that in the quest to achieve China's economic advancement there is no fundamental contradiction in a socialist economy operating with market exchange. Deng first proposed this reassuring but possibly contentious claim in 1962, in a speech to a conference of the Communist Youth League. At this time, whether the cat is black or white, it was decidedly a black or a white socialist cat. Since the post-1978 reforms, designed and led by Deng, the difference between these cats is not simply in the color of their coats but more importantly in the methods they employ in catching mice and how the mice they catch are distributed to the kittens. Deng's own view was that market exchanges may indeed operate in a socialist economy, just as economic planning is often employed in capitalist states. A market economy, then, may operate with socialist characteristics, or as Deng put it at the Twelfth National Party Congress in 1982, the introduction of market incentives, including the retention of profits by enterprises and the introduction of performance bonuses for workers, was no more nor less than 'socialism with Chinese characteristics'.

The transition from a plan-dominated to a market-infused economy in China, during the period from the late 1970s to the late 1980s, involved not only major institutional change, but also revisions in the meaning of such key terms as 'market', 'plan', 'ownership', 'prices', and 'wages'. When Deng first introduced his black and white cats in the 1960s and through to the mid-1980s, the notion of a market, in which commodities exchange through the medium of money, applied to a narrower range of possible transfers than were commonplace outside of China. Under socialist conditions, labor, for instance, could not be a commodity, nor could state-owned natural resources; consumer goods could be commodities, but not capital goods. Yet, there was wide agreement at this time that markets and commodities are compatible with socialism. An article published in 1979 summarized a view widely held in China during this period, namely, that 'the antithesis of socialist planning is not the market but spontaneity and anarchy in production, and that the antithesis of the market economy is not the planned economy but ... the subsistence economy' (quoted in Hsu 2005: 29). By the mid-1980s, with a broadening of the concept of market to accommodate the reality in China of capital, labor, and technology functioning as commodities in both the newly instituted Town and Village Enterprises (TVEs) and in those enterprises which operated in China's newly created Special Economic Zones (SEZs) in which non-national (mainly Hong Kong) Chinese ethnics engaged in production for export (Naughton 2007: 271–82, 406–10), the growing dominance of market exchange generated further conceptual and institutional changes that continued to transform both China's economy and how it was thought about.

There are three market-related concepts that underwent change during this period that are useful barometers of institutional change. These are the concepts of 'competition', 'information', and 'bankruptcy'. Everyone is likely to agree that markets involve competition. Indeed, the virtue of competition in China's newly marketized economy was to eliminate inefficient enterprises. The creation of 'multiple channels of distribution', in which producers in different sectors of the economy, including state-owned enterprises (SOEs), collectively-owned enterprises and also privately-owned enterprises, compete in the same market had the effect of forcing producers to be attentive to consumers' demands, of aligning production with social needs, and also, eliminating socially-costly enterprises and inferior products. Socialist market competition, then, supports the state's development strategy, and if it does not support that strategy, then it becomes what was known as 'pernicious competition' (Hsu 2005: 39–41). In this sense, then, the difference between socialist competition and capitalist competition is that they are respectively cooperative and antagonistic (Hsu 2005: 42). One aspect of cooperative competition that characterizes a socialist market, according to this terminology, is that as firms do not produce for private profit, they will share technical information with each other, rather than withhold it from each other.

While the notion of cooperative competition as a characteristic of socialist market relations was widespread during the early 1980s, the reality, that firms refused to share technical information with their competitors, quickly led to institutional catch-up. Chinese market competition through its impact on information flow was therefore revealed to be decidedly capitalistic rather than socialistic. And yet, for market price signals to work effectively, whether the markets are red or blue, the availability of market information must be unhindered. There was thus generated at this time a new role for the socialist Chinese government, to provide reliable economic data and impose sanctions against the production and dissemination of unreliable, false, or misleading economic data. This requirement, consequential on the 1980s marketization, is in sharp contrast to the party-state's prior information practices. In this sense, the adoption in 1983 of the Statistics Law of the People's Republic of China, at the Third Meeting of the Standing Committee of the Sixth National People's Congress, can be regarded as a significant capitalistic departure. The strong legal sanctions against the fabrication or falsification of statistical data by individuals or government agencies, in the Law's Chap. 5 on Legal Responsibility, set a standard not only facilitating market engagement, but also the rule of law, given the Law's provisions of legal enforcement (see Liu 2012).

Finally, capitalist market competition implies the possibility, indeed, the real prospect of bankruptcy. What Marx (1976: 433, 436) calls the 'coercive law of competition' both forces capitalists to strengthen their productive capacities through capital accumulation, as indicated above, and at the same time it eliminates those less successful than others in doing so, leading to their bankruptcy. In socialist China, on the other hand, it was not possible for enterprises to suffer bankruptcy. Prior to the 1980s, failing enterprises were subsidized by state resources so that they could continue to provide employment to a workforce, irrespective of how poorly they performed. The desirability of permitting the bankruptcy of nonperforming enterprises, in order to conserve state resources, was first raised in 1983 (Hsu 2005: 44). The Enterprise Bankruptcy Law of the People's Republic of China was passed in 1986. This was part of a number of related reforms introduced in the same year, which included a system of unemployment insurance for workers who lost their job through employer's bankruptcy, as well as a labor contract system that tied employment to the market viability of the employing enterprise (Ngok 2016: 240–41). While bankruptcy law has thus operated in China since 1986, with a new iteration of the Enterprise Bankruptcy Law effective since 2006, the incidence of bankruptcy remains remarkably low. It has been reported that in 2009 there were 2434 bankruptcy applications accepted by Chinese courts, whereas there were at the same time 1,473,675 accepted by US courts; and the Chinese bankruptcy numbers have declined since the enactment of the 2006 law (Jiang 2014: 559).

While the Chinese economy continues to be described officially as a socialist market economy, the overwhelming consensus in the scholarly literature and in popular opinion is that it is best described as capitalist. Indeed, since the decision of the Fifteenth National Congress in 1997, to legitimate the role of private business in setting the national economic trajectory, the socialist market economy has ceded leadership to capitalist forces. And yet the appellation 'capitalist' is itself thought to provide an unsatisfactory summary of China's economy for a number of reasons. The role of the state in the management of the economy, through its continuing control of enterprises regarded as essential to the national economy and through other means of setting prices and operating as a visible hand at least paralleling the market's invisible hand (Heilmann and Melton 2013) has led to the idea that China's market economy is state capitalist. This is only one of a number of characterizations of capitalism with Chinese characteristics.

The development of the post-Mao economic reforms has been achieved in significant ways through China's participation in the global capitalist economy. It is appropriate to note, though, that the clear beginnings of market reform emerged during the late 1970s in the rural sector by peasant households privately operating on their own behalf against the background of collective agriculture and through overcoming or ignoring cadre opposition (Faure 2006: 73–82). The so-called Household Responsibility System was officially adopted, however, when it was realized how successful its implementation was in raising productivity. Parallel with this development was the advent of the TVEs, noted earlier, that were formed after the abolition of Communes in 1982 through the conversion of commune workshops into profit-led flexible production units. The TVEs were not only self-consciously market actors in their own right but were of interest to foreign investors, especially from Hong Kong, Taiwan, and overseas Chinese communities (Vogel 2011: 446–47). The setting up of Special Economic Zones in the 1980s in order to capitalize on the benefits of direct foreign investment, including technology transfer and the introduction of new managerial forms, was only the beginning of China's incorporation into the global economy. The full realization of this part of China's economic transition was realized at the end of 2001 when China joined the World Trade Organization and was more fully integrated into the capitalist global economy.

A CHINESE CAPITALISM

The implications of late development for economies such as China's from the 1980s have long been recognized as including the availability of advanced technologies without a need for the 'late starter' itself to replicate the developmental stages undergone to achieve those technologies that took place in the more advanced sectors of the global economy. This idea was pioneered by Thorstein Veblen in his account of the 'advantages of backwardness' enjoyed by England in the seventeenth century relative to more advanced Continental European industrial production; he describes the benefits of a 'late start' as the 'peculiar advantage in being able to borrow what their neighbours had worked out' (Veblen 1946: 164; see also Veblen 1966: 187–88, 194). This idea, that 'in its technological borrowing the backward country was to utilize decades or even centuries of [the advanced country's] progress' (Gerschenkron 1962: 362–63), is now part of the folklore of comparative political economy. Among other things, this general proposition has been taken to entail that 'the timing of a political economy's entry into the global capitalist system directly influences the shape of its capitalism' (McNally 2012: 754). While Veblen and Gerschenkron refer only to technology, a similar point has thus been made regarding organization. In a classic study of the 'social structural grounds [of] the correlation between the time in history that a particular type of organization was invented and the social structure of organizations of that type which exist at the present time' (Stinchcombe 1965: 143), Stinchcombe (1965: 168) shows that:

> ...organizational types generally originate rapidly in a relatively short historical period, to grow and change slowly after that period. The time at which this period of rapid growth took place is highly correlated with the present characteristics of organizations of the type.

Stinchcombe explains this phenomenon in terms of the social resources available at the time of origin.

The historical period during which China fashioned its market institutions and joined capitalist globalization coincided with the dominance in Anglo-American politics of Thatcherism and Reaganism. The policies of these right-wing political leaders and their economic agendas of reducing the role of government in economic management, reducing taxation and state expenditure, and enforcing private property rights and market determination of resource allocation are widely described as neoliberal. On the basis of the 'advantages of backwardness' notion in conjunction with Stinchcombe's research findings on the consequences for organizational structure of the historical time of formation, it is possible to hold that the form of China's capitalism would correspondingly be neoliberal. Indeed, this is essentially David Harvey's argument, that China's market reforms 'just happened to coincide—and it is very hard to consider this as anything other than a conjunctural accident of world-historical significance—with the turn to neoliberal solutions in Britain and the United States' (Harvey 2005: 120). Harvey immediately goes on to say that the 'outcome in China has been the construction of a particular kind of market economy that increasingly incorporates neoliberal elements interdigitated with authoritarian centralized control'.

The rise of neoliberalism that Harvey refers to drew upon circumstances in American and British polities and economies that were not general and certainly could not be attached to Chinese conditions. While the contribution of the SOE sector to China's GDP has declined since the beginning of marketization, SOEs remain central in economically strategic areas, including energy, transport, and communications, and since 2003 they have been collectively managed by the state-owned Assets Supervision and Administration Commission of the State Council. Similarly, while neoliberalism is orientated to the dismantlement of state-provided welfare, the Chinese government is developing new welfare policies. Originally introduced to cope with the problems of workers unemployed through closure of failed SOEs, state-provided welfare now has extended in scope and cover, even though it has a long way to go to meet the full needs of its population, especially the elderly in rural areas. A recent overview summarizes the situation as follows:

> China's welfare development since its economic reform in 1978 has been to build a new welfare system that is compatible with its mixed economy under the name of socialism with Chinese characteristics. Although there were some positive adjustments to China's welfare policies, its current welfare system is mainly market oriented and urban biased that has excluded many disadvantaged groups from accessing decent social services. (Chan 2016: 11)

The limitations of the present welfare system in China do not derive from neoliberal indifference, however, but from the problems of creating national cover against a background of a prior partial, local, and unstable welfare provision that operated during the Mao period (Wang 2009).

These points are made here simply to suggest that application to China of terms that arise out of non-Chinese contexts are unlikely to be helpful in understanding Chinese developments. Indeed, the nature of the Chinese economic system after the changes initiated by the 1978 reforms, how these reforms may be characterized and the likely trajectory of the economy, has itself given rise to a growth industry of commentary and assessment that generally agrees that China's economy is capitalist but not quite like US or British or German or Japanese capitalism. This is not the place to review this literature, vast and diverse and unresolved as it is. What can be taken from the academic and journalistic discussion of the Chinese economy, though, is the fact that there is overwhelming recognition that the Chinese economy is indeed capitalist and also that it is distinctive in its capitalism and distinctive in a Chinese way. One of the chief aspects of this distinctiveness relates to the importance of the family's underlying role in China's transition to capitalism (Whyte 1995). Another feature of the Chinese economy is that in the economic relations between businesses, in the relations between business and the party-state, and also in the relations between Chinese and foreign corporations, what is known as *guanxi* is unavoidable (see, for instance, Boisot and Child 1996; Chow 1997; Guo and Miller 2010; Lee and Anderson 2007; McNally 2011; Nitsch and Diebel 2008; Standifird and Marshall 2000; Wank 1996). *Guanxi* refers to personalist favor exchanges which, in China, underlie the organization of business relationships and the relations between entrepreneurs and officials (Barbalet 2017).

One recent Weberian account describes Chinese capitalism, primarily because of the continuing role of the Communist Party in its development, as 'a form without spirit and without a carrier stratum that is able to promote a new civil spirit based on freedom, calculated risk-taking, responsibility and sustainability' (Schluchter 2014: 28). The taxonomy of the ideal type that was described above is taken here to be the measure of Chinese capitalism today. But given the dynamic of the present-day Chinese economy, the experimental pragmatism of its leadership (Ang 2016), and the short historical span of its development to the present time, this seems to be an approach which ignores the particular characteristic features of Chinese economic development. Consider one source of accumulation in China over the past 30-odd years. The appropriation of farmland for urbanization provides developers with enormous profits. Villagers themselves have no legal right to transfer land for compensatory use; they have only the right to use and supervise the use of land. The state, on the other hand, has the legal right to expropriate land which is under collective ownership. The state, in this case, is local government, which transacts with developers. Land that has been expropriated is compensated for not by the government, but by the potential user who purchases the 'land user right' from the local state authorities. Compensation is legally set to make up for the loss of crops on the ground, and to assist the village collective in relocating the agricultural population affected by land expropriation; that is all (Cai 2003; Guo 2001; Walker 2006). As compensation to villagers is not based on the market value of the land for urban development, developers are able to make enormous profits. In April 2015, the US finance magazine *Forbes* published a list of China's 400 US dollar billionaires. Second from the the top of the list is a real estate investor with assets of US\$ 29.6 billion. In fact, the single biggest industry group of these 400 billionaires is real estate, comprising 80 individuals. From Weber's perspective, this would be a cut-and-dry instance of political capitalism, irrational and outside of the range of modern capitalism. But it cannot be that simple.

In his ideal-type conceptualization of modern capitalism, Weber stipulates that a principal condition for formal rationality of capital accounting is the 'appropriation of all physical means of production [including] land ... as disposable property of autonomous private industrial enterprises' (Weber 1981: 276). Marx (1976: 877–95) said it rather differently. In his discussion of the 'Expropriation of the Agricultural Population from the Land', an account of what he calls the primary accumulation of capital, Marx effectively considers the underlying social process of the eviction of peasant producers from their means of production, an appropriation that Weber's just-mentioned formal accounting measure requires. The method employed in Scotland, mentioned here by Marx, was different than the one used in China, but the effects are similar:

> Between 1814 to 1820 these 15,000 inhabitants, about 3,000 families, were systematically hunted and rooted out. All their villages were destroyed and burnt, all their fields turned into pasturage. British soldiers enforced this mass of evictions, and came to blows with the inhabitants. One old woman was burnt to death in the flames of the hut she refused to leave. It was in this manner that [the Duchess of Sutherland] appropriated 794,000 acres of land that had belonged to the clan from time immemorial. She assigned to the expelled inhabitants about 6,000 acres on the sea-shore—2 acres per family. (Marx 1976: 891)

Marx (1976: 932–35) later shows that in colonial Australia yet another method was employed to achieve the separation of agricultural producers from their land, one in which the colonial administration placed an artificial price on land sufficiently high to prevent purchase by English working-class immigrants. In this way, a labor supply is assured for employers who, by virtue of that fact, may proceed to accumulate capital.

It is too simple a point to claim that rudimentary typologies are inadequate to characterize economic systems that change and develop and go through stages of formation. The development of modern capitalism in China has hardly begun, from its beginnings in the late twentieth century. The value of a Weberian ideal-type analysis for understanding this process will be proportionate to its imaginative application to something that is still incipient, in process and cannot be confined to the calibration of simple measures unconnected from a long-term historical perspective.

CONCLUSION

In the course of the discussion in the chapters above, beginning with the apprehension of China in Germany during the nineteenth and early twentieth centuries and Weber's interest in exploring the conditions of the origins of capitalism, Weber's reflections have been a constant source of consideration for our understanding of Chinese thought and practices. Through the prism of Weber's writing, it has been possible to expand our understanding of not only Confucianism but also Daoism; not only the conception of self and self-interest in China but also religion and magic. Weber's vision is unified and expansive. In a sense, to agree with him confines us to the compass of his sources and to his own purposes. To challenge him, on the other hand, is to have the advantage of beginning from a position of his insight and erudition and drawing upon what he neglected or could not know in extending further along the path on which he set out.

Much of what is written above has been in disagreement with Weber, and yet, the disagreement was in conversation with his rich, detailed, and extensive texts. Whatever is of interest in the chapters above was derived from conversation with Weber. In that sense, our debt to Weber is enormous, indeed essential; he defined a subject matter and a way of presenting it that invites engagement. While that engagement in this instance has been almost wholly critical, it is no mere rejection of Weber's original contribution, for that contribution is a provocation, and therefore, an unavoidable starting point. In science, there is no last word; social science is no different in this regard. Weber cannot have the last word, nor can any critical commentary on Weber provide the last word, ad infinitum.

REFERENCES

Aho, James. 2005. *Confession and Bookkeeping: The Religious, Moral, and Rhetorical Roots of Modern Accounting*. Albany: State University of New York Press.

Ang, Yuen Yuen. 2016. *How China Escaped the Poverty Trap*. Ithaca: Cornell University Press.

Balazs, Etienne. 1964. 'The Birth of Capitalism in China'. Pp. 34–54 in his *Chinese Civilization and Bureaucracy: Variations on a Theme*, translated by H.M. Wright and edited by Arthur F. Wright. New Haven: Yale University Press.

Barbalet, Jack. 2008. *Weber, Passions and Profits: 'The Protestant Ethic and the Spirit of Capitalism' in Context*. Cambridge: Cambridge University Press.

Barbalet, Jack. 2017. 'Dyadic Characteristics of *Guanxi* and their Consequences'. *Journal for the Theory of Social Behaviour*. First on line: 23 January. DOI:https://doi.org/10.1111/jtsb.12133.

Boisot, Max and Child, John. 1996. 'From Fiefs to Clans and Network Capitalism: Explaining China's Emerging Economic Order'. *Administrative Science Quarterly*. 41(4): 600–28.

Cai, Yongshin. 2003. 'Collective Ownership or Cadres' Ownership: The Non-agricultural Use of Farmland in China'. *The China Quarterly*. 175: 662–80.

Chan, Chak Kwan. 2016. 'Rebuilding a Welfare System for China's Mixed Economy'. Pp. 3–13 in *China's Social Policy: Transformation and Challenges*, edited by Kinglun Ngok and Chak Kwan Chan. London: Routledge.

Cheng, Linsun. 2003. *Banking in Modern China, Entrepreneurs, Professional Managers, and the Development of Chinese Banks, 1897–1937*. Cambridge: Cambridge University Press.

Chow, Gregory C. 1997. 'Challenges of China's Economic System for Economic Theory'. *American Economic Review*. 87(2): 321–27.

Elvin, Mark. 1973. *The Patterns of the Chinese Past*. Stanford, CA: Stanford University Press.

Elvin, Mark. 1984. 'Why China Failed to Create an Endogenous Industrial Capitalism: A Critique of Max Weber's Explanation'. *Theory and Society*. 13(3): 379–91.

Faure, David. 2006. *China and Capitalism: A History of Business Enterprise in Modern China*. Hong Kong: Hong Kong University Press.

Gerschenkron, Alexander. 1962. *Economic Backwardness in Historical Perspective: A Book of Essays*. New York: Praeger.

Guo, Xiaolin. 2001. 'Land Expropriation and Rural Conflicts in China'. *The China Quarterly*. 166: 422–39.

Guo, Chun and Miller, Jane K. 2010. 'Guanxi Dynamics and Entrepreneurial Firm Creation and Development in China'. *Management and Organization Review*. 6(2): 267–91.

Hamilton, Gary G. 2006. 'Why No Capitalism in China: Negative Questions in Historical Comparative Perspective'. Pp. 50–74 in his *Commerce and Capitalism in Chinese Societies*. London: Routledge.

Harvey, David. 2005. *A Brief History of Neoliberalism*. Oxford: Oxford University Press.

Hansen, Valerie. 1995. *Negotiating Daily Life in Traditional China: How Ordinary People Used Contracts, 600–1400*. New Haven: Yale University Press.

Heilmann, Sebastian and Melton, Oliver. 2013. 'The Reinvention of Development Planning in China, 1993–2012'. *Modern China*. 39(6): 580–628.

Hoekman, Bernard M. and Mavroidis, Petros C. 2015. *World Trade Organization (WTO): Law, Economics, and Politics*, 2nd Edition. London: Routledge.

Hsu, Robert C. 2005. *Economic Theories in China, 1979–1988*. Cambridge: Cambridge University Press.

Huang, Philip C.C. 1990. *The Peasant Family and Rural Development in the Yangzi Delta, 1350–1988*. Stanford: Stanford University Press.

Jiang, Yujia. 2014. 'The Curious Case of Inactive Bankruptcy Practice in China: A Comparative Study of U.S. and Chinese Bankruptcy Law'. *Northwestern Journal of International Law and Business*. 34(3): 559–82.

Kraus, Willy. 1991. *Private Business in China: Revival between Ideology and Pragmatism*, translated by Erich Holz. London: Hurst and Company.

Krüger, Dieter. 2010. 'Max Weber and the Younger Generation in the *Verein für Sozialpolitik*'. Pp. 71–87 in *Max Weber and his Contemporaries*, edited by Wolfgang J. Mommsen and Jürgen Osterhammel. London: Routledge.

Lee, Edward Yiu-chung and Anderson, Alistair R. 2007. 'The Role of Guanxi in Chinese Entrepreneurship'. *Journal of Asia Entrepreneurship and Sustainability*. 3(3): 38–51.

Lin, Z. Jun. 1992. 'Chinese Double-entry Bookkeeping before the Nineteenth Century'. *Accounting Historians Journal*. 19(2): 103–22.

Liu, Xin. 2012. *The Mirage of China: Anti-Humanism, Narcissism, and Corporeality of the Contemporary World*. New York: Berghahn Books.

Marx, Karl. 1976. *Capital: A Critique of Political Economy, Volume 1*, Introduction by Ernest Mandel and translation by Ben Fowkes. Harmondsworth: Penguin Books.

McNally, Christopher A. 2011. 'China's Changing Guanxi Capitalism: Private Entrepreneurs between Leninist Control and Relentless Accumulation'. *Business and Politics*. 13(2): 1–29.

McNally, Christopher A. 2012. 'Sino-Capitalism: China's Reemergence and the International Political Economy'. *World Politics*. 64(4): 741–76.

Naughton, Barry. 2007. *The Chinese Economy: Transitions and Growth*. Cambridge, MA: The MIT Press.

Nitsch, Manfred and Diebel, Frank. 2008. 'Guanxi Economics: Confucius meets Lenin, Keynes, and Schumpeter in Contemporary China'. *Intervention*. 5(1): 77–104.

Ngok, Kinglun. 2016. 'Modern Chinese Welfare Arrangements and Challenges Ahead'. Pp. 239–59 in *China's Social Policy: Transformation and Challenges*, edited by Kinglun Ngok and Chak Kwan Chan. London: Routledge.

Parsons, Talcott. 1968. *The Structure of Social Action: A Study in Social Theory with Special Reference to a Group of Recent European Writers*. New York: The Free Press.

Peng, Yusheng. 2005. 'Lineage Networks, Rural Entrepreneurs, and Max Weber'. *Research in the Sociology of Work*. 15: 327–55.

Pomeranz, Kenneth. 2000. *The Great Divergence: China, Europe, and the Making of the Modern World Economy*. Princeton, NJ: Princeton University Press.

Rawski, Thomas G. 1989. *Economic Growth in Prewar China*. Berkeley: University of California Press.

Richardson, Philip. 1999. *Economic Change in China, c. 1800–1950*. Cambridge: Cambridge University Press.

Rowe, William T. 1998. 'Domestic Interregional Trade in Eighteenth-Century China'. Pp. 173–92 in *On the Eighteenth Century as a Category of Asian History: Van Leur in Retrospect*, edited by Leonard Blussé and Femme S Gaastra. London: Ashgate.

Selznick, Philip. 1948. 'Foundations of the Theory of Organization'. *American Sociological Review*. 13(1): 25–35.

Schluchter, Wolfgang. 2014. 'How Ideas become Effective in History: Max Weber on Confucianism and Beyond'. *Max Weber Studies*. 14(1): 11–29.

Schultz, Walter J. 2001. *The Moral Conditions of Economic Efficiency*. Cambridge: Cambridge University Press.

Schumpeter, Joseph A. 1966. *Capitalism, Socialism and Democracy*, 5th Edition. London: George Allen and Unwin.

Schumpeter, Joseph A. 2008. 'Capitalism'. Pp. 189–210 in *Essays on Entrepreneurs, Innovations, Business Cycles, and the Evolution of Capitalism*, edited by Richard V. Clemence with a new Introduction by Richard Swedberg. New Brunswick: Transaction Publishers.

Standifird, Stephen S. and Marshall, R. Scott. 2000. 'The Transaction Cost Advantage of Guanxi Based Business Practices'. *Journal of World Business*. 35(1): 21–42.

Stinchcombe, Arthur L. 1965. 'Social Structure and Organizations'. Pp. 142–93 in *Handbook of Organizations*, edited by James G. March. New York: Rand McNally.

Veblen, Thorstein. 1946. *The Instinct of Workmanship, and the State of the Industrial Arts*. New York: The Viking Press.

Veblen, Thorstein. 1966. *Imperial Germany and the Industrial Revolution*. Ann Arbor: University of Michigan Press.

Vogel, Ezra F. 2011. *Deng Xiaoping and the Transformation of China*. Cambridge, MA: Harvard University Press.

Walker, Kathy Le Mons. 2006. '"Gangster Capitalism" and Peasant Protest in China: The Last Twenty Years'. *Journal of Peasant Studies*. 33(1): 1–33.

Wang, Shaoguang. 2009. 'Adapting by Learning: The Evolution of China's Rural Health Care Financing'. *Modern China.* 35(4): 370–404.

Wank, David L. 1996. 'The Institutional Process of Market Clientelism: *Guanxi* and Private Business in a South China City'. *The China Quarterly.* 147: 820–38.

Weber, Max. 1949. '"Objectivity" in Social Science and Social Policy'. Pp. 50–112 in *The Methodology of the Social Sciences,* edited by Edward A. Shils and Henry A. Finch. New York: The Free Press.

Weber, Max. 1960. *The Religion of India: The Sociology of Hinduism and Buddhism,* translated and edited by Hans H. Gerth and Don Martindale. New York: The Free Press.

Weber, Max. 1964. *The Religion of China: Confucianism and Taoism,* translated and edited by Hans H. Gerth, with an Introduction by C.K. Yang. New York: The Free Press.

Weber, Max. 1978. *Economy and Society: An Outline of Interpretive Sociology,* edited by Guenther Roth and Claus Wittich. Berkeley: University of California Press.

Weber, Max. 1981. *General Economic History,* translated by Frank Knight with a new Introduction by Ira J. Cohen. New Brunswick, NJ: Transaction Books.

Weber, Max. 1991. *The Protestant Ethic and the Spirit of Capitalism,* translated by Talcott Parsons. London: Harper Collins.

Whyte, Martin King. 1995. 'The Social Roots of China's Economic Development'. *The China Quarterly.* 144: 999–1019.

Wilks, Stephen. 2013. *The Political Power of the Business Corporation.* Cheltenham: Edward Elgar.

Yuan, Weipeng, Macve, Richard and Ma, Debin. 2015. 'The Development of Chinese Accounting and Bookkeeping before 1850: Insights from the Tǒng Tài Shēng Business Account Books (1798–1850)'. *Working Paper No. 220.* Department of Economic History, London School of Economics and Political Science.

Zelin, Madeleine. 2004. 'Economic Freedom in Late Imperial China'. Pp. 57–83 in *Realms of Freedom in Modern China,* edited by William C. Kirby. Stanford: Stanford University Press.

Zelin, Madeleine. 2009. 'The Firm in Early China'. *Journal of Economic Behavior and Organization.* 71(3): 623–37.

INDEX

© The Author(s) 2017
J. Barbalet, *Confucianism and the Chinese Self*,
https://doi.org/10.1007/978-981-10-6289-6

Printed in the United States
By Bookmasters